From Broadway To Hollywood

The Musical And The Cinema

Printed by: Staples of Rochester, Kent

Copyright: Robert Matthew Walker, 1996.

Designed by: David Houghton

Photographs: The Kobal Collection, London.

Published by: Sanctuary Publishing Ltd, The Colonnades, 82 Bishops Bridge Road, London W2 6BB

ISBN: 1-86074-145-2

From Broadway To Hollywood

The Musical and the Cinema

by Robert Matthew-Walker

To Lionel Bart

Contents

Part III

Yesterday, Today And Tomorrow

Foreword

The subject of the musical film is a fascinating and glamorous one, and in many respects any book on the subject has to be largely subjective. Largely, but not completely so. Ask any film musical buff to come up with their top ten favourite films and the chances are the elements of agreement will be generally broad. The same is probably true of almost any other subject where personal choice forms a major part in the selection process – if asked to supply lists of the top ten greatest painters or philosophers, dramatists or composers; the greatest plays, novels, poems, paintings, symphonies – and so on – each of these artists, thinkers or art-forms may find a similar measure of agreement among us.

But ask for 30 or 40 or 50 selections, and then subjectivity really takes over. It may be that the longer the selection lists get, the more the selectors reveal aspects of themselves – but what are these aspects, and are they of any significance to others? Even if we can broadly agree on the top ten best musical films of all time, we may find ourselves put on something of a spot if asked to describe in some detail precisely why they appeal so strongly to us.

One of us may admire the music above all; another, the film-making craft; a third, the performance of a favourite artist; and a fourth enthusiast may praise some other aspect. It may

well be that the comprehensiveness of the best musical films – almost all of the elements that make up the film are themselves so excellent – sets them apart from less accomplished offerings. Even within the broadly similar lists of top ten musical films, each of us will prefer one element above another – and we may not even agree on those.

The long and short of it is that a book such as this cannot help but be a personal selection – the more so when the total number of Hollywood musicals on film runs into several hundreds. What I may have seen or heard in a film may not be that which similarly appeals to you; in which case, I crave your indulgence, for I have been an avid watcher of film musicals for 50 years, ever since I first saw Doris Day sing 'It's Magic' in what was – so far as Great Britain was concerned – the film of the same name (the original American title was *Romance On The High Seas*) in 1948. When I at last met Doris Day in Century City, Los Angeles, in 1974, my childhood dreams had come true: she was the personification of what I thought girls of her age should be – when I was a boy.

Now, having watched films for 50 years is no guarantee of having understood them, nor is it any reason for you to take my opinions more seriously than your own. But what I crave from you, as my reader, is the realisation that because of my experience in having seen so many such films, my personal perspective may shed some light on your own.

In this regard, I trust we can all agree that we can learn from each other. I do not claim that my opinions are more important than yours, merely that I hope you will consider them just as valid. I bring my own experience and insight to this subject, and you bring yours, and my opinions are made up not only from having watched a lot of films for many years, but also from having met and spoken with a goodly number of composers, lyricists, artists, film-makers, record producers and experts on the film musical, in the course of a varied life.

It is to these people that I offer thanks and acknowledgments, on another page, in a big way: for without their creativity no-one would have any opinions to express at all on this subject. Such a list is also necessarily subjective – for we tend to seek out the people we think we are going to like most, such as Doris Day, for example, and ignore those with whom we instinctively feel we might not get on (in which cases I have been almost invariably proven wrong: many of the people I thought I might not get on with have turned out to be charming). It is very likely the case – as in mine – that, for whatever reason, any author compiling a list of acknowledgments in a book which relies to some extent on matters of fact is haunted by the fear of having omitted a source he should have acknowledged. In this instance, however, I am consoled by the knowledge that some of my sources would consider it more discreet to allow such comments to remain anonymous.

Not that the reader will find anything too contentious in these pages. After all, film musicals surely have one prime aim – the 'feel-good factor'. We should leave the cinema or rise from our chair at the end of seeing a musical in a much better frame of mind than when we began watching it. I certainly did in 1948, having seen and heard Doris Day, and have done so often since. If the best of these films do not leave us feeling better for having seen them, then whose fault is that? Is it ours? Or the movie-makers'? We can all justify our own behaviour, but a half-century of watching films of all kinds has taught me one thing – if somebody likes something that I do not, my understanding is all the greater in the long run if I take the trouble to find out just what it is that others have found so attractive, and what it is that I overlooked – in which case, what might mean something to them might mean something to me also.

The format of this book takes two parts; the first is a broad outline of the film musical in historical terms, lighting upon various aspects of its development. The second is concerned with a detailed consideration of a number of the finest examples of the genre – necessarily subjective, if my previous criteria are applied, but hopefully nonetheless worthwhile. Broadly speaking, I trust the amount of space allotted to each gives some indication of the merit I attach to them. The first part is therefore chronological, and the second alphabetical.

It may seem a truism to say that the essence of the film musical is music, but it is necessary to state that opinion near the beginning of this book rather than towards the end. The main ingredient of film drama is drama, as comedy is of film comedy. So it is with music and the musical. In this regard, I make no apology for concentrating where necessary on the music at what might sometimes appear to be the expense of other elements. This is, on such occasions, deliberate, and the reader must not therefore complain if, in their opinion, too little space has been given to other elements in these instances.

I have also tended to concentrate upon the theatrical productions to a degree which the film buff might find disconcerting. If a film is made of a show which at first saw life as a theatrical production, then we should consider the result wholly as film and as nothing else. By and large, I incline to this view, but in the case of our subject it is clear that the one could not have come into being without the existence of the other. If the film, by its very nature, lays claim to being a kind of permanent record, and the theatrical production which inspired it has long since vanished into thin air, then that which we cannot immediately recall deserves more of our detailed attention. Quite apart from anything else, the original theatrical production will have contained all the ingredients which combined to make the show a hit – it follows, therefore, that if the show in question created a big impact, then the elements that contributed to that success have to be considered, in a way that is not always true of the film version.

In the concluding chapter of a book on the British composer Havergal Brian, I made the point that although human beings can be stupid, as we have seen all too often in the 20th-century, they can be wise also. We should agree that it is better to exercise wisdom in preference to stupidity. Similarly, our humanity, so often as a consequence of our own shortcomings, is prone to experience much unhappiness in the world, but we all know that it is far better, surely, for us to pursue happiness.

The pursuit of Happiness is enshrined in the second paragraph of the American Declaration of Independence, and it might not be entirely coincidental that through the twin channels of 20th-century American popular cultural entertainment – the Broadway musical and the Hollywood film, from which so much has sprung – that a very great deal of happiness, pure and simple – and some of it not so simple – has been given to the world. In the course of this book, let us pursue it together.

Robert Matthew-Walker
London, SE12
May 1996

Acknowledgments

My thanks are due to many friends and other people with whom, over the years, I have conversed and corresponded on the subjects of musicals. Sadly, some of them are no longer alive, but they are listed here, in memory as well as in thanks. Barbra Streisand, Doris Day, Julie Andrews, Hermione Gingold, Jean Simmons, Leonard Bernstein, Richard Rodgers, Richard Adler, Goddard Lieberson, Vera Zorina, Alan Jay Lerner, André Previn, Lionel Bart, Maurice L. Oberstein, Richard Asher, Ken Glancy, Paul Myers, George Korngold, Charles Gerhardt, Madeleine Kasket, Mike Batt, David Kernan, Ned Sherrin, Tony Tweedale, Stephen Sondheim, Thomas Z. Shepard, Cyril Ornadel, Martin Moritz, Rex Bunnett, Mike Fletcher, Herschel Burke Gilbert, Mark Eynon, Penny Braybrooke, Ray Jenks, Erik Johnson, Geoffrey Solomon, Nigel Lea-Jones, Shimon Cohen, Clauson Braithwaite and Stephen Camp.

Part I
The Rise Of The Film Musical

Chapter 1

Prelude

Our subject is two-fold: film and music. More specifically, it is about how one art-form has been reinterpreted through another to produce a third. To have made such a statement 100 years ago would have given rise to incredulity, when both the film and the stage musical were in their respective infancies. Most people, at the dawn of the 20th-century, would have considered moving pictures to be nothing more than a flickering peep-show, a piece of reportage – and they would have been correct. There were few people indeed who thought that the arrival of film had brought about the birth of a new art-form in its own right. Such people might very well have expressed a similar view of the stage show with music, exclaiming, "A new art-form? Art? Certainly not!" Old habits and prejudices die hard, for – regrettably – it would appear that there are still those who think that way today.

I live in south-east London and, more often than not, if I have to travel to Town, I will drive through New Cross and pass New Cross Gate Station. At that point, just opposite the station, there begins a block of buildings in the direction of old Hatcham. Even today – some 90 years or so after it must have been painted – an old sign at the top of the end wall of the block can still be made

out. It reads: 'The Flickerless Cinema'

This was where 'The Flicks' was – the popular name for 'The Flickerless Cinema', an early movie house which showed films that *didn't* flicker in the manner of the pioneering peep-shows. The films thus shown were made and projected in a way that began to depict, for the first time, clearer moving images, images that involved the viewers – for there was less interference to come between him or her and the screen. The 'flickerless' system was better, and an improvement to which the public readily responded.

If, in the earliest days of the cinema, the sheer novelty of seeing images of everyday life soon began to wear off, what was to replace them? Well, we might think we all know the answer to that, for it was two-fold. On the one hand, these everyday images were replaced with travel films of foreign lands – people could actually see what was going on in other countries rather than having to read about such events, or even having to bother to learn to read – for, in the absence of talking pictures, the slides containing text, explaining locale or action, would more often than not be read out loud by the more literate members of the audience to others less well-educated than themselves. On the other hand, dramatised stories equally would replace those early bits of everyday reportage. These dramas were of all kinds, including a lot of comedy and sometimes fantasy, and they made 'stars' of the actors and actresses who appeared in them: these were the things that both attracted and, thereby, fascinated those early cinema audiences.

There was, of course, one essential aspect missing from these dramas, to which we have already alluded: sound. This came later, along with colour and other technical innovations, all of them further attempts in making the unreal real. But one thing that the early film-makers found quite remarkable, and which, in its own way and in its utter simplicity, transferred the peep-show element of film-making into an art-form, was the manner in which stories could be told.

To explain this, we should step back a little perhaps and consider another 20th-century invention which has come to dominate our lives: broadcasting. In some ways, the rise of broadcasting and the rise of film have been very similar, quite apart from having been developed within a decade or so of each other; their eventual coming together, in sound projection, was perhaps to be expected. However, the essential difference between broadcasting and film is that whereas film has become – indeed, because of its nature, could not help but become – an art-form, a principal new art-form in the 20th-century, broadcasting could not have so become, and therefore cannot be so considered.

The central characteristic of what makes an art-form an art-form is that, through it, creative artists can communicate things which cannot be communicated in any other way or by any other art-form. This central fact dawned upon the early film-makers, and it was this which made film-making capable of being raised to the level of art.

No such claim can be made of broadcasting.

Broadcasting is a medium, nothing else, for there is nothing in broadcasting that cannot be communicated in another form. So if we claim that film is an art-form, what was it that these early film-makers discovered about film, about what they did, that was capable of raising it to the level of art?

It was the juxtaposition of image. Or, rather, the juxtaposition of moving images in telling a story. Early film-makers discovered that if they had to shoot one part of a story, in which a character had to leave his room and go to a shop, for example, they were obliged to show him leaving the room, closing the door, going down stairs, out of the front door, along the street until he came to the shop, and going into the shop. All of this narrative took time, not only in the making but also in the showing, and such redundant additional footage slowed up the story-line to an unacceptable extent

The early film-makers were forced to consider making this dramatically-empty additional footage because their audiences could not, at first, take the juxtaposition of images that might have shown, to begin with, a man deciding to go to a shop to buy something and then – suddenly, to those early audiences – being in the shop, without any linking scenes to show him actually getting there. To them, it was nonsense. As such juxtapositions could not happen in real life, for we cannot jump from our room to the shop (however much time we may like to save by being able to do so), so the audiences were confronted with something that was beyond their experience.

There are well-documented accounts of members of early cinema audiences trying to run round the back of the screen in order to find out what had gone wrong, or complaining that because the linking footage was not in the film's narrative, they were being short-changed. So far as their experience of drama in those days was concerned, no stage play could do this. What they were being shown was true-to-life, with proper perspective and distance – methods of staging which were quite beyond theatres, no matter how well equipped.

This aspect was unique to film, and was something that the stage could not provide – certainly not with regard to any fast scene-changing in those days, however much film has come to be used in theatrical productions to effect such a change. Even if a contemporary stage-production had approximated to such sudden juxtapositions, film had one other utterly new concept to offer the creative artist. This was the absence of the concept of distance. In short, film could use the 'close-up'. Film could show a person walking down a street, from a distance, and immediately juxtapose that with a shot of the character's face, to show direct emotion – and by filling the entire screen with the character's face, the emotional impact was by far the greater. Therefore, one could express things through film in a way which was unique to that medium, things which could not be expressed in any other way.

No matter how dramatically good, or dreadfully ham, stage actors and actresses at the turn of the century were, a theatrical production could never show characters for a dramatic moment in close-up as film can. The same is true today, of course. Now, this comment should not be taken as a criticism of stage drama, merely as a statement of fact, but a fact that took some time to be absorbed by early film-makers.

By the end of the first decades of the 20th-century, it was clear that in terms of popular entertainment the film-show was here to stay. Films were sometimes projected in ordinary theatres, on the same bill as live acts, but those who could accurately foresee the way things were likely to go were concerned that the rise of film would lead to the decline of live theatre.

In some respects, they were right, but in others they were not. Many live theatre shows, of a mundane and ephemeral kind, ultimately were killed off in this way, even if they took several decades in the dying, but film came to live alongside the theatre as a valid art-form in itself, in much the same way as those who predicted that the development of gramophone records and, later, broadcasting, would replace live concerts and opera-going. On the contrary. It can be argued, and probably proved, that the twin communication media of records and broadcasting have helped not only to sustain the broad art of music, but, as an aid to musical appreciation, have actually increased the size of the audiences for these types of music.

Nevertheless, theatre continued to have several important advantages over film: sound and colour.

Films were silent, and only – except in a few experimental efforts – in black-and-white, whereas a staged show would contain not only speech, of course, but also could have music. The show's costumes and sets would also be in colour. The one art medium (to stretch a point) that benefited from both the rise of film and the response of the theatre was music. Silent cinemas, even the more modest ones, such as 'The Flicks' at New Cross Gate, would have at very least a resident pianist to play music to accompany the soundless films. Larger, purpose-built 'picture palaces', would have orchestras and, later still, cinema organs were installed – and those vast electric cinema organs, being on-site, would last well into the age of the 'talkies' (some into the early 1960s), their purpose having changed by then to entertain audiences between screenings.

There was, therefore, film music of one kind or another from the earliest years, its function being emotionally to heighten the dramatic moment. Necessity being in all other respects a mother of invention, the hey-dey of the cinema saw also the hey-dey of the film score.

For it proved to be a curious and, in many ways, a deeply tragic, combination of social and political circumstances that led to a number of outstandingly gifted young European composers, many of them Jewish and thus forced to leave Nazi-dominated Europe – if they were fortunate to escape with their lives – end up in Hollywood to help provide the necessary film music for the seemingly never-ending output of an industry that could barely keep up with the world-wide demand for the product it had itself created. The late 1930s and the whole of the succeeding 20 years marked the hey-day of the classic film score – although we can find examples of great film music having been written both before and after that period.

Previously in the theatre world the competition from film – even from silent, black-and-white movies – was a major factor which led to a reappraisal of what the theatre was capable of providing in terms of popular entertainment. Far from a conscious effort on the part of those 'in the theatre world', it was, as is always the case with success, the luckily bold identification and seizing of main chances by a few dynamic and committed individuals: and in this instance, in the United States in the first decades of the 20th-century, another combination of circumstances provided the favourable and fertile ground from which has sprung the undoubted masterpieces of the American musical theatre.

In the first place, as we have seen, there was the burgeoning threat from film. In the second place, it was a result of the bringing together of millions of immigrants to the USA in the closing years of the 19th-century and the opening years of the 20th. For, by 1917, the population of the United States had topped the 100 million mark for the first time, and more than one in ten of the population had actually been born in Europe.

This had been migration on a scale never before seen in history, and the far-reaching results were equally breathtaking. Jewish pogroms in Russia in the 1880s and 1890s had caused many families and individuals to flee to America. We shall note, in the course of this book, just how many composers of popular music that have always been regarded as essentially 'American', had either been born in Russia, or were born to parents of Russian extraction.

Perhaps, if none of the events which caused these families to flee their homeland had happened, we might be speaking of a Russian 20th-century music theatre. Yet talent, no less than genius, needs a sympathetic environment in which to flourish – otherwise, it withers and dies. The USA possessed, as it has always striven to possess, a social culture made up largely of personal freedom and of capitalism within a republic. Russia, in the early years of the 20th-century, may have provided an environment for great art, music, ballet and drama, but it was essentially an insular environment, whose patronage stemmed from the Romanoff Royal Family downwards.

What America additionally possessed was what was to become its own music – jazz – which in turn derived from older, and sadder, immigrant cultures of a minority to which personal freedom had more often been denied. Elements from black music – jazz being itself an amalgam of various musical strands – were to be taken and refashioned by white musicians of European extraction.

Musicians, composers, theatrical people of all kinds, along with millions of what were to become their fellow-countrymen, had passed through the immigration centre of Ellis Island in New York on their journey to making and remaking their own way in the new world. Suddenly, by 1920, America was awash with talent, and – as a direct consequence of the Great War of 1914-18 – found itself, for the first time, the richest single country in the world with regard to its valuable raw materials. The USA additionally possessed the means to turn its raw materials into merchantable commodities and manufactured goods. Consequently, America was also, for the first time in its history, a major power in world affairs. But if internal politics in the USA in the decade of the 1920s tended to favour isolationist policies, the exact opposite was true in the case of American popular culture.

The British Empire had spread the English language around the world. English was also the language of America, so that all aspects of popular culture, certainly that which was transported throughout the globe by the modern means of mass communication, would, if emanating from the USA – through the earlier spread of the English language and the still-potent influence of the British Empire – find a ready and receptive world-wide audience.

Gramophone records, too, carried all kinds of music – and the language in which the music was sung – to audiences who would otherwise neither have had the chance of hearing the music for many years, nor ever hear it at all. A portable gramophone in rural areas could bring the latest music to all and sundry, and singers who otherwise might have worked for a long time to establish their careers found themselves world-famous within months, rather than years.

Composers benefited, also: George Gershwin's 'Swanee', written at the age of 20 and taken up almost at once by Al Jolson, was the singer's first major hit – Jolson's recording sold more than two-and-a-quarter million copies world-wide, in the days before electrical recording. When Gershwin first visited Britain, in 1924, the English immigration officer at the port of Southampton, on examining his passport, said: "George Gershwin?

Are you the man who wrote 'Swanee'?" The officer's comment greatly pleased the composer, as well it might.

By 1924, if Gershwin was famous in Britain and in America as the man who wrote 'Swanee' (it was also the year of the 'Rhapsody In Blue' and, later, the show *Lady, Be Good*) it was nonetheless also true that in those days movies were still without sound. But not for long. It was the same Al Jolson who, in popular terms, brought talking pictures to the world in 1927. He was, of course, merely the man who spoke them, unwittingly it seems, but that simple statement "Wait a minute, wait a minute – you ain't heard nothing yet!" opened the floodgates. What is undoubtedly also significant is that the film in which he spoke these words was a musical, *The Jazz Singer*, in which the music itself was to be heard on film in the movie theatre. What makes this single act of speech additionally significant is that *The Jazz Singer* was a film musical – in other words, not a Broadway show turned into a film but an original screenplay on a musical subject.

It is impossible to overestimate the effect on audiences of hearing Jolson speak on film. That it created a sensation is beyond doubt; audiences – particularly for the film's opening night, most of whom were film people – were themselves dumbstruck at what they witnessed on screen and heard. Once the initial shock had sunk in, some cheered, some applauded, some cried and some were saddened that a true universal language – the silent film drama – was being overtaken by the very spoken language that was a cause of so much misunderstanding and consequential strife in the world. But no-one who witnessed it could be in any doubt as to the direction that movies had taken. There was no going back.

After 1927, therefore, sound (combining both speech and/or music) and film were indisputably linked, apart from the efforts of a few reactionary diehards, and, with the arrival of colour some years after that, film-makers had all the ingredients they needed for great leaps forward in their art. It meant, without question, that films could be made of theatrical productions – and thus provide, for the first time in history, the final solution to what had been up to then an insoluble theatrical problem.

For film could do what the theatre never could: film offered the possibility of a permanent record being made of a performance. The run of a successful show on Broadway, or anywhere else for that matter, has, *ipso facto,* to come to an end. No show runs forever – although, with several recent examples, it has begun to seem as though there may be exceptions to this rule. Later generations of theatre-goers can only speculate as to the wonders of legendary productions of the past, and the memories of those who saw these shows may be tinted various hues as time goes by, or their memories may be at fault in the recollection. Still photographs, and also original cast recordings, will help to recapture the flavour, but once a production has closed – that is the end of it. If you did not see the show during its run, you have missed it forever.

Film changed all that. It offered the chance of capturing, once and for all for future generations, a permanent record of great performances by the best, and the most popular, actors, actresses and singers of the day. If many such opportunities were missed or simply not taken, that is the way of human behaviour, but it did offer that chance.

Nevertheless, as a result, two things have happened. The first is that many fine films *have* been made of musical shows that were originally written for the theatre, and some of these will be examined in varying degrees of detail in the latter part of this book. The second is that sound, almost from the beginning as we saw in the case of *The Jazz Singer,* afforded the possibility of making musical films that were conceived with the screen, and not the stage, in mind.

It may seem paradoxical, but such appears to be the nature of the best of this second type, that several musical films have been made into convincing theatrical shows. If it has not always been the case that such 'musicals-from-films' have been successful in the theatre, the fact remains that if the very existence of those 'cross-overs' does not demonstrate the inter-dependence of the two art-forms, and by inference the validity of the film musical as an art-form within an art-form, then nothing does. It is the nature and purpose of this book to examine how these various art-forms have interacted over the years, and continue to interact.

As we approach the dawn of a new millennium, with all the modern means of communication and film-making at our disposal, there is a very strong case to be made out for remaking films of the great musicals of the past, a subject to which we shall return at the end of this book. Within the last quarter of the 20th-century, the lasting qualities of earlier Broadway musical shows have been demonstrated afresh in new productions – some of which have enjoyed exceptionally successful runs. If these shows have a validity and reviviscence that far outlasts the age in which they were created, and in so doing can delight newer theatrical audiences, there is no reason to suppose that, done well, they cannot do the same thing for new generations of movie-goers.

Chapter 2

The Dawn Of An Era

On April 14, 1894, the first public showing by Thomas Alva Edison of the Kinetoscope was demonstrated at 1155 Broadway, New York City. Although there may be some doubt as to whether the Kinetoscope had been invented by Edison in 1891, this public demonstration showed the system in a confined format, almost as a peep-show. Nonetheless, moving pictures for a fee-paying public had been shown to be a practical possibility. The development of a projector, which showed moving pictures on a screen, was not long in coming. On April 23, 1896, Thomas Edison demonstrated the Vitascope projector, which had actually been invented by Thomas Armat, who was present on that occasion, but was content to let the famous Edison take the popular credit. By the end of the century, moving picture houses, or cinemas, had been established in major cities throughout the western world.

The growth of the early cinema is both a fascinating subject, and a significant one, too, for the impact of the movies in the 20th-century was arguably the most important social development of all – certainly until the arrival of television.

1155 Broadway is situated just above Madison Square Park near the junction with 28th Street. It was a small building in 1894 and, 102 years later, the building that stands on this spot houses a much more recently-built sports store, with no mention of the important event that took place there in 1894.

If the last decade of the 19th-century saw the arrival and early development of the motion picture film, it may not have been such an extraordinary coincidence that Edison chose to demonstrate moving pictures in their infancy on the very street whose name has become synonymous with another great American invention – the musical theatre. The Kinetoscope that Edison demonstrated led, eventually, to the Hollywood motion picture industry, but Broadway – in all its forms and all its magical meanings – was already there.

Whilst we may be able to pinpoint with some degree of accuracy the era in which motion pictures became a fact of life, no such year or date can be considered to be that in which the musical was born. Whatever the provenance of the 20th-century musical – the play with music, the light opera or the revue which grew, or any combination of these or a half-dozen other types of theatrical productions – it evolved, rather than was invented. It became at heart – as we have indicated before – an American theatrical phenomenon, and as such had to have emanated from Broadway.

America was born from immigration. The extraordinary melting-pot that became the United States was made up of waves of immigrants, the majority from Europe – being Jews, Protestants and Catholics and those without religion – together with others from the Far East across the Pacific, and, most tragically of all, the slave trade from Africa. All of these people had to seek their destiny in a new environment. In spite of this amazing coming-together of races and cultures, a coming-together which eventually blended into a more or less recognisably American way of life, the principles upon which America was founded – which principles have curbed and directed its evolved system of jurisprudence as the basis for a civilised free society – were those upon which every ethnic strand in the American melting-pot could agree.

In which case those principles embody the hopes and aspirations of all men, who were, according to the country's most precious declaration, created equal. The slate, for every immigrant, was wiped clean – the United States, if you could get into the country, offered the chance for a new beginning, and the President's office could, in theory, be inhabited by anyone able to call themselves an American.

If the vast majority of American immigrants came from Europe it was only to be expected that they brought with them European ways of thinking and the appurtenances of various European ways of life. This was as true in art and entertainment as it was in fashion, styles of dress and law-making, but America offered not just a place in which Europeans could flourish, it also offered something else – the chance to be influenced by different cultures to produce something new that was acceptable to all.

In addition, America was big and rich. It could absorb millions of people – and did – as well as support this growing population; once more, it offered opportunity and the means to realise ambition. To many of the immigrants, fleeing a Europe torn apart by, and entrenched in, war and misery, New York must have seemed the gateway to a promised land, the more so as they contemplated the powerful image of the Statue of Liberty on Bedloe's Island, the unveiling of which had been witnessed by more than one million people on October 28, 1887.

But if, as the American Declaration of Independence states, we are all created equal, we do not grow up that way. Equality of opportunity is not the same as equality of achievement, for each of us is different, has different capabilities, which make us in the best sense – to use a word which has in modern parlance come to mean something damning – élite.

The moment we talk about people being different or élite, we are at the threshold of a door which opens onto controversy, a modern controversy which is one of the more dispiriting results of the explosion in mass-communication of the last quarter of the 20th-century. The controversy centres upon the commonly-held concept of the word élitism, which holds that the use of the word makes it 'normal' for a majority of people, in the words of the late Hans Keller, to express "an emotive, derogatory, pseudo-democratic, almost psychotic denial of the fact that all men are not equal".

Nor did those immigrants come to America with uncluttered minds; they brought with them their unequal talents, the miracle of which was that America enabled them to pursue their talents unencumbered by many of the social conventions which, in their native countries, might have tended to squash them.

The musical part of our subject is that of the theatre, and for Europeans in the 19th-century the three centres for music theatre were London, Paris and Vienna. These have always been major cities with relatively large populations that provided work during the day and entertainment at night, and their growth as centres of music tended to spring, by and large, from being ruled by Royal Families who encouraged music at their courts alongside the other arts.

This encouragement was nothing more than the realisation, conscious or otherwise, that to make music – even at its most primitive, through singing – is a natural human means of expression. The members of some European Royal Families were musically gifted – it could hardly otherwise have been the case, considering the large numbers of children that were often born to such families – and the royal courts would vie with each other for superiority in all fields. Music – and the other arts – could flourish in such patronising circumstances, and it did, long before critics were thought of. For the critic was the consumer: if the court did not like your music, you were out of a job, and often out of a home, and out of the city as well.

In the United States in the 19th-century, no king ruled, and no king – Ludwig II excepted – or court in Europe could support a coterie of various artists as their forefathers had done. Royal patronage of that kind did not exist in America, and the only patronage that meant anything was the patronage of the paying public. The consumer became king.

However – as we have seen – the public was not all the same: they had come from many different backgrounds, spoke different languages, worshipped in different ways and even if they were obliged to discard many of their differences for the common good, they alone decided where they spent their money.

Musicians of all kinds soon learned that what might have gone down well in Paris might not go down too well in Little Italy or neighbouring Bowery, or what had wowed them in London meant much less in Harlem or Morningside Heights. And so the melting-pot of America, as exemplified by New York and, more specifically for our purposes, the theatre district around Broadway, found itself the means by which new forms of entertainment, with wide appeal, could be created. The élitism was being expanded to a bigger market.

Considered purely as a matter of luck, Edison's Kinetoscope demonstration and the development of motion pictures could not have come at a more opportune moment or occurred in a more suitable city. The luck was to make a positive virtue out of a technical drawback. In other words, the fact that films were silent would attract all – there were, quite literally, no language problems – and the additional fact that the American economy was growing at an enormous rate, fuelled to some extent by the Spanish-American War of 1898, provided greater disposal income for a growing, and working, population.

The social and economic circumstances in the United States at the turn of the century therefore were highly favourable for the development of new means of entertainment, in the more popular musical theatre as much as elsewhere. The Metropolitan Opera House at Broadway and 39th Street had opened in 1883 and had soon become established as one of the world's major opera houses. New York also boasted two fine symphony orchestras – the Philharmonic, founded in 1842, and the New York Symphony, founded in 1878 – as well as much else besides in terms of the musical arts.

But whereas the symphony orchestras and opera houses of New York had to rely on European repertoire, the popular musical theatre theoretically had no such restrictions. True, it was irrigated from the three rivers of Paris, Vienna and London in its formative years, but it soon ceased to be sustained entirely by offerings from these cities. There had been early examples of musical shows – from the founding of the first theatre in America, built at Williamsburg, Virginia, in 1716 – but these were almost invariably of material that had originated in Europe, and, more likely, in London.

There is a lot of documentary evidence showing that America in the 18th-century had a reasonably thriving music theatre life, to which was added in the early 19th-century shows of a more indigenous character – the minstrel shows, the first truly American music theatre entertainment. This has more of an historical significance than an aesthetic one, but minstrel shows did develop into a whole evening's entertainment.

The historical significance was that this was the first time in history that African and European cultures met on a permanent basis, with each influencing the another. The result, as could well be imagined, was a new music, but it was hardly sophisticated, and the entertainment it supported was aimed wholly at semi-literate working-class audiences.

Whilst the growth in popularity of music theatre continued alongside vaudeville – a branch initially of the English music-hall, which was basically a succession of different stage acts, singing, dancing, juggling, comedy sketches and the like – there was a move towards the combination of drama, music and dancing (both solo and in formation) into a reasonably unified whole.

Perhaps the most significant ground-breaking show to achieve this was *The Black Crook*, a remarkable retelling of the ur-Faust story by Charles M Barras. This opened at Niblo's Garden Theatre in New York on September 12, 1866 and ran consecutively until the end of January, 1868. The cast was the largest ever seen in America up to that time, and the show was by all accounts a massive, expensive and breathtaking piece of theatre, the success of which was due in no small part to the timelessness of the story.

The music was culled from various sources; most of it was new, and included songs, ensemble pieces, orchestral parts and ballet music. Nonetheless, for all its innovation and spectacle, it was a very expensive show to mount and to sustain, and it failed to open any theatrical floodgates. In addition, not all theatres were of the size or possessed the machinery to mount such a production.

But it had shown what could be done, and the notion of an entire evening's drama supported, and indeed punctuated, by music had planted seeds in various theatrical brains. The principle had been established in New York, and new material – not necessarily so expensive to mount, nor indeed indigenous to America – could be produced.

As is so often the case, the moment somebody does something somewhere, somebody else is found having been working on something similar at the same time. For *The Black Crook* did not spring fully-formed, Janus-like, upon the New York stage – it contained elements that were familiar to European audiences of the day – indeed, some of its performers had been brought in from Europe specially for the show.

The first all-American unified show, with music by one composer, came in 1874. This was *Evangeline*, a jocular caricature of HW

Longfellow's narrative poem which had been published in 1847. The poem is set in Arcadia, precursor of modern-day Nova Scotia, and tells the story of Evangeline Bellefontaine and her love for Gabriel Lajeunesse, a love that is separated by fate and is only reunited at the end of their lives with Evangeline a nun, and Gabriel now a dying victim of the plague in Philadelphia.

The composer of this very successful humorous adaptation, the book of which had been written by Joseph Goodwin, was Edward E Rice (1848-1924) about whose early life little is known until the appearance of *Evangeline*. Rice is reported as having written the show with the intention that it could be considered as "a burlesque diversion to which an entire family might be taken, in lieu of the imported entertainment at which only the black sheep from every fold might be expected".

This comment reflects general concerns at the time regarding the growth in the big cities of cheaply frivolous shows with music, which were often deliberately made quite unsuitable for family entertainment to attract a certain type of customer. Rice came to make a lot of money from his wholesome 'burlesque diversions' – not 'burlesque' in the meaning of the term's later application, referring to shows of the low type that Rice condemned – but an interesting sidelight on his method of working was that he could barely read or write music. He would pick out his tunes on the piano, for a transcriber to notate and often harmonise, while Rice would give explicit instructions for orchestration and other matters. In this, Rice was the eminent precursor of the methods of working of Irving Berlin, amongst others.

Rice formed his own touring company, and eventually wrote seven shows of a similar structure, including a quatercentenary commemoration of Columbus's discovery of the New World, *1492*, which was first heard early in 1893. By this time, the success of a popular song by David Braham, 'The Mulligan Guard', about a military company of Irish extraction in the American Civil War, had led to a series of shows being written, based on the character of Dan Mulligan – but these were hardly at all suitable as being of a type to which "the entire family might be taken".

It was a British import, Gilbert and Sullivan's *HMS Pinafore* which hit Boston at the end of 1878, and later New York, that added new impetus to the burgeoning musical theatre on Broadway. The combination of William S Gilbert and Arthur Sullivan had been the idea of Rupert D'Oyly Carte, who brought the two disparate men – disparate in age, size and temperament – together in 1871, to form an artistic union of incomparable originality and lasting influence, and in 1876 formed a light opera company specifically to perform their works. The partnership would also make all three men wealthy.

HMS Pinafore was their third collaboration and their first major success. It had opened in London in May 1878 and enjoyed more than 700 consecutive performances. In America, it caused a sensation, so much so that within a year Gilbert and Sullivan had travelled to New York in a largely successful attempt to protect their copyrights and to give an official performance of the show, for up to 40 unauthorised ones had been given in America within a year, as well as giving a preview of their next work, *The Pirates Of Penzance*.

The success in America of Gilbert and Sullivan led to a new vogue for things European, especially English and French, for one very important influence on Sullivan's music was the composer Jacques Offenbach, who had created virtually single-handedly the genre of French light operettas, the success of which had made him an international figure. Offenbach was to die in Paris in October 1880, leaving his masterpiece, *The Tales Of Hoffmann*, all but finished.

During the following decade, American composers found it difficult to break through the fashion for European musical shows; but the early 1890s saw a change in public taste. America had begun to assert its own individuality, as we have also seen in the unveiling of the Statue of Liberty, in preparations for the forthcoming 400th anniversary of Columbus and in the Chicago World's Fair of 1893.

Two of the first native shows to achieve popularity were *A Trip To Chinatown* by Percy Gaunt, set in contemporary San Francisco, and Reginald De Koven's comic opera *Robin Hood*, which deserves revival today. Both of these works appeared in 1891, and could stand alongside contemporary imports; the door was opening again for American composers.

One of the first American shows at this time to achieve renown was *The Belle Of New York* by Gustave Kerker, a musical show which scored a bigger success in London than it did in its native city. This was in 1897, by which time the great Victor Herbert – a symphonic conductor of considerable attainment and a composer of serious concert works, as well as being a cellist of international repute (he premiered Brahms's *Double Concerto* in the USA), had begun to write his series of operettas. Herbert wrote more than 40 before his death in 1924 at the age of 65, including the brilliant *Babes In Toyland* (1903) and *Naughty Marietta* (1910).

In between these shows came what has come to be recognised as the first wholly American musical comedy: *Little Johnny Jones*, by George M Cohan. It was also a show in which Cohan wrote the book, music and lyrics and in which he starred. The show first appeared in 1904, and was set in contemporary times. With such songs as 'Yankee Doodle Boy' (better known as 'Yankee Doodle Dandy') and 'Give My Regards To Broadway', the Broadway musical can truly be said to have finally arrived.

Chapter 3

From Broadway to Hollywood: Silence To Sound

The story of how, at the dawn of the 20th-century, a sleepy suburb called Hollywood, with a population of not more than several thousand people on the outskirts of the growing California city of Los Angeles, became the movie capital of the world is as extraordinary as that of any of the films subsequently made there.

By all rational standards, the notion of selecting such a place, thousands of miles from the financial and entertainment heart of the country – New York City – was absurd. In many ways, looking at it with the benefit of hindsight, such a choice did not, on the face of it, make sense – were it not for two most important, and over-riding, reasons: climate and space.

As we have seen, Edison had exhibited moving pictures in the mid-1890s in New York, on Broadway; the sudden, unprecedented growth in public demand for movies led to an equally sudden and unimagined growth industry to make and provide them, and as the cinemas were initially confined to major cities, it made sense to make the movies as close to the cities as was practicable.

Quite apart from the logistic advantages of such close proximity, New York had a large body of actors and actresses who could be called upon and taken out to, say, New Jersey for the day and brought back to New York at night, although the more established serious members of the acting profession rather disdainfully looked down upon this dramatic upstart at first.

Many of the early cowboy films, certainly following Edwin Porter's *The Great Train Robbery* of 1903, were made in neighbouring New Jersey, not in the Wild West. If this seminal 12-minute film was the first great American movie – and it was – there are various aspects of when it was made and of the film's creation itself that ought to be mentioned.

The first is that by this time, with the advantage of silent pictures, picture houses in the USA – and all over the world – were showing films made in various countries, particularly Britain. It was a very early British thriller, a similar 'robbery' film, entitled *Daring Daylight Robbery*, that provided the initial inspiration for *The Great Train Robbery* – Edwin Porter worked for the company which had the rights to show this British film in the USA. It must be at once admitted, however, that his American movie was a superior and more exciting product in every way than its British predecessor.

The second point is that *The Great Train Robbery* was also shown in 1903 in some theatres in colour. This was not as a result of any early technical photographic innovation with regard to primitive cinematography, but to the far-sighted vision of those who rightly thought that a hand-coloured film would create an even bigger impact – as it did.

The problem, of course, was that hand-colouring every frame was both a lengthy and expensive undertaking, and in spite of the amazement with which the early audiences saw the hand-coloured 'prints', the film is best remembered for its black-and-white impact, in which form it is still shown today all over the world. The film-makers also learned something of the need for good continuity: in one scene, in the station office, a man shot dead in the previous scene moves in the next one, before he 'lays down dead' again.

But *The Great Train Robbery,* shot in only two days, showed the way forward in no uncertain terms. Furthermore, what was also learned by the early years of the century was that a film, once seen by a regular audience, was not something that the same audience wished to see exhibited week after week, again and again. The films soon became akin to ancient history for the rapidly sophisticated, and demanding, early audiences, those who wished to visit the movie houses on a regular basis. The audiences would willingly return to the same theatre if a new film was to be shown: the demand was there, and had to be met.

This meant making a lot of films, but technically this was not such an easy undertaking, for the cameras needed a good and reliable source of light. Almost all film-making had to be done out-of-doors, for even those scenes which purported to take place indoors were shot on sets built in the open air.

The climate of the north-eastern states of America is varied, and sunlight – the best and most reliable source in those early days – cannot be guaranteed. In addition, sets had to be built, and space was needed in which to build them. What was ideally required was a place close to a city, and therefore near to major railroad connections, which enjoyed a sunny climate almost all the year round, with little rainfall, and with a lot of flat unused acreage nearby – therefore making this land cheap to acquire – and close to mountains and deserts if possible, where English was the spoken language. It also had to be within the United States.

One place fitted these requirements – Los Angeles. It was still a long way from New York – five days by railroad – but the film processing could be done there, close by, and the finished movies shipped by rail to all major cities within a day or so of each other to coincide with a nationally-advertised release. Suddenly, a potential major distribution problem was no longer a problem, although older figures were slow to grasp the opportunity which the younger showmen and entrepreneurs were about to seize in the Los Angeles suburb of Hollywood.

From around 1908, when Thomas Edison had formed the Motion Picture Patents' Trust in New York in an attempt to monopolise the growing industry, primitive film studios and sets were quickly erected in the surrounding area of Hollywood, which within a matter of months had grown to more than 300 square miles. It rarely rains in Southern California – Los Angeles is built upon a desert – and the natural abundant sunshine meant there would be no natural interruptions in film-making.

The native Hollywoodians were resentful of the newcomers: theatres and bars had been illegal there for decades and it was by no means unusual for hotels to bar actors and actresses from their premises: the sign 'No dogs, no actors' was a permanent fixture at the Hollywood Hotel.

Their resentfulness was not entirely unreasonable: the film-makers would take over large areas of the suburb, and the city if need be – as the early films make plain – in order to shoot their movies, with little or no consideration for the people who lived there, folk whose taxes had gone to provide the streets and police force which the film-makers were using, free of charge, for their dangerous car-chases and so on without so much as a nod to the city authorities.

The early years of the film industry were not free from violence: Edison's Trust resorted to strong-arm tactics, and some Hollywood film-makers hired gangs of enforcers to 'persuade' locals to allow their neighbourhood to be used for filming. There was also rivalry between the fledgling film companies, and a certain amount of early commercial espionage took place as the more unscrupulous film-makers attempted to steal all kinds of property – physical as well as technical and intellectual.

A group of brilliantly-gifted independent entrepreneurs, acting as a consortium but retaining their commercial individuality, took on Edison's Trust in the courts and won; they knew, as the hidebound Trust did not, that the new film-stars, large-scale films, and highly luxurious movie theatres – the first of which was opened in New York on 1913 with all modern facilities – were the way forward for an industry which, by 1920, had become the fifth largest in the United States.

With the Trust's restraints removed legally, the way was clear for the industry to flex its muscles artistically and to begin to produce large-scale, full-length movies which had an enormous impact and influence upon the millions of people who flocked to see them. In addition, of course,

shorter films – often of slapstick comedy – also enjoyed a world-wide reputation. Hollywood had certainly arrived and had become a financial mecca for the aspiring artist of all kinds, if the stories of the salaries paid were true.

Such stories were often exaggerated, but the money involved was clearly considerable, and attracted its share of less than admirable characters. A part of Hollywood had become synonymous with the more licentious aspects of life – alcohol abuse and drug-taking had become very common for some actors and actresses, and sexual appetites of all kinds were readily catered for – sometimes blatantly so – with the gratuitous excitement of underground pornographic movies adding a salaciously thrilling layer.

The sharp turn to the political right in the United States, which began with the election of President Harding in 1920, was also personified by the Prohibition of the sale of intoxicating liquor and the establishment of 'the new morality' the same year. After several unsavoury reports of Hollywood immorality and the extraordinary sexual scandal surrounding the movie star Fatty Arbuckle in 1921 (in which he was falsely accused of rape, a charge relentlessly pursued by the powerful Hearst press, for reasons more to do with the owner's paranoia than simple justice) led to growing demands for censorship in movies, and a greater moral leadership to be shown by the movie-makers, in which demands the Hearst press also played a prominent role.

The industry combined to meet these challenges by forming its own censorship office, headed by a member of President Harding's cabinet and Presbyterian church leader, Will Hays. With such a figure to oversee the moral content of movies, and with the sacrifice of a number of figures in the industry, who may or may not have been amongst the leading perpetrators of immoral conduct, the industry had saved itself, and indeed in so doing made itself more respectable.

By the mid-1920s, the technical innovations in the movie industry had enabled full-length movies to be made on a whole variety of subjects that attracted audiences throughout the world. Major studios had emerged from the demise of the Trust and the amalgamation of smaller companies, and the distribution outlets for their product had also been rationalised and brought to a fine art. A great deal of money was being made, and the future looked bright indeed.

But the movies still lacked sound. Thomas Edison – who else? – had attempted to marry sound with moving image in the 1890s by combining early film with cylinder recordings, but the problem of synchronisation between the two incompatible systems proved insoluble. At New York's Rivoli Theatre, at the junction of Broadway and West 39th Street, Lee de Forest showed sound-on-film shorts in April 1923, but these were devoted to vaudeville acts. The major studios were not interested; they argued that their world-wide markets would be decimated if speech were added to silent movies, and their own experiments in the second decade of the century were unsuccessful. By this time also the movie business was heavily financed, and the cost of changing to sound stage studios would be enormous. Finally, not all silent movie stars could command the world-wide following they currently enjoyed if their occasionally exaggerated manner of acting had to be toned down for more normal portrayals including the spoken word.

And so the big studios tended to leave sound alone, but the then comparatively small production company set up by the Warner brothers, Sam and Jack, pushed ahead with their plans to make sound-on-film a viable commercial possibility. In 1926 they issued a two-hour movie, *Don Juan*, starring John Barrymore in one of his finest roles, with Mary Astor, Myrna Loy, Warner Oland and Estelle Taylor, and brilliantly photographed by Byron Haskin, which had a synchronised music score by William Axt.

Axt was an outstanding musician who, born in New York City, had studied music in Berlin and conducted for Oscar Hammerstein I's Grand Opera Company in Manhattan – a serious rival to the Metropolitan, to which it was sold in 1910 – before conducting on Broadway and joining the staff of the Capitol Theatre, which had begun to specialise in spectacular musical accompaniments to silent films. In 1925, Axt wrote a score for arguably the greatest of all silent films – MGM's *The Big Parade* – a two-hour feature which became the biggest grossing silent movie ever. Axt wrote his score in collaboration with David Mendoza; the music was printed and distributed along with copies of the film to movie theatres across the country. Incidentally, in 1933, Axt was to be music director for an MGM film called *Broadway To Hollywood*.

But for *Don Juan* in 1926 the movie company went one better with regard to Axt's music – his score was electrically recorded on 78rpm discs which were played in synchronisation with the film's reels. The effect was astonishing, for electrical recording had only become a viable possibility the previous year and was not then within everyone's experience. To have heard this score played by an invisible symphony orchestra and relayed on large electrical speakers – even though the music was not a part of the film's print – for the audiences, this combination showed the way forward with considerable impact.

That same year of 1926 Fox Studios, using a technique not unlike that shown to be practicable by Lee de Forest, began making and distributing newsreels with occasional sound. These events were, however, merely tantalising developments in the journey towards talking pictures, for in spite of demonstrating the technical possibility of sound-on-film, the single most important feature was still lacking: dialogue.

After *The Jazz Singer* had been shown for the first time with such sensational success in October 1927, completely vindicating the faith in the future that this innovation by the Warner brothers had demonstrated, less than nine months later more than 300 movie houses in the United States had been wired for sound, and were already showing the first, inevitably somewhat rudimentary, talking pictures.

Almost at once, audiences for movies throughout the country – and soon, abroad – reached all-time record levels, for they had, in fact, been falling for a number of years following the growth of broadcasting in the mid-1920s. The studios lost no time in re-equipping, at considerable cost, to sound movie production. Some studios borrowed heavily from the banks, but within two years from the first screening of *The Jazz Singer*, that is, by October 1929, the Wall Street Crash had inaugurated the Depression, a world-wide catastrophic slump which closed banks, bankrupted firms and individuals, threw millions out of work for many years, and brought the film industry – as well as virtually all others – to its knees.

Although background music had been a part of the early 'talking' pictures, the sound-recording technique on film was still in its comparative infancy, and whilst it was possible for studio microphones in the late 1920s to pick up dialogue with a certain accuracy, the quality of music recording on film was far less good in comparison with speech.

This meant that the musical ingredient in the early sound films was not as well served as it should have been; in addition, distortion was a feature of much music on the early talking soundtracks, and it was to solve this particular technical problem that within a few years the quality of all sound on talking pictures (music, sound effects and dialogue) had improved considerably, to the point where it was perfectly possible for a large symphony orchestra to be recorded on film without an unacceptable level of distortion.

Many film studios had made considerable profits in the boom years of the 1920s; some were, therefore, inured to a degree from the initial effects of the Depression, despite their heavy borrowings and other costly investments when sound came. But if they could continue to make films, the studios had to make their money in the traditional manner – from a paying audience. With millions now out of work, and with movie theatres closing down in large numbers all over the country, the outlets and opportunities for the same level of earlier profits were now much reduced.

People who are unhappy do not wish to be reminded of their misery when they seek entertainment; they have a genuine desire to pursue happiness, and the movie industry responded to the social effects of the Depression with a raw energy and infectious positivism in a way that united the country at a time when it was unlikely that any other medium – with the possible exception of broadcasting, as exemplified by the 'fireside chats' of the Democratic President Franklin Delano Roosevelt, who in 1932 swept away twelve years of Republican administrations – could have achieved. What made the film industry's output so important at this time is something that all generations could witness for themselves: the movies provided a permanent record, which broadcasting could barely match. And so it was that by the end of 1930 – and certainly by 1933 – the mood of the people not only demanded a genuine escapism but also could be satisfied by the enormous advances in recording techniques of the previous three years or so. Sound had arrived, and with it the possibility of fusing speech with music to make the Hollywood musical. The subject? Broadway, of course.

Chapter 4

The Early Years: 1929-1939

The first true Hollywood musical appeared in 1929. It was not *The Jazz Singer*, nor the immediate follow-up to that film, *Lucky Boy* – starring George Jessel, one of Jolson's biggest rivals – which, it seems, was based very closely on *The Jazz Singer*. The onset of talking pictures, and talking pictures with music, led to a number of filmed musical revues, in which famous stars would be heard talking as well as singing. These could hardly be termed 'musicals' in the generally accepted sense of the term.

It was left to MGM – which became, as it turned out, arguably the greatest studio ever to have produced musical films – to make the first Hollywood musical. This was *Broadway Melody*, shot at the end of 1928, and screened for the first time in February 1929. It created something of a sensation, for it was literally the first 'All-Talking! All-Singing! All-Dancing!' (as it was advertised) movie ever made – the first Hollywood musical – as well as being the first talking picture undertaken by MGM. The dialogue was by James Gleason, the photography was by John Arnold, and the director was Harry Beaumont.

There was much in this film that was extraordinarily original, not least in the making.

The songs were all new, specially written for the movie by Nacio Herb Brown and Arthur Freed, and when it came to shoot 'Wedding Of The Painted Doll' Irving Thalberg was not impressed by the takes, and ordered it redone. But as the only unacceptable thing in the first takes was the dancing, not the music, the movie's sound engineer, Douglas Shearer, suggested it be retained and during the retakes played back to the dancers to get their choreography as Thalberg wanted. In this way, the film could be edited to match the pre-existing music. This was indeed what happened, setting a standard for the filming of musicals which has remained ever since. The noises made by the metallic-fringed costumes were also picked up, even by the comparatively primitive microphones in use in those days, so they were done away with. There were various other production problems, which were solved as the shooting continued, very much on a hand-to-mouth basis, but the MGM staff were amongst the best in the business, and their solutions sometimes gave the director new ideas for filming. The result is a fine movie, interesting in many ways – and not least for starring Charles King, a leading Broadway performer in the musical theatre, who, although he appeared in six further films, never made the transition to movie star.

The story of *Broadway Melody* concerns two sisters and the girls in a Broadway chorus; the sisters are Bessie Love and Anita Page, both of whose affections are directed towards Charles King as Eddie. In the end, after several adventures, Eddie chooses Queenie (Anita Page), affording Bessie Love a scene of touching sentiment, which is acted with no little skill. Love, who had been one of the biggest attractions in silent pictures, was one of the rare stars to make a successful transition to talkies. She was nominated for an Academy Award in 1929, and the movie justly won that year's Oscar for Best Picture.

Broadway Melody, whilst not, strictly speaking, being a film of a Broadway musical, was nonetheless about the staging of musical shows on Broadway, and as a movie it showed what could be achieved by a sympathetic and talented production team. It also made the audiences feel good.

By 1929 one of the leading Broadway composers was Sigmund Romberg, born in Hungary but living in America since before the outbreak of World War I. He was a prolific and successful composer of light operettas – not so much 'musicals' in the then-current vogue, which tended to be rather thin plays with music in a contemporary setting. Romberg's best works were those with a far-away background: far away from America, that is. In this regard, his finest scores are *The Desert Song* and *The Student Prince*.

It was the former that was chosen by Warner Brothers to be the first filmed operetta; the lure of Arabia had been very strong for Europeans and Americans in the first third of the century, from the real-life aura of Lawrence of Arabia to Rudolph Valentino's *The Sheik* of 1921 and the production of James Elroy Flecker's *Hassan* in London in 1923. Sigmund Romberg's 1926 setting of *The Desert Song* carried with it, therefore, a built-in audience interest.

The show was Oscar Hammerstein's first collaboration with Sigmund Romberg, although the lyricist had enjoyed a notable run of successes in operettas with various composers, particularly Rudolf Friml. The setting of the story of *The Desert Song* is French Morocco, and tells of the Scarlet Pimpernel-like figure, similarly called The Red Shadow, who – when he is not a bandit leader – is the somewhat wimpish son of a general. The Red Shadow is loved by two women; one a sophisticated French lady and the other a native girl. John Boles took the lead, Carlotta King and Myrna Loy were the two women (respectively) and the movie was daringly directed by Roy del Ruth.

The daring quality was that certain sequences were shot in Technicolor, and this – combined with the all-talking, all-music aspects – proved a quite exceptional draw. In many ways the film possesses some historically important features, but it is let down badly by the sound quality, which was poor – even for its day, the more disappointing in that it came from the same studio that two years earlier had electrified audiences with *The Jazz Singer*.

The following year came MGM's reply: *The Rogue Song*, after an operetta by Franz Léhar that was first produced with tremendous success in Vienna in January 1910, *Zigeunerliebe* (Gypsy Love). This film is a curious one; clearly meant to answer *The Desert Song* (the titles are similar, and the plot tells of a Russian bandit), it starred the great American baritone Lawrence Tibbett, then a great favourite with the New York Metropolitan Opera in his first film role and also included an early outing from Laurel and Hardy. The movie was directed by the great Lionel Barrymore and Hal Roach and the musical direction was by the outstanding Dmitri Tiomkin. On paper, this movie seems particularly interesting, but it seems that no known copies are in existence.

Another lost musical from 1930, also seeming to jump on the same bandwagon, is *The Vagabond King*, taken from a very successful operetta by Rudolf Friml of 1925. By all accounts, this version, which starred Dennis King, was very disappointing, King getting in the way – almost literally – of Jeanette MacDonald's Katherine. Both *The Desert Song* and *The Vagabond King* were remade in the 1950s with greater success, but one hopes that original copies may survive somewhere and be found capable of restoration.

In 1927, the American composer Harry Tierney, under the auspices of the great Florenz Ziegfeld Jr, produced his finest stage success, a musical comedy called *Rio Rita* with a book by Guy Bolton and Fred Thomson, the first film version of which was made two years later by RKO Pictures, and which also starred John Boles and the young Bebe Daniels as Rita. In 1942, MGM remade the musical, substantially changed to accommodate Bud Abbott and Lou Costello in the main starring roles.

The film musical took several strides forward in 1929 with the release of a new vehicle, written expressly for the screen by the end of 1929. This was *Sunny Side Up*, and it starred Janet Gaynor and Charles Farrell in a modern-day romantic comedy. However many strides this movie took forward with the ebullient Janet Gaynor at her best, it also took several steps backwards with the somewhat inept characterisation from Farrell.

Another film musical from this year was Paramount's *The Love Parade*, which starred Jeanette MacDonald (her first film) and the young romantic Frenchman Maurice Chevalier, a quite pleasant creation directed by Ernst Lubitsch from an adaptation by Ernest Vajda and Guy Bolton of a

play *The Prince Consort* by Leon Xanrof and Jules Chancel.

The significance of this rather faded movie lies in the casting and direction, for MacDonald and Lubitsch were together for *Monte Carlo* in 1930, a film which is otherwise unremarkable apart from the final sequence 'Beyond The Blue Horizon' – this is one of the musical cinema's finest and most influential early segments, a convincing demonstration that this was indeed a new art-form, which received another considerable reinforcement in 1931 in Lubitsch's *The Smiling Lieutenant*.

This remarkable film starred Chevalier, and was based upon Oscar Strauss's best operetta, *A Waltz Dream* which dates from 1907 and is a work characterised by a succession of superb melodies, a touching sentimentality and a wryly satirical humour. The result is a quite brilliant film, which also starred Claudette Colbert, Miriam Hopkins and George Barbier as the King of Flausenthurm, although some experts consider that the movie is not entirely beyond reproach. By 1932, the theatrical skills of Rouben Mamoulian had already led him to Hollywood. This exceptionally-gifted man had been born of Armenian extraction in Tiflis, the capital of Georgia, in 1898, but the turmoil brought by the Armenian massacres in the final years of the Ottoman Empire led to his family moving to Paris and Moscow, in which cities Rouben studied, before coming to England – as part of a Russian dance company – in 1920, and staying to continue studies at London University. In 1923, he emigrated to the USA, where he remained until his death in Los Angeles at the age of 89. Rouben Mamoulian was one of the most significant and gifted of all 20th-century producers and directors for the American musical stage, and in 1929 he had already directed his first feature film, *Applause*, for Paramount. A distinguished series of movies directed by Mamoulian followed – not so many, however, for he had a reputation for being somewhat difficult to work with – including *Love Me Tonight* of 1932, also for Paramount, which has been described by Leslie Halliwell as being "The most fluently cinematic comedy musical ever made", and by Ted Sennett as "one of the true masterpieces in the musical genre, and a film of durable wit, beauty and sophistication".

With such plaudits – and there are many more – it is somewhat surprising that this film, and Mamoulian's reputation, are not better known to to general film-going public, but – like several other masterly film musicals from this era, from different hands – *Love Me Tonight* is so completely a film that it simply could not have been transferred to any other medium without significant losses. It stars Jeanette MacDonald and Maurice Chevalier alongside a splendid cast, and the most important – purely cinematic – feature is the lead into the song, 'Isn't It Romantic?' and the song itself, which is begun by Chevalier and then taken up by a whole succession of passers-by, irrelevant to the story, and passed from one to the other until finally it arrives at Jeanette MacDonald, a Princess who eventually joins forces with Chevalier. The significance of this filmic business and its premonition of the movie's unfolding plot, to say nothing of its utter originality and subsequent influence on later film-makers, following the release of the movie on August 13, 1932, are quite exceptional.

The songs were by Richard Rodgers and Lorenz Hart, and it was the first movie for which this matchless team specially wrote: they include three of this team's finest songs, 'Isn't It Romantic?', 'Lover', and the title song, the first and last being duets for MacDonald and Chevalier. 'Lover' was the big hit, written solely for MacDonald; Chevalier's own song, 'Mimi', was not quite in the same class. The success of this score led to Rodgers and Hart writing exclusively for Hollywood movies until 1935.

The success of the film, and that of Paramount's other musical success of 1932 *The Big Broadcast*, did not go unnoticed by the studio's rivals, either. At Warner Brothers, despite their earlier finger-burning forays into the genre, the company's head of production Darryl F Zanuck decided – without the permission of the Warners themselves – to give the film musical another shot.

In 1929, Zanuck had produced a so-so film musical, in crude colour, about Broadway backstage dramas called *On With the Show*. Using this movie as a general blueprint, but determined to capitalise upon the prevailing mood for quality musicals and add new elements of street-wise, modern-day verismo, away from Europe and Ruritania, Zanuck put together a team of quite exceptional artists.

The result was a movie that was both contemporary and timeless. *42nd Street* starred Dick Powell, Warner Baxter, Ruby Keeler (Al Jolson's wife), Bebe Daniels, Ginger Rogers and George Brent, as well as a further clutch of outstanding players. The story concerns a Broadway producer who is trying to put on a show, the troubles which assail him and other production members and the dramas of the cast as they jockey for position in the show and in their lives. In the event, the show is a great success.

The music and lyrics were by Harry Warren and Al Dubin, and include one of the best of their early numbers, 'You're Getting To Be A Habit With Me' which is brilliantly performed by Bebe Daniels. But every element in this wonderful film is outstanding; the dialogue crackles and is often extremely funny, the outside world of the

Depression is never far away and adds an element of present-day reality that gives a tensile strength to the story itself. However, Zanuck's finest stroke of genius was in hiring Busby Berkeley as the choreographer, and as the director of the dance routines. In *42nd Street* it is the sensational choreography, the extraordinary use of a Broadway *corps de ballet* in a veritable kaleidoscope of dazzling photography and choreography which leaves the audience sated with pleasure.

The impact of *42nd Street* reverberated throughout the movie industry – and continued to do so 60 years later. In 1980, a very successful stage version of the movie opened on Broadway, which ran for eight years; it later successfully transferred to London. But the hit of *42nd Street* was immediately capitalised upon by Warners who in 1933 reassembled Powell and Keeler, Ned Sparks, Ginger Rogers, Harry Warren and Al Dubin – and also with Busby Berkeley as choreographer – to remake their 1929 movie *Gold Diggers Of Broadway* as *Gold Diggers Of 1933*.

The new version represents several advances on the earlier film, although that had the interest of being another early Technicolor movie – the *Gold Diggers Of 1933* was in black-and-white, as *42nd Street* had been. The story again centres upon young theatrical hopefuls on Broadway, and such songs as 'We're In The Money' personified the chasing of dreams – for the characters as well as for their audience, who are poignantly brought into sharp relief in the 'Remember My Forgotten Man' finale, with its direct tug at the emotions surrounding World War I soldiers now forgotten by contemporary society. Busby Berkeley's brilliant photographic choreography repeated the success of *42nd Street*'s more breathtaking aspects, as he was to do yet again in *Footlight Parade* – Warners' third film musical of 1933.

Once more, Dick Powell and Ruby Keeler, with Joan Blondell from *Gold Diggers Of 1933* and songs by Warren and Dubin (with other writers) – together with Busby Berkeley – were conjoined by the Warner Brothers studio for another variation on the putting-on-a-musical-on-Broadway theme. *Footlight Parade* may not have been as groundbreakingly original as *42nd Street* was – indeed, it could hardly have been, given all the criteria – but it remains a splendid film, notable for outstanding dialogue and for the star, James Cagney, here making his 14th movie but his first true leading role.

But *42nd Street* resounded throughout Hollywood. Most studios were anxiously looking for some formula to restore their fortunes in the depth of the Depression, and RKO was determined to out-do Busby Berkeley, through the imaginations of its producers Lou Brock and Merian C Cooper. The story they chose was a thin one on which to hang a musical intended to trounce *42nd Street* – it was about an American dance band and its leader (who was also an early aviator) whose success in Rio de Janeiro causes the leading lady to have to choose between him and her Brazilian boy-friend.

If the story was somewhat innocuous, made more up-to-date by the aviation interest, the other ingredients seemed reasonable for early film musical success. The score was by Vincent Youmans, a gifted but ultimately tragic figure for whom tuberculosis forced retirement in 1934 at the age of 35 yet not before he had scored the biggest musical comedy success of the 1920s on Broadway, *No, No, Nanette*. He was a major coup for RKO in 1933, and provided a fine score for the movie, including 'The Carioca', 'Orchids In The Moonlight' and 'Music Makes Me'.

The leading stars in the movie were billed as Dolores Del Rio, Gene Raymond and Raul

Roulian, but the film has passed into cinema history as being the first appearance on the screen of Fred Astaire and Ginger Rogers, whose dancing of the 'Carioca' atop seven white grand pianos is a sensation – as was flouting cinema convention by fading the film out not on the stars, but on Astaire and Rogers.

Before this fade, the highlight of the movie is the dance number performed by chorus girls strapped to the wings of airplanes flying over the city of Rio de Janeiro, while Astaire sings below them. Of course, trick photography was used, but it works so well that it remains highly convincing.

It was the combination of the aerial finale and the electricity of teaming Astaire and Rogers that ensured the fame of *Flying Down To Rio*. In other respects, the movie lacks the brash movement of *42nd Street*, and that film's contemporary relevance. However, the Astaire and Rogers combination was here to stay.

This could not have come at a more opportune moment for either partner. Astaire had enjoyed considerable success on stage in New York and in London in partnership with his sister Adele in the 1920s, but she had recently retired to marry. Fred was alone, and felt he had little to offer on his own; he was not good-looking, his acting ability was ordinary and his singing voice was equally mundane. But he could dance, and he travelled to Hollywood to seek a break into movies. It was not straightforward, but all he needed was the break. His agent at the time, Leland Hayward, managed to get him signed to RKO, but his first Hollywood movie was for MGM with Joan Crawford in *Dancing Lady*.

The break for Astaire – and for Ginger Rogers – came with the 'Carioca' in *Flying Down To Rio* in 1933. A year later, and Astaire and Rogers made the second of the ten films in which they were to star together, the first in which they had undoubted top billing.

This was *The Gay Divorcee*, a major adaptation of a successful Broadway musical by Cole Porter in which Astaire had starred in 1932. The title was changed by RKO, owing to possible censorship susceptibilities, and most of Porter's music was jettisoned as well, even if the incomparable 'Night And Day ' was retained.

The story is set in the English seaside town of Brighton, where in a grand hotel an author, Guy Holden (Astaire), who is also a keen dancer, is mistaken for a professional co-respondent by a lady (Rogers), who is anxious to divorce her husband. The leading roles and the supporting cast play their parts to perfection, but the music is the outstanding ingredient, alongside the breathtakingly assured dancing of the duo.

The realisation of 'Night And Day' is one of the great settings in all film musicals, and the big production number, 'The Continental', with its large troupe of dancers in evening dress, is overwhelming, not just in its choreography by Hermes Pan but also in its length. It lasts for almost 18 minutes and was by far the longest musical number in any film up to that time.

For the first time on screen, Astaire had found his true persona, as a nonchalant charmer, which was to mark him out for almost the rest of his career. The real innovation in this movie was that of a couple in love, dancing their emotions and feelings almost in balletic terms, something that Warner Brothers, and Busby Berkeley, had not apparently considered.

In 1934, Berkeley worked on two further Warner musicals, one of which was *Wonder Bar*, in which Al Jolson starred – but without Ruby Keeler – together with Kay Francis, Dolores Del Rio, Ricardo Cortez and the by-now ubiquitous, but always outstanding, Dick Powell. The songs were also by Warren and Dubin, and Busby

Berkeley's choreography was fully up to his own high standards, especially in the astonishing 'Don't Say Goodnight' sequence.

The other musical film was *Dames* (which was originally to have been titled *Gold Diggers Of 1934*), and – yet again – it starred Joan Blondell, Dick Powell and Ruby Keeler, and the imaginative ZaSu Pitts, whose comedy timing added much to the movie's charm. If it may be thought that yet another variation on the Broadway theme could have been one too many, especially with a broadly similar cast, the fact remains that the musical content, as much as the quick-fire repartee and choreography, continued to be of high quality – especially the staging of Warren and Dubin's classic 'I Only Have Eyes For You', a dream sequence which turns into a fabulous jigsaw puzzle. Up to now, the Warner series of musical films of the early 1930s had been marked out by a number of outstanding ingredients, but the most innovative in terms of film had been Busby Berkeley's choreography, which, from *42nd Street* onwards, he had been allowed to direct on screen. He hankered after directing an entire movie, and was given the chance in *Gold Diggers Of 1935*.

Yet another 'Broadway' film musical, once more with Dick Powell in the lead and with songs by Warren and Dubin, Busby Berkeley now had earned the chance to show what he could do. It is a fascinating movie, and – although parts of the story drag a little, no doubt due entirely to Berkeley's inexperience in this aspect of film-making – in 'Lullaby Of Broadway' the director excelled himself. Here, the choreography reaches heights of cinematic art which have never been topped, for – apart from the brilliance of the conception itself and the manner in which it was executed – the 'message' is that the allures of success on Broadway will, almost invariably, lead to tragedy. In addition, the 'The Words Are In My

Heart' sequence, choreographed to no less than 36 moving grand pianos which combine to form one gigantic instrument, is another highspot in this extraordinary film-maker's career.

Berkeley's career still had several surprises in store although he never directed an entire movie again. *Gold Diggers Of 1937* (which actually appeared in 1936) was directed by Lloyd Bacon who had directed *42nd Street* – and, probably consequently, had a rather harder edge than some of the intervening musicals from this studio. Once more, Dick Powell and Joan Blondell starred, and Harry Warren and Al Dubin were joined by 'Yip' Harburg and Harold Arlen; Busby Berkeley continued to amaze in a military-style kaleidoscope with Joan Blondell leading 70 dancing girls in formation. The last of the *Gold Diggers* series was the 1938 offering, *Gold Diggers In Paris*, directed by Ray Enright and also containing Berkeley choreography. This had songs by Warren and Dubin, and also songs by Johnny Mercer; but Dick Powell, Joan Blondell and Ruby Keeler were not in the cast. In 1935, Ruby Keeler had made the only movie in which she appeared starring opposite her husband, Al Jolson. This was *Go Into Your Dance*, a pleasant enough romp but without so very many redeeming features, apart from the irrepressible Jolson style of performing and Keeler's contrasting lightness of touch.

Powell continued to make musicals for Warner Brothers, perhaps the most interesting being *Broadway Gondolier* of 1935, which had all the right ingredients – except perhaps the essential one. With Powell and Blondell, and a good supporting cast, with songs by Warren and Dubin and directed by Lloyd Bacon, the only thing it lacked was Busby Berkeley.

The continuing success of Warners' musical team inevitably led to a formula-style which found itself in a rut. There was no such danger in the initial Astaire-Rogers movies, although a certain risk-taking in using pre-existing stage material as a basis carried with it the possibility of failure. There is always a danger in adapting for the screen something which had been a success in the theatre or elsewhere, rather than creating something wholly for movies from scratch – as was the case with *42nd Street*.

The next Astaire and Rogers movie from RKO came in 1935, an adaptation of Jerome Kern's *Roberta*, which was a very recent musical show, having opened on Broadway on November 18th 1933. It was remade in 1952 by MGM as *Lovely To Look At*. A problem here was that neither Astaire nor Rogers received top billing in the movie, which went to Irene Dunne as a Russian princess who works for a Paris fashion house which is inherited by Randolph Scott, Astaire's friend in the movie – Astaire being a band leader. Ginger Rogers plays Countess Schwarenka, who is a little down on her luck, and sings at the Café Russe. Two new songs were added for the movie, although they were not written by Kern, but by Dorothy Fields with lyrics by Oscar Hammerstein II and Jimmy McHugh (the show's lyrics were by Otto Harbach), but were not at all out of place – 'Lovely To Look At' and 'I Won't Dance' – alongside such masterly Kern songs as 'Smoke Gets In Your Eyes', which provided one of the dancing team's finest moments.

Despite the Astaire-Rogers team seemingly not warranting top billing in *Roberta*, the very next RKO movie, released during that same year of 1935, showed them to be the biggest box-office attractions of the age. The splendid *Top Hat*, with music specially written for this, his first film score, by Irving Berlin, has one of the greatest musical film scores ever written: songs such as 'Isn't This A Lovely Day To Be Caught In The Rain?', 'Cheek To Cheek' and 'Top Hat, White Tie And Tails'

together raised this movie into the immortal class. The setting, Hollywood's view of London, is a wonderland of wealth and privilege, worlds away from the universal Depression that still was the daily grind for the overwhelming majority of cinema audiences. The plot, such as it is, is wafer-thin, but the dancing and singing – to say nothing of the quality of the music – and that almost inexplicable chemistry from Fred and Ginger added several new qualities to the genre. *Top Hat* demonstrates, as no other film musical of the 1930s does to the same degree, the possibility of creating a lasting movie of this type without colour – although shot in black-and-white, the colour is in the film itself.

It has been suggested – not without reason – that the sheerly glamorous settings of Fred Astaire and Ginger Rogers movies up to then might have brought about a backlash on the part of the public – even if the box office receipts showed no such reaction – and that the more mundane setting of their next movie for RKO, *Follow The Fleet* of 1936 was driven by these considerations. Even so, the chemistry again worked its wonders – Astaire is a sailor who teams up with his old dancing partner Ginger Rogers (a dance-hall hostess) when his ship docks in port.

Once more Irving Berlin provided the songs, and once again he handed in an outstanding score: 'We Saw The Sea', 'Let's Face The Music And Dance', 'Let Yourself Go' – these are but three of the seven new numbers he wrote for the film. Perhaps the problem with this movie, which is still a stunning example of the genre, is its profligacy of talent: seven songs in one film is a lot, if the film was not originally a musical. Consequently, at 110 minutes (and with more songs than *Top Hat*, which was about 10-15 minutes shorter), *Follow The Fleet* gives the impression of being just a little too long for the material.

Much less than a year later, Astaire and Rogers were back in the studios of RKO for *Swing Time*. This did not exactly recreate the glitzy world of *Top Hat*, but it was rather more in that vein than *Follow The Fleet*; this time, however, the songs were by Jerome Kern and Dorothy Fields, and once again, the quality of the music has ensured another masterly film of its type: such titles as 'The Way You Look Tonight', 'A Fine Romance', and the opening number, 'Pick Yourself Up' – an absolutely outstanding beginning to the movie – would have graced any show, in the theatre or on the screen, and – at just over 100 minutes – the film exhibits none of the dangers of longueur as could be levelled against *Follow The Fleet*, although in one number, for the only time in his career, Astaire blacked up for 'Bojangles Of Harlem', a brilliant piece of solo dancing that for social reasons could hardly be countenanced today.

The duo were now at the peak of their profession. In 1937, as we shall see, they made a series of films so speedily as to be echoed only in the 1960s by Elvis Presley – and without the same style or panache. Their next RKO movie was *Shall We Dance*, a movie that, in many ways, restored the couple's social fortunes on film in that it takes place amongst the higher echelons of society. It is also a significant film for rather more lasting reasons: this was the finest movie for which George and Ira Gershwin had written the score. It was, as could perhaps have been expected, fully up to the standards of Irving Berlin and Jerome Kern's earlier work for Astaire and Rogers, and contains – in the three great numbers, 'They All Laughed', 'Let's Call The Whole Thing Off' and 'They Can't Take That Away From Me' – some of the Gershwins' best work. However, a level of criticism has been made of this film: it is said to contain too much repetition of earlier work; at

one point Astaire dances with a new partner (Harriet Hoctor) for one song; and its length at just under two hours appeared to others to be getting out of hand. In other words, an element of self-indulgence was thought to be setting in. These criticisms may or may not be true: what cannot be denied is that here was a film that was eminently enjoyable and is still very much worth seeing today. 'They Can't Take That Away From Me' was nominated for an Academy Award.

But *Shall We Dance*, for all its qualities, was still in danger of becoming yet another chapter in the duo's career, and both Astaire and Rogers felt that their individual talents should be recognised in movies where they did not automatically have to appear opposite one another. There was, by all inside accounts, no animosity in this: they both felt they needed a change.

And so it was that within a few months Astaire without Rogers made *A Damsel In Distress* with George Burns, Gracie Allen and a somewhat disappointing Joan Fontaine (Miss Fontaine's dancing skills were manifestly not in the Astaire class on the one duet she had with him). But the score was again provided by the Gershwins, and there were three very good solo spots for Astaire in another Hollywoodian view of London – 'A Foggy Day', 'Nice Work If You Can Get It' and 'I Can't Be Bothered Now'. The most enduring segment in the film, however, is the brilliantly choreographed scene in an amusement park, in which Astaire, Burns and Allen are quite outstanding.

Ginger Rogers, meanwhile, had been hard at work on her first solo starring film, *Vivacious Lady*, appearing opposite James Stewart. This was a fine romantic comedy, and showed that Ginger could well act this kind of role without the prop of choreography, but it was not a musical.

The individual points having been made, RKO

reunited the team in 1938 in *Carefree*. George Gershwin had died suddenly in July 1937 at the age of 38; Irving Berlin provided the music for this reunion, but even if the plot was a cut above some of the earlier ones in terms of dramatic possibilities, the music was not quite in the same class and it is clear – even today – that the earlier magic the two had brought uniquely to the screen was ebbing away. It was even clearer then, and in 1939 RKO brought them together for the last time: in 1949 MGM reunited them for *The Barkleys Of Broadway*, but their last RKO picture was a biopic *The Story Of Vernon And Irene Castle*. This told of a famous American husband and wife dance team of the early years of the century, whose career was cut short when Vernon was killed as a pilot in World War I. The rather cumbersome title, which – it appears – was insisted upon by Mrs Castle herself, undoubtedly told against the box office appeal of the movie, which – in the nature of things, as it is based on true events, with many of the protagonists then still living – is not at all a bad film. The central fact, that Astaire and Rogers were not creating characters made in their own image, but were recreating pre-existing ones, made this film somewhat disappointing for dyed-in-the-wool fans, but it is nonetheless a worthy movie, true to its subject, and permitting its lead stars the chance to show they could act very well.

The smash that *42nd Street* had become, as we have already noted, was hardly lost on rival studios. In the first half of 1934, the already financially-troubled Fox Studios had released *Stand Up And Cheer*, which was such a blatant attempt to make money out of the Depression – and to exhort Americans to get happy about it – as to be almost breathtaking in the inherent crassness of its ethos. In this movie, the US Government has a Secretary of Amusement, who decides to enjoin the whole country (it seems) in putting on a show that will make everyone happy. Perhaps we are being too hard on what were undoubtedly good intentions, but the interesting thing about this film is not that its story is so vacuous – there were plenty of other good film musicals at the time which did not stretch the intellect – or that some of its most impressive moments are carbon copies (inevitably rather blurred or faded) of Busby Berkeley routines, but that a young lady appeared in it who stole the show. She was six years old, and her name was Shirley Temple, to whom we shall return later, in a general discussion of her movies starting with *Bright Eyes*, also from 1934.

If the influence of Berkeley was notable in *Stand Up And Cheer*, it was even more palpable in *George White's Scandals* of 1934. This was nothing more than a peg on which to hang several acts, but it starred Rudy Vallee and marked the debut of Alice Faye – the two became lovers in real life, and their explosive combustion can be discerned on screen in no uncertain terms. But neither film could entirely save Fox Studios, who in 1935 merged with 20th Century pictures. In turn, 20th Century had just made a musical film of its own, *Folies Bergere* with Maurice Chevalier, one of the best and most innovative musical films of its day. It is not a brash movie, but a literate and intelligent one, and has all the production values allied to a script that, for its day, was remarkably forward-looking in its attitude to sexual innuendo.

As it happened, the resultant commercial union made 20th Century-Fox one of the big players in motion pictures, and the new company's first film musical *Thanks A Million* was a shrewd mixture of established star (Dick Powell), good book (Nunnally Johnson), excellent direction (Roy del Ruth), good songs (Gus Kahn) and a new slant for musicals – politics. This was not an entirely new subject, however, for the

Gershwins had used it in *Let 'Em Eat Cake*. Compared with the all-or-nothing power of the Astaire-Rogers musicals of the time, the 20th Century-Fox movies were subtler, if no less light-hearted and lively.

In 1936 the headlined pursuit of John Barrymore by Elaine Barrie was used as the basis for *Sing Baby Sing* which tells of a drunken Shakespearean actor who fancies a night-club singer to distraction. The music was good, from various sources, and Alice Faye and Adolphe Menjou were brilliant, as were the Ritz Brothers (as always): there was a great deal of humour in this committee-written script, as in the next 20th Century-Fox musical, *Wake Up And Live*, which was likewise based on a current story. This film is about a feud between a radio commentator and a band leader (hence the music) and also starred Alice Faye, after Ben Bernie and his Band and Walter Winchell had taken top billings.

1936 also saw the debut of Sonja Henie, the Norwegian ice-skating champion, in *One In A Million*, the first of several musicals, of – it has to be admitted – gradually declining appeal, all based around her skating skills. Henie had a charm and winsome personality, but she could not act, and her best film by far was her first.

Another Alice Faye 20th Century-Fox musical of 1937 was *You Can't Have Everything*, more notable perhaps for Gypsy Rose Lee's screen debut (as Louise Hovick, her real name), but the more important movie was *On The Avenue* (Park Avenue) with Dick Powell, Madeleine Carroll and the Ritz Brothers, and with a stylish score by Irving Berlin, including 'I've Got My Love To Keep Me Warm'. It was written by Gene Markey and William Conselman, and directed by the gifted Roy del Ruth, and, at a little under 90 minutes, has a pace and vibrancy which lifts it into the superior class.

However, in 1937 the highest paid actress in Hollywood was not yet ten years old. This was Shirley Temple, who for 20th Century-Fox made a series of endearing musical films that were notable for her absolute charm and considerable screen presence, allied to her outstanding gifts as a singer, dancer and actress. It may seem strange to claim all of these characteristics for a nine-year-old to later generations, but the proof is there – in the movies themselves – and in the money she was paid.

Her 1934 movie *Bright Eyes* was the first in which the adorable little mite starred and which provided her first hit – 'On The Good Ship Lollipop'. It told the story of an orphan who is torn between various foster-parents. The sensation was at once capitalised upon by 20th Century-Fox, who put substantially more money in Shirley Temple's next film, *The Little Colonel* of 1935, set in the American South after the Civil War, which has an unusual colour sequence set in the largely black-and-white movie. In the next few years, Shirley Temple made seven more movies – *The Littlest Rebel*, *Curly Top*, *Poor Little Rich Girl*, *Captain January*, *Stowaway*, *Heidi* and *Little Miss Broadway*. It has to be said that the films hardly advanced the genre, but they were superb vehicles for a major talent, the like of which was utterly unique in every sense of the word. After 1938, Shirley Temple's appeal began to wane, but by then she had made a contribution to film musical history that will endure for as long as movies are shown.

It was 20th Century-Fox in 1938 that made, in *Alexander's Ragtime Band*, one of the finest fictionalised screen biographies. This starred an unusual but remarkably successful team, Alice Faye and Tyrone Power, and was chock-full of some of Irving Berlin's most famous songs – no less than 26 of them! – in a movie that made a great star of Alice Faye, just in time for 20th

Century-Fox, as Shirley Temple's appeal had begun to wane. In the next few years, Faye was to appear in a number of less-than-inspired film musicals, even if none of them was by any standards a bad movie. *Alexander's Ragtime Band* remains, however, a great film.

It is a curious fact that the studio that perhaps came to mean most for many people in later years with regard to Hollywood musicals, MGM, was not in the forefront of the genre in the early-to-mid-1930s. The impact of Warners' *42nd Street*, as we have seen, was considerable, right across the industry – and in 1933 MGM jumped on the almost literal bandwagon with *Dancing Lady*, a vehicle for Joan Crawford based, none too subtly, on *42nd Street itself* – backstage shenanigans and the occasional song. Joan Crawford made a reasonable fist of the part, but her talent lay more clearly in dramatic roles.

However, MGM had found itself in the forefront of making films of operettas of yesteryear: they began in 1933 with *The Merry Widow*, which had been first produced in Vienna in 1905, the film version starring Jeanette MacDonald and Maurice Chevalier. There were well-reported differences between the co-stars – effectively, the score is slanted almost entirely in the direction of the female lead – and the older English language version was updated (but not too much). Despite good performances and good production values (and a lot of money) the film was not the great success Louis B Mayer had hoped it would be. Nonetheless, it was an excellent vehicle for Jeanette MacDonald, and in the next MGM operetta, *Naughty Marietta* from 1910, she was starring alongside the man with whose name she would forever thereafter be professionally inextricably linked: Nelson Eddy. This was an enormous success, taking more in box office receipts than almost any other musical

film up to that time.

This was the combination MGM had been looking for: Rudolf Friml's *Rose-Marie* was next; or, rather, was used as the basis for a story which varied in no little way from the original. But the outstanding original music – notably the 'Indian Love-Call' – became synonymous with MacDonald and Eddy for the rest of their lives. Their next operetta was Sigmund Romberg's *Maytime* which proved to be arguably the best of their films, considered purely as film, and in the May Day country fair the couple excelled themselves.

By 1934, the slowly building career of a young singer under contract to Paramount Pictures had risen to the point of take-off. He was Bing Crosby, who in the previous few years had appeared in a number of inoffensive, and nonetheless innocuous, movies in which he sang the occasional song. In that year, however, he made a first-class musical comedy for Paramount, *Here Is My Heart*, plus an excellent supporting cast with Kitty Carlisle, Roland Young, Alison Skipworth, Reginald Owen and Akim Tamiroff. This was not exactly a sensation, but it did good business, and ensured a starring role in the film version of Cole Porter's *Anything Goes*, which was made in 1936, and is considered in further detail in Part II. Further Bing Crosby Paramount musicals to follow in the next few years were *Pennies From Heaven* (which had Louis Armstrong), *Mississippi* (with WC Fields in a film-stealing role), *Rhythm On The Range*, *Waikiki Wedding*, *Double Or Nothing* and *Sing, You Sinners* of 1938. During this period, Crosby established himself as the archetypically artless and flippant star who is fazed by nothing and always seems to come out on top, even if his beginnings were humble. He had starred in *The Big Broadcast Of 1936* (in the 1938 *Big Broadcast* movie, Bob Hope made his Hollywood debut – although Bing Crosby was not in that film), and the 'year'-type musical movies had become something of an annual fashion parade. If Paramount had the *Big Broadcasts*, MGM had the *Broadway Melodies*.

In *Broadway Melody Of 1936* Eleanor Powell made her MGM debut; this followed – at seven years' distance – the success of the original 1929 *Broadway Melody*, and remains a pretty good movie in its own right, becoming arguably Powell's very best film. She was more than ably supported by Robert Taylor (who actually sings in the movie), Jack Benny and by Buddy and Vilma Ebsen. 'Sing Before Breakfast' is a gem.

The movie was directed by Roy del Ruth, and he was re-engaged for the first of the two follow-ups; *Broadway Melody Of 1938* – not quite in the same class, in spite of having some major talent on board, including Sophie Tucker and Judy Garland along with Buddy Ebsen and Eleanor Powell and George Murphy. For the 1940 edition, he was replaced by Norman Taurog, who made the very best of some less than inspired material, although he enjoyed the luxury of having Fred Astaire and Eleanor Powell as the lead team.

The major MGM musical film of 1936 was *The Great Ziegfeld*, a quite splendiferous screen biography of the undoubtedly great American impresario, Florenz Ziegfeld, who had died in 1932, and who was more than affectionately remembered in this three-hour epic, in which William Powell played Ziegfeld. The film is only of value to the extent of being so ludicrously over-long, and for containing several production numbers of quite spectacular extravagance. One of Ziegfeld's greatest finds was Eddie Cantor, who made a number of occasionally quite brilliant musical films for Samuel Goldwyn productions in the late 1920s and 1930s. The first Cantor-Goldwyn film was *Whoopee*, released in 1930, and more notable for marking the film debut of Busby

Berkeley as choreographer. Perhaps the best Cantor movie was *Kid Millions*, of 1934, in which he plays a young man from the slums who inherits a million dollars and thereafter proceeds to enjoy life.

The spending of money had become something of an MGM trademark in film musicals, not always with the result of showing suitable returns on the investment, but in the film version of *Rosalie* in 1938, which also starred Eleanor Powell, alongside Nelson Eddy, the studio pulled off one of the best movies of the genre at that time. This included new material by Cole Porter, in particular 'In The Still Of The Night', which alone would have ensured the commercial success of any film.

Nelson Eddy without Jeanette MacDonald had been pre-empted the previous year (1937) when Rudolf Friml's first operetta, *The Firefly* which dates from 1912, was filmed with MacDonald co-starring with Allan Jones. Friml was certainly then very much alive, and he contributed to the film version a new song, which became one of the most popular he ever wrote – the world-famous 'Donkey Serenade'. Eddy regarded Allan Jones as a serious rival, his fears being confirmed by Universal's outstanding film of Jerome Kern and Oscar Hammerstein II's great *Show Boat*, which they had made in 1936, starring Jones and Irene Dunne. with Paul Robeson singing the role of Joe.

But the public still hankered after Jeanette MacDonald and Nelson Eddy, who were reunited twice in 1938 – for *The Girl Of The Golden West*, with music by Romberg (by no means one of their better films) and for *Sweethearts*, their first Technicolor movie, and in fact MGM's first all-colour film for nine years. A little on the long side (exactly two hours), this is for many people the best film they ever made. The score was by Victor Herbert and it is clear that, for once, the bickering of the story line (two musical stars are constantly at loggerheads) found perfect personifications in the duo's portrayals. In the early 1940s Jeanette MacDonald and Nelson Eddy made three more films together, but each marked a decline on its predecessor. By that time, the film musical had taken several giant steps forward.

For in 1939 came the greatest film musical of all time, *The Wizard Of Oz*. So important was this movie for a whole host of reasons, that in strict terms, it has no place in this book, for it most assuredly did not begin on Broadway or any other place of like ilk. It remains a masterpiece, an endearing, fabulous piece of fantasy and wonderland, of beauty and hauntingly simple songs, of homespun philosophy all brought to immortal life by the cinema at its best – doing something which could not be done in any other way. Indeed, quite apart from making Judy

Garland immortal (it had to happen sooner or later, and it were better it were sooner), *The Wizard Of Oz* has had an influence way beyond that of almost all other movies. There can surely be no question that it influenced not only other film makers, but also theatrical producers, too. It has also exerted influences on almost all later generations of children and adults.

With *The Wizard Of Oz* it was soon evident that a new era had dawned. By 1940 the Hollywood musical had reached the height of its early success, and with the dawning of a new decade, made more uncertain by the outbreak of a war in Europe that would soon spread around the world, audiences across the globe looked to the cinema to help them pursue the happiness they felt was theirs by right. A golden age was shortly to dawn to help millions of them in that self-evident pursuit.

Part II

From A Golden Age

Chapter 5

Anything Goes

The musical *Anything Goes* is unique in that it was filmed twice, 20 years apart, with the same star taking the male lead in both movies. It is one of Cole Porter's finest scores, and therefore, by implication, one of his finest sets of lyrics, yet in the filming most of his original material was jettisoned and replaced by songs from other writers.

The show *Anything Goes* has been described with justification as possibly the quintessential 1930s Broadway musical – a superb antidote to the drab miseries of the Depression years. Not that the show reflects being born out of the economic climate of the early 30s for it is almost literally an escapist story – 'almost literally' as it takes place on an Atlantic liner sailing from New York to England.

Some years earlier, such pure escapism might have generated a backlash, but in 1934 the signs of an American recovery were there – Roosevelt had been elected President in 1932, and by 1934 his New Deal had begun; Prohibition had been repealed, the National Industrial Recovery Act (NRA) had been implemented, John Dillinger was killed, Al Capone was behind bars and the power of the Chicago gangs had been broken; things were looking up. But in Europe, following Adolf

Hitler's election in Germany the previous year, the outlook was not so rosy – Hitler had taken supreme power and the Saar would soon be returned to a Greater Germany, the seeds of the Spanish Civil War had been sown and the Italian war with Ethiopia showed, in no uncertain fashion, the way things were going to go.

From whichever side of the Atlantic one looked at it, the need for some form of escapism was real, and this show, more than any other in Cole Porter's output until *Kiss Me, Kate* (qv), summed up his outstanding genius as a writer of shows for the musical theatre. It may be that Porter's own privileged background had shielded him from the ravages of the Depression, but he was not so insensitive to what was going on as to ignore the consequences entirely. What he knew was that it was probably not within the confines of musical comedy to make light of these difficulties; his contribution to the pursuit of happiness was to make people feel better – to lighten their lives in some way – an admirable, and profoundly artistic view: not 'reflecting' life, but showing how life might be enhanced. He was not alone in thinking along these lines, for the admirable Gershwin brothers team of George and Ira had attempted much the same thing in their shows *Pardon My*

Donald O'Connor in Paramount's 1955 production of *Anything Goes*.

English and *Let 'Em Eat Cake*, both of which appeared in 1933 but, equally, both shows had flopped: perhaps they were not right for their time, but for whatever reason, they were the last musicals for the theatre this team were to write. The grand opera *Porgy And Bess*, to which we shall return on other pages, does not come into this category.

If the Gershwins had retired from the scene by 1934 then Cole Porter was getting into his stride, following the success of his 1932 show *The Gay Divorce* and the lesser-regarded *Nymph Errant* of 1933. In this pursuit, he was ably assisted in *Anything Goes* by the great Guy Bolton and PG Wodehouse, all three driven initially by the enthusiasm for the project of the powerful Broadway producer Vinton Freedley, who had had his fingers burned in the *Pardon My English* failure but was keen to get a vehicle for the major star he had engaged for his next production – Ethel Merman. The Gershwins had turned the idea down, and so had the other great Broadway team of Rodgers and Hart, but Porter accepted with alacrity.

There is a great story concerning the initial meeting between Cole Porter, Guy Bolton and PG Wodehouse in Le Touquet, south of Boulogne-sur-Mer, where the three were to discuss progress on the show. Wodehouse – at whose house the meeting took place – did not have a piano, so they went to a local bar which had one, at which Porter played several of the songs he had written, including 'I Get A Kick Out Of You' and 'You're The Top', but a drunk customer complained and asked Porter to "play something good".

The drunk was not alone: Vinton Freedley was not enamoured of the book, which was originally – as his idea – about a shipwreck; then Guy Bolton was rushed to hospital in Brighton with a burst appendix so neither he nor Wodehouse –

who was then engaged upon other work – could work on the rewrite. In fact, *Anything Goes* was PG Wodehouse's last work for the musical theatre.

Time was running out when, against all odds, and with other theatrical luminaries Howard Lindsay (who was to produce the show) and Russel Crouse drafted in to help, new songs written (including the title number) and others dropped, the show finally opened at the Alvin Theatre on West 52nd Street on November 21, 1934.

By all accounts, it was the glitziest opening night since the Depression began and, apart from Ethel Merman, *Anything Goes* starred William Gaxton, Bettina Hall and Victor Moore. It ran for 420 performances – very good in the mid-1930s – and almost seven months after it debuted on Broadway, the show opened in London on June 14 at the Palace Theatre, produced by CB Cochran and directed by Frank Collins and with the French star Jeanne Aubert in the lead role, whose name was changed from Reno Sweeney to Reno Lagrange in deference to her nationality and her accent. Mlle Aubert co-starred alongside Jack Whiting, Adele Dixon and Sydney Howard, and, although the score was much admired in London, it ran only for a little under nine months. Nevertheless, it was sufficient for Cole Porter's music to have taken several steps upwards in the appreciation of the British public.

That same year, Paramount made the movie. Produced by Benjamin Glazer and directed by Lewis Milestone, this is another of those American film musical comedies of the 1930s in the mould of *42nd Street*. Like that masterpiece, it is also in black-and-white, but, unlike it, it lacks consistent electricity. Ethel Merman recreated her stage role, the original Reno Sweeney, delivering her three outstanding songs – 'Anything Goes', 'I Get A Kick

Out Of You' and 'You're The Top' with unabashed vitality and skill, and Bing Crosby played Billy Crocker, the personable young man who stows away on the liner to be near his sweetheart, Hope Harcourt (played by Ida Lupino in the movie). Charles Ruggles played Moon-face Mooney a character who first appears disguised on the liner as a clergyman. As it turns out, he is on the run to Europe as America's Public Enemy number 13).

A disappointing aspect of the movie is that only three of Porter's original songs were retained for it. This was not such an unusual facet of Hollywood filming of musicals as might first appear 60 years later, nor has the practice entirely disappeared, but it is a shame that the complete score was not used. The additional material was by Leo Robin and Frederick Hollander (their songs were 'Shanghai-di-ho', 'My Heart And I' and 'Hopelessly In Love'), by Leo Robin and Richard Whiting ('Sailor Beware'), and Hoagy Carmichael and Edward Heyman ('Moonbeam').

If the show was possibly the quintessential 1930s musical, the film was not. It is difficult to put one's finger on the reason, but perhaps it boils down to the show not being one that would transfer well to the screen. This is a surprising disappointment, for the locale – an ocean liner – would seem to be more suited for cinematic treatment than a theatrical staging.

There are some delicious moments, but at heart Ethel Merman was at her best in front of a live audience, where her infectious enthusiasm could be felt – almost tangibly – across the footlights. She was not the same person, talented and attractive though she was as an all-round performer, before a camera. In spite of some excellent moments, the film was not the equal of the show.

Nor, it has to be said, was the 1956 remake, also by Paramount, and also starring Bing Crosby. This was in VistaVision and in Technicolor and was directed by Robert Emmett Dolan.

Chapter 6

Brigadoon

One of the more remarkable aspects of 20th-century American popular musical life is that most of its greatest exponents were either born in Europe or were first-generation Americans. One of the former composers was Frederick Loewe, who was born in Vienna on June 10, 1904 into a very musical family. His father was Edmund Loewe, a noted operatic tenor of his day, and he was related to Ferdinand Loewe, a pupil of the composer Anton Bruckner and a gifted symphonic conductor.

Young Frederick himself was classically-trained: he studied the piano with Busoni and D'Albert, and composition with Emil von Reznicek. He seemed destined for a classical career, but already at the age of 15 he had composed a song called 'Katrina', which has a line claiming her to be 'the girl with the best legs in Berlin'.

However, it was classical music that brought Frederick Loewe to the USA – although he stayed after tragic circumstances obliged him to. He accompanied his father on a concert tour of America, but soon after their arrival his father died suddenly, leaving the young Frederick alone and penniless.

Forced on to his own devices, the youth showed considerable presence of mind. He earned money as a boxer, mailman, horse riding instructor and cowboy, as well as an itinerant musician. His first songs for Broadway shows date from the mid-1930s but he had spasmodic success. He was also trying to make a career as a concert pianist, but when he met , by chance, Alan Jay Lerner in 1942, they hit it off immediately despite their difference in ages and background.

Alan Jay Lerner had been born in New York on August 31, 1918; his family was prosperous and literate. It is said that his father, a highly successful chain-store owner, would ensure that Alan went to every new Broadway show as it opened, and it so happened that his mother had taken singing lessons with the mother of Richard Rodgers. Alan's mother also ensured that her son received a wide cultural education – which was enhanced by his enrolment variously at Choate College in Connecticut, Bedales' Public School in England, the Juilliard School of Music in New York and at Harvard University.

This was an education, indeed, and Alan Jay Lerner came to love European art, and perhaps British art above all, in each of its manifestations. Whilst some have pointed out that this love can be discerned in almost every one of Lerner's subjects

Cyd Charisse and Gene Kelly in the MGM film of *Brigadoon*.

for his collaborations with Frederick Loewe, the fact remains that in *Paint Your Wagon* he set that show in the Wild West of the 19th-century. Another unusual facet of Lerner's subjects is his fascination for the metaphysical – there is, it seems, almost an 'other-worldliness' about his choice of subject-matter which sets him somewhat apart from his contemporaries. A useful byproduct of this fascination for the composer is that it provides a much wider range of expression. The composer is stretched, as it were, beyond the rather more often met with emotions of love and jealousy.

Be that as it may, and we shall consider these aspects of his work later on in this book, it may well have been Frederick Loewe's own European classical background that first attracted him to Alan Jay Lerner. Nonetheless, the first collaboration between them, *What's Up?*, which appeared towards the end of 1943, proved to be disastrous. As Lerner himself later admitted: "*What's Up?* was not even promising."

Their second collaboration, *The Day Before Spring* appeared 18 months or so later; this was markedly more successful by comparison, although it did not set Broadway on fire. It contained two good songs, 'I Love You This Morning' and 'A Jug Of Wine', but is otherwise unremarkable.

With Frederick Loewe and Alan Jay Lerner's third collaboration, however, they struck gold. This was *Brigadoon*. With this, the mystical side of Lerner's nature came into its own. It tells the metaphysical story of a mythical Scottish town – Brigadoon – which comes to life only once every 100 years, which event occurs during a stay by two American tourists. One of these visitors, Tommy, falls in love with a local girl, Fiona, although he is already spoken for in his home town in America, and it is only through some further magicking,

that the visitors are able to leave Brigadoon at last, before it returns to its place in history, and escape home to the present-day.

But back in America Tommy breaks off his engagement and manages to persuade his friend Jeff to go back to Scotland with him to find Fiona. When they return their search appears fruitless and when they are on the point of giving up, Mr Lundie, the old schoolmaster of Brigadoon appears, and explains that Tommy's love for Fiona is so powerful that it has broken the spell of the 100 years' sleep. Mr Lundie has come to take Tommy back with him to Brigadoon, and they disappear from view, Tommy now returning forever to his Fiona, an event wrought by the power of love.

This is a story of some power, and in many ways was just what Broadway had been waiting for. It contains some elements of the supernatural and folk-lore, a yearning, nostalgic look backwards to a mythical golden age in which everyone was good to each other. This escapism was just what was needed in the immediate post-war years, a point not lost on Rodgers and Hammerstein either in *Carousel*, which bears a family resemblance to *Brigadoon* in its changes of time and place, in its supernatural element and in its setting in a stylised community of long ago.

The producer on Broadway (almost a last gasp for the show's creators, but in the event a perfect match) was Cheryl Crawford and the director was Robert Lewis. The show starred David Brooks as Tommy, Marion Bell as Fiona and George Keane as Jeff, but another star was the choreography by Agnes de Mille, which Alan Jay Lerner said was "To our everlasting good fortune".

But a problem for Lerner and Loewe (and everyone else connected with the show) was that another show, on a not dissimilar subject, had opened on Broadway a few weeks before, so the market for whimsical Gaelic leprechaun-cum-magic-cum-fantasy had been scooped by Yip Harburg and Burton Lane. Their show was *Finian's Rainbow* which outsold *Brigadoon* in New York but flopped badly in London, whereas the West End run of *Brigadoon* was notably longer than its Broadway equivalent. *Finian's Rainbow* is a good show, with a fine score and excellent individual songs: 'Something Sort Of Grandish' and 'Old Devil Moon' for examples, but it was not filmed until 21 years later, by which time the magic of the original had long gone, even though it marked Fred Astaire's final appearance (at the age of 69) starring in a musical.

However, if *Brigadoon* was upstaged on Broadway – but only relatively so, for it ran for almost 600 performances at the Ziegfeld Theatre, after it opened on March 13, 1947 – as mentioned above, it took to London admirably. It opened at His Majesty's Theatre on April 14, 1949 with Philip Hanna and Hiram Sherman as Tommy and Jeff, and – a daring piece of casting – the operatic soprano Patricia Hughes as Fiona. All was well in this production.

The story naturally afforded Frederick Loewe the chance to write some characterful music in a locale outside of the USA; his score is a delightful amalgam of modern-day music with what might be termed 'Scottish-tourist' – but it works, admirably. The real hit of this show is 'Almost Like Being In Love', one of the first great post-war songs and a well-deserved standard popular song. This alone would have made a hit show out of almost anything, and with *Brigadoon* the team of Lerner and Loewe had finally arrived.

The MGM film version, produced by Arthur Freed, has been almost universally panned for one reason or another, but it is not a bad movie. Its main plus points are the brilliance of Gene Kelly, Cyd Charisse and Van Johnson, and if the direction of Vincente Minnelli has been quite strongly criticised at times for being uncertain, and the sets for not being real, such subjective views overlook the essential whimsicality of the material which seems to cry out for just the kind of unreal settings it gets. Anything directed by Minnelli has to be worth watching, and even those who dislike the film overall have to admit that the movie contains some excellent moments – in particular, the opening shot, which shows the town appearing out of the mists. Shot in Cinemascope and rare Ansocolor, the combination gives a unique feel to this film which sets it apart from almost any other, for, whatever happens from now on – after the film has begun – we are in a magical world, where realism has no place.

Chapter 7

Cabaret

In 1930, the 26-year-old Englishman Christopher Isherwood, having decided to abandon his medical studies at King's College in London, went to Germany to teach English there. He had already, as a student, tried his hand at what he really wanted to do, which was to write novels, and in Berlin, in the concluding years of the post-war Weimar Republic, he found a rich seam of material to mine.

This was the period just before Hitler came to power in January 1933, which was also the year in which Isherwood left Germany, but not before his stay had provided him with the inspiration for such novels as *Mr Norris Changes Trains* and *Goodbye To Berlin*, and the eponymous character for one of his more enduring stories, *Sally Bowles*, which appeared in 1937.

Two years after that story appeared, Isherwood emigrated to the USA. In Hollywood, he soon earned a living as a scriptwriter for MGM before he eventually took American citizenship in 1946. His literary work is original and distinguished, and covers a wide range, but his years in Berlin produced his most famous work – so far as the general public is concerned.

After the Second World War, several of Isherwood's Berlin stories were adapted by John Van Druten and made into a successful Broadway play, *I Am A Camera* in 1951, which was later none-too-well filmed in England in 1955, starring Julie Harris, Laurence Harvey and Shelley Winters.

The story was semi-autobiographical and told of a young English man in Berlin in the early 30s who has a platonic relationship there with a somewhat wanton and reckless English girl, Sally Bowles. The story, with its rather unique character and intriguing locale, continued to exert a strong fascination for various people, including Howard Prince, who it seems had hankered to make a musical out of it for some time before he mentioned it one day in the early 1960s to the writer and lyricist Joe Masteroff, who had had no little success earlier with the musicals *She Loves Me* and *The Warm Peninsula*.

Masteroff sketched out a scenario, but this was not to everyone's taste (including his own) and he and Prince decided to go back to the original Isherwood material rather than stay with the play. Prince had in mind to approach Sandy Wilson, the British composer whose 1920s-pastiche *The Boy Friend* had been a surprising success on both sides of the Atlantic in the mid-1950s. *The Boy Friend* had also been the vehicle which first

Joel Grey recreated on film the part of Emcee in *Cabaret*.

brought Julie Andrews to Broadway.

However, in the event, it seems that Wilson's projected music – he actually fully sketched several numbers – lacked the hard-edge which Prince thought the treatment would demand. With no hard feelings on either side, Prince turned from Sandy Wilson to John Kander and Fred Ebb, a young Broadway team of composer and lyricist, whose undoubted talents had not yet produced the major show of which their admirers knew them to be capable.

Not for the first time in Prince's career – and certainly not for the last – his choice proved particularly astute, for he had chosen a team who were not only prepared to mould their own creative personalities to the nature of the job in hand, but also capable of doing so. This was a crucial attribute, for all the elements of the show were to be under Prince's control to a degree hardly ever seen before in the work of a Broadway producer and director.

The cabaret of the title is both a venue, the Kit Kat Klub, and a parallel for the drama – a reflection, in other words, of early 1930s society in Berlin. The notion of a hard-edged cabaret was Prince's own, recalling a venue he knew in Stuttgart during his military service in the US Army in the early 1950s. This night-club was infamous for having, among other things, a Master of Ceremonies – the Emcee – whose face was whitened, whose lips were painted bright red and who wore large false eyelashes.

This bizarre, all-seeing, all-knowing character was to exert a strong influence on Prince's ideas for staging the show, which was also based to some degree on the bitterly ironic drawings of the German artist George Grosz – who, like Isherwood, was later to become an American citizen – which attacked the bourgeois middle-class as the Weimar Republic drew to its close.

As Prince's plans progressed, his manner of staging was beginning to resemble that of the left-wing theatre-pieces of Berthold Brecht and Kurt Weill, which came to dominate the avant-garde Berlin theatre movement of the late 20s and early 30s, the more notable being *The Threepenny Opera* and *The Rise And Fall Of The City Of Mahagonny*, and characterised by a hard-edged, direct approach both in music and production values. Many of these original Brecht-Weill shows starred Kurt Weill's wife, Lotte Lenya.

After the Nazis came to power, Weill and Lenya fled Germany. They went first to Paris, and then to America, where Weill pursued a new career as a composer for Broadway and Hollywood. Kurt Weill died in 1950, but his widow, the possessor of a distinctive, untrained gravelly voice, outlived him by 31 years. Lotte Lenya continued as an artist with a wide performing range, including that of film actress. Her notable roles for the cinema were as the Soviet Colonel Rosa Klebb in *From Russia With Love* and as the calculating procurer in *The Roman Spring Of Mrs Stone*. It was Lotte Lenya's devotion to her husband's work, and the immense popular success of the Marc Blitzstein Broadway version of *The Threepenny Opera* (one of the Brecht-Weill Berlin scores that was virtually unknown in America during Weill's life), including the transcontinental hit of 'Mack The Knife' by Bobby Darin, that kept his music alive until its gradual re-evaluation finally established him as a major figure.

Lenya was of course still active in the mid-1960s – *From Russia With Love* had appeared in 1963 and brought her to a new world audience – and she had the performing style Prince was looking for in her blood. Indeed, it can be argued that Lotte Lenya herself was perhaps the major star who actually created this performing style. Prince approached Lenya with a proposal for her to appear in *Cabaret*, and her agreement to play Fraulein Schneider came as an immense coup for him.

John Kander was born in Kansas City in 1927 and studied music at Oberlin College and Columbia University. His first love was the musical theatre, and his initial jobs were as rehearsal pianist, arranger and conductor. In 1962, he met Fred Ebb, the lyricist – five years Kander's junior – and their first songs proved highly successful, including 'My Colouring Book'. Their first musical together, *Flora, The Red Menace*, was not such a success, although it was the vehicle which first brought Liza Minnelli to Broadway.

This proved to be a fateful show: Prince saw it on Broadway, and *Flora*'s song-writing team (and, as it happened, much later, the show's leading lady) were brought in to create the music for *Cabaret*. Jumping somewhat ahead in our chronology, the *New York World Journal Tribune*, reviewing *Cabaret*, claimed that "One thing that never lapses is Prince's sense of theatre" – a reference to Prince's notion that a cabaret show, played before an audience seated at tables, will often involve the audience to some degree. To involve the audience in the theatre, manifestly not seated at tables, Prince conceived the notion of hanging a mirror on stage, facing the audience, and thereby reflecting their images back to them, and, to some degree, involving them in the action.

The story of *Cabaret* begins on New Year's Eve, 1930, in Berlin. Politics is in turmoil, the country's economy is in a parlous state, and – as people seek to escape from their daily misery – they frequent the many night bars in the city which cater for every taste. One of these is the Kit Kat Klub, where the Emcee welcomes the clientele.

At this time, Clifford Bradshaw, a young American writer, meets Ernst Ludwig, a young German, who recommends a modest lodging house, which is run by Fraulein Schneider. Even so, the rent is more than Clifford can afford, but Fraulein Schneider agrees to take less money, so the American moves into his room and begins work on his new novel.

But the pull of Berlin night-life proves irresistible; unable to concentrate, he goes to the Kit Kat Klub, in time to see Sally Bowles wow the audience with her song, 'Don't Tell Mama', during which performance she sees the young stranger. Afterwards, she makes herself known to him, as the arrival of New Year is celebrated in suitable style.

The next day in Clifford's room Ernst – who seems to have some hidden political affiliation – is having his first English lesson, when suddenly Sally Bowles arrives, full of excuses, but failing at first to reveal the real reason for her visit – she has been thrown out and has nowhere to stay. Clifford is at first somewhat put out, but he soon learns that roommates of either sex are quite common in Berlin – through the relationship between Fraulein Schneider and one of her lodgers, Herr Schultz, who runs a greengrocer's shop, and treats her to a rare whole pineapple.

Back at the Kit Kat Klub, the mood changes as the emergent tide of nationalism begins to surface, but for Sally and Clifford their relationship continues, unaffected by outside events. Sally is, in fact, pregnant, and as they will soon need a larger income Sally accepts Ernst's offer of a rather shady job for Clifford.

The political mood gets darker, according to the Emcee, yet the friendship between Herr Schultz and Fraulein Schneider continues unabated. The nature of their relationship is exposed when another lodger, Fraulein Kost, who rents herself out by the hour to German soldiers in her room, sees Herr Schultz leaving the landlady's quarters. Thinking on his feet, Herr Schultz claims to Fraulein Kost that he and Fraulein Schneider are to marry.

The idea is not unappealing to either of them, and they hold a party to celebrate their engagement during which Herr Schultz, a little the worse for drink, reveals his previously somewhat suppressed Jewish origin; this is not received too well by everyone, and Ernst arrives, openly wearing a swastika armband. The next day, the window of Herr Schultz's shop is smashed.

The Nazis can no longer be ignored, and Fraulein Schneider feels she has to break off her engagement with a Jew. This greatly upsets Sally and Clifford, and he, realising the way that things are likely to go, determines to take Sally away from Berlin. But Sally is unphased by political matters; her life and her career are in the capital, at the Kit Kat Klub, to where she now goes.

Clifford decides to fetch her, but when he arrives at the club, he and Ernst argue and Clifford is attacked by some Nazi thugs. He is dragged away, but Sally goes on with her act. For Clifford, this is the last straw: the following morning he is packing his bags when Sally arrives and tells him she has had an abortion.

There is nothing left for him, so he goes, leaving her train ticket – which he knows she will not use. On the train, he muses over the sights and sounds of the Berlin he knew, which he knows will soon be gone for ever. It is possible Sally realises this, too, as she sings her title song, 'Cabaret', with an inner meaning she had never given it before. She cannot leave, and will have to take her chance in the new Germany. "Did it all happen?" asks the Emcee.

This wonderful story affords the lyricist and composer some tremendous opportunities, not least in the variety for musical treatment, and John Kander especially responded with a score of considerable richness and immediate appeal. Some may feel that there is an element of post-Weill influence, and in certain respects it is difficult not to agree, but where Kander shows his originality is in the sheer positive vitality that shines out from the score time and time again. The show appears to be musically driven from first note to last, and is wholly exceptional in that the score does not sag at any moment.

The original production opened at the Broadhurst Theatre on West 44th Street on November 20, 1966 with sets by Boris Aronson, costumes by Patricia Zipprodt; the choreography was by Ronald Field. The brilliant orchestrations were by Don Walker. The cast included Jill Haworth as Sally Bowles, Joel Grey as the Emcee and Bert Convy as Clifford Bradshaw. Herr Schultz was played by Jack Gilford, and Fraulein Schneider by Lotte Lenya.

The impact of the show was considerable; the press was uniformly enthusiastic and although there were early changes in the cast the show ran successfully for 1,165 performances. It won no fewer than eight Tony Awards and 15 months later, the London run opened at the Palace Theatre on February 28, 1968 with exactly the same production team as had been responsible for creating Cabaret on Broadway. The London cast included Judi Dench as Sally Bowles, Kevin Colson as Clifford, Lila Kedrova as Fraulein Schneider, Peter Sallis as Herr Schultz and Barry Dennen was the Emcee; although well enough received, this production ran for just eleven months.

Four years later, in 1972, the film of Cabaret was released. If the music of this movie was essentially the same as that in the show, and the story retained something of the broad outline, the film was very different in many respects. This was an ABC Pictures/Allied Artists movie and proved to be just as successful as a film as the Broadway show had been as a theatre piece.

One of the main changes in Jay Allen's screenplay was to make Sally Bowles much more the central character of the drama, and not the Emcee, whose place in the show had been that of the pivot around which all other events rotated. Liza Minnelli was chosen to play Sally Bowles, thereby making the character an amoral American girl, and not a London 20s 'flapper-girl' Chelsea-ite.

As a result of this central dramatic change from the show, the focus of the film is more widely spread; whilst Sally is given a greater prominence, the cabaret remains central both to itself and to reflecting her own character and adventures; but the social background against which the interlocking drama is played also assumes much more significance. This last aspect is a practical consequence of filming on location, a change which could never have been adequately shown on the stage. Nor is this a question of travelogue: it is the social, street-life background which is given greater emphasis, the inexorable rise of Nazism.

Clifford Bradshaw became Brian Roberts, an English student type, played by Michael York, whose ambivalent sexuality is more akin to the tenor of the original stories – it would have been difficult, if not impossible, so to depict his character in earlier dramatisations. Sally's German friends in the movie are Fritz Wendel (played by Fritz Wepper), a gigolo keen to improve his English, so to better his chances with lady tourists; Natalia Landauer, a wealthy Jewish lady on whom Fritz has designs, and finally the worldly Baron Max von Heune. The young Baron takes Sally and Brian under his wing and, in return, takes each of them to bed.

As a consequence of these dramatic changes, the characters are all, to a greater degree, shown to be inherently more vulnerable: the stronger the Nazi background is depicted, the more we know them to be threatened. So when finally Sally decides that she cannot leave Berlin and go to England to live with Brian, her decision, and her final song, have a more profound impact.

In this regard, such impact would be relatively meaningless were it not for the portrayal of Sally by Liza Minnelli, who gave the performance of her life and, in so doing, finally shook off the spectre of her mother, Judy Garland. Liza Minnelli's combination of worldly hedonist and touching vulnerability is both exactly right for the part and the more affecting for being so exceptionally well brought off.

The film, directed by Bob Fosse (who was also responsible for the choreography) won eight Academy Awards, including those for him, for Liza Minnelli and for Joel Grey, who recreated on film the part of the Emcee he had made his own on Broadway. The score was not retained intact; but two fine new songs by Ebb and Kander were added – 'Money, Money' and 'Mein Herr' – to part replace those which were dropped.

The show was outstanding and highly original; the film, based upon it but changed in several material respects, was equally so. The result is a rare chapter in this book: both stage and screen versions are masterly and each can stand independently of the other.

Chapter 8

Camelot

With the opening of *My Fair Lady* in February 1956 the team of Frederick Loewe and Alan Jay Lerner had reached its zenith; no subsequent collaboration of theirs was to reach the heights of this masterpiece. The music they wrote for the 1958 film of *Gigi* was a fine score by any standards, and their last big show together – planned from the outset as a stage work – to have had any major success, *Camelot*, was not quite in the same class.

Nonetheless, *Camelot* retains the affection of many people, and of it Lerner himself said: "In some ways I like *Camelot* better than almost anything I have ever written." It is not difficult to see why – certainly from Lerner's point of view. In the first place, compared to the work he had to do on *My Fair Lady*, the story of *Camelot* did not come with an awesome dramatic pedigree. In *My Fair Lady*, Lerner had to perform a literary tightrope act: he had to create dialogue and lyrics which were compatible with the existing dialogue of one of the greatest masters of the English language, existing dialogue which was known the world over. The measure of his success in that work is a tribute to Lerner's linguistic skill.

With *Camelot*, Lerner was freer as a creative artist in his own right. It is also true that the story itself was closer to his own mercurial spirit, a spirit which found itself attracted both to British history and also to the metaphysical. It gave his own creative imagination a looser rein, in which he could exercise a greater control than in many of his earlier collaborative efforts.

The provenance of the show *Camelot* began in August 1958. Alan Jay Lerner, his latest project with Loewe (*Gigi*) now successfully completed and whilst not consciously looking around for a new subject for a musical, for he had one or two other matters of a personal nature to deal with, read a review of *The Once And Future King* by TH White. White was almost solely known as a writer of children's literature, and he was deeply affected by coming into contact, at an early age, with Malory's *Morte d'Arthur*. White's most famous work is to be found in his retelling of the Arthurian legends in a series of books, *The Sword In The Stone*, *The Witch In The Wood*, *The Ill-Made Knight* and *The Candle In The Wind*, the last appearing in the same year as *The Once And Future King* which was a revision of the earlier books in the tetralogy. White was a pacifist, and profoundly believed that the Arthurian legends were a corollary for our own times, being "a quest for an antidote to war", as he put it.

Camelot, perhaps better suited for the medium of film than stage.

Having noted the publication of *The Once And Future King*, Lerner was astonished to receive a call soon afterwards from Moss Hart, in which the theatrical director commended the self-same subject as the basis for Lerner and Loewe's next musical.

Times were beginning to change in America, and, by influence, in the rest of the world. The rise of rock-and-roll in 1956, the dazzling success of *West Side Story* in 1957, the cult of James Dean following his death at the age of 24 – the personification of inarticulate rebellious youth – each betokened, alongside other straws in the wind, the changes that the first post-war generation were to make to world society. Change was not merely needed, it was virtually inevitable: the world's leaders were all old men – President Eisenhower in the USA, Prime Minister Macmillan in Britain, General de Gaulle – the first President of the French Fifth Republic, Chancellor Adenhauer in West Germany and First Secretary Khruschev in Soviet Russia – men who represented, and spoke for, older generations.

No-one, it appeared, was to speak for youth, until the arrival of a 42-year-old Democratic Senator who catapulted across the world's media by his sensational win in the 1960 New Hampshire primary elections for the Presidential race that year. Eisenhower, coming to the end of his second term, could serve no longer as America's President, and the world was electrified at the dawn of a new decade by this handsome young politician who seemed to promise so much.

Kennedy's election address claimed that "the time of a new generation had come" and for the thousand days that he was President his administration certainly gave all the appearance of "a new generation" in power – but not so immature that it could not handle the Cuban missile crisis with genuine statesmanship.

Kennedy's assassination in November 1963 brought the dazzling dream to an end. The Kennedy presidency had been compared to Camelot – the court of the legendary King Arthur – in its sense of idealism, and, in a curious combination of circumstances, aspects of the Lerner and Loewe *Camelot* show came to be associated with the Kennedy years.

If Lerner and Moss Hart, together with a mutual friend, Bud Widney, had all become enthused about the prospect of a musical on the Arthurian legends, Frederick Loewe was not initially at all impressed: "That King Arthur was a cuckold. Who the hell cares about a cuckold?" But as he was asking the question of Alan Jay Lerner, he clearly asked the right man. "There was something about *Camelot*," Lerner said, "more than any other play I have written, that was too much a part of me to be objective." With this commitment, Loewe was eventually persuaded to take on the project.

Lerner had the greater task at first: to condense and select from TH White's tetralogy sufficient material to make a coherent dramatic whole which would be suitable for musical treatment. That he succeeded, eventually, is much to his credit – although the show, in one of its try-outs, ran for more than four hours at first. It was later trimmed to under three hours, and – as we shall see – was further shortened.

However, as Lerner himself recalled, "From the first day that pen was set to paper, *Camelot* was plagued by enough misfortunes to send all connected with it into the desert for 40 years." The litany of misfortunes began with Adrian, the designer, who "came out of retirement, and when he had completed only half of his work died of a heart attack". In the months before rehearsals began, Lerner himself fell seriously ill, but "the day after it opened, I went into hospital for ten days and the day I returned to work, Moss Hart [the show's director] suffered a serious heart attack and never saw the play again until four months after its New York opening".

The health of leading members of the cast thankfully remained unaffected by fortune's outrageous slings and arrows, as Richard Burton as King Arthur, Julie Andrews as Queen Guenevere (as her name is spelled) and Roddy MacDowell as Mordred – the three English leads (shades of *My Fair Lady*) – and Robert Goulet as Sir Lancelot, all retained good health.

Lerner amusingly commented that *Camelot* on Broadway became known as a 'medical' more than a 'musical'. He went on: "Thanks to the high degree of professionalism of Richard Burton, Julie Andrews and dear Roddy MacDowell, who held the company together while the play was being rewritten and restaged, *Camelot* opened only a week late on December 3, 1960 [one month after John F Kennedy had been elected 36th President of the United States] to the most star-studded audience in memory. People literally flew transcontinentally and transatlantically to attend the premiere. I remember the last person to rush to his seat before the curtain rose was Noel Coward, who had arrived from London late that afternoon." It was a Saturday.

But Moss Hart, the show's director was still in hospital. With the success of *My Fair Lady*, and more recently the film of *Gigi*, behind them, the advance ticket sales were at one time the best Broadway had ever seen, which guaranteed – at the very least – a run of several months. But the show did not open to universally enthusiastic reviews; if it was to continue to run successfully, some rewriting and surgery might be necessary.

Thankfully, Moss Hart had recovered sufficiently to return to the show for which he was still billed as director. On seeing it now for the first time, he persuaded Lerner to cut around 20 minutes from it, making it a much tighter proposition. At around the same time, there was an hour-long CBS television tribute on the Ed Sullivan Show to Lerner and Loewe commemorating the fifth anniversary of the opening of *My Fair Lady*, which included excerpts from *Camelot*. As was already well-known, and as President Kennedy had conclusively shown the previous year, television exposure was a key to fame; as Alan Jay Lerner commented: "The following day, the pre-opening line returned to the box office and *Camelot* ran for over two years, almost that again on tour, and its success was repeated across the Pacific and Atlantic." Moss Hart died soon after.

The story of *Camelot* begins, after the overture and opening male chorus set the scene, with the arrival of Guenevere to be married to King Arthur. The entire court comes to greet her, except the King, who appears unsure of himself and hides behind a tree. The Queen-to-be is also understandably uncertain, and slips away: she and the King come upon each other, and to their mutual relief they find they are attracted to each other.

Merlin, the magician and mystic, believes that Guenevere's arrival will prove disastrous for his protégé the King and the Knights of the Round Table, a group devoted to high-minded principles, but before he can caution Arthur, Merlin is himself spirited away by Nimue, a curious elf-like sprite. Across the English Channel, in France, a youthful knight called Lancelot has learned of the Round Table and, attracted by its precepts, determines to come to England to join the Knights.

At Camelot, Lancelot is made welcome by Arthur. Although the newcomer has a lot to learn, not least in the art of gentilesse, as his vanity jars somewhat, the courtiers forget his selfishness as they proceed to celebrate 'The Lusty Month Of

May'. During the festivities, Queen Guenevere takes an instant dislike to the newcomer, and proceeds to turn the Knights against Lancelot. Arthur cannot understand this, but when Lancelot is challenged at a tournament by three Knights his defeat of the first two and slaughter of the third works a miracle. For the third Knight is brought back to life by Lancelot's remorse – at which event, Queen Guenevere realises her growing love for the young Frenchman.

Lancelot feels likewise, and, not to allow passions to grow, he asks to be sent abroad for a while. After two years, he returns, but his love for the Queen is still strong, and Arthur, sensing the position, determines not to precipitate matters, which are made more complicated by the arrival of Mordred, King Arthur's illegitimate son. Mordred despises the principles of the Round Table Knights, and determines to depose his father, who is captured in this strategy by Morgan le Fey for a night in the enchanted forest.

Whilst Arthur is absent from the court, Lancelot visits the Queen in her room; Guenevere will remain faithful to her husband, but the couple are surprised by Mordred and some Knights: during the melée Lancelot escapes, but the Queen is arrested on a charge of treason and is sentenced to be burned at the stake.

Arthur returns, and finds himself unable to interfere with the course of justice, even though it is his wife that will die. In the nick of time, Lancelot rescues Guenevere; his action runs counter to the principles of the Round Table and the King has no choice but to punish Lancelot. In France, Arthur finds the lovers, and sees them separately before the battle; he forgives them both and as Guenevere plans to stay in a nunnery an English boy, Tom of Warwick, who has followed the Knights to France and is inspired by their ideals, tells King Arthur that when he grows up he wants to become a Knight of the Round Table. Arthur realises that his ideals will now live on after him, and, with this inspiring thought and hope for the future, the story ends.

Camelot ran for 873 performances on Broadway but has been revived many times since. In 1996 it was chosen to be performed in a new production in the Grand Temple of Freemason's Hall in London as part of that year's Covent Garden Festival of opera and the musical arts, a particularly apt venue, given the ritual nature of much Masonic business.

But by the time the show opened in London at the Drury Lane Theatre on August 19th 1964, with a cast that included Laurence Harvey as Arthur, Elizabeth Larner as Guenevere, Barry Kent as Lancelot and Nicky Henson as Mordred in a production by Jack Hylton with Sir Robert Helpmann as director and choreographer, President Kennedy had been dead for nine months.

Alan Jay Lerner proudly recalls that two quatrains of the song 'Camelot' had become associated with the Kennedy era, quotations becoming the titles of two books about the President – *A Fleeting Wisp Of Glory* and *One Brief Shining Moment*.

Frederick Loewe's score is a good one, and as with the rising three notes that unite the songs of *My Fair Lady*, a rising three-note figure – a major triad – runs through *Camelot* as a leitmotif, fitting the word, and its associated meanings, like a glove. A curious point is that this same figure is woven through much of the battle music, and its falling inversion, altered, makes some of this music sound very much like that which Sir William Walton had written for the battle of Agincourt in Laurence Olivier's film of Shakespeare's *Henry V*. The point has sometimes been made, with more than a grain of truth, that – memorable though the best of his songs are – there is little that is distinctive about them, in the way that a Gershwin or Jerome Kern, Irving Berlin or Cole Porter melody will often be immediately recognisable as being by that composer, and no-one else. Loewe's genius, and that is not too great a claim, was his uncanny ability to mould his ideas to the job in hand in such a way that one becomes aware not of the composer as a creative personality but of the aptness of the music sung by the character at the particular dramatic moment. In this way, in this 'art that conceals art', Loewe was able to give his scores a kind of symphonic unity that other composers rarely achieved. He could create a totally integrated score, not run a string of great songs together which would have been hits no matter for which drama they may have been provided.

By mid-1966 both the original Broadway and London runs of *Camelot* had come to an end, and – as had become very much the custom – Hollywood now entered the scene, almost literally. The film, a Warner Brothers presentation, and produced by Jack L Warner, was outstandingly well cast, but as also had become the custom, with entirely new leading players. King Arthur was Richard Harris, who in this film discovered he had a distinctive and more than passable singing voice. Guenevere was played by Vanessa Redgrave, Franco Nero was Lancelot and David Hemmings was Mordred. Other parts were played by Lionel Jeffries and Laurence Naismith as Merlin. Franco Nero's songs were dubbed for him by Gene Merlina.

If the casting was outstanding, the technical and production staff were equally fine; Joshua Logan's direction was spot-on, the photography by Richard H Kline contributed superbly to the overall effect and the design and costumes by John Truscott and the art direction by Edward Carere could not have been bettered, a point echoed by their peers for the last three named gentlemen won Oscars for their work on this film.

Alan Jay Lerner wrote illuminatingly of the change from stage to screen in 1967, by which time the partnership had long since come to an end. Loewe had had heart problems, and decided to retire, to enjoy the fruits of his labours, unencumbered by more creative pressures from Broadway.

And so Lerner was able to play by far the major role in the screen adaptation, which was, he said, "One of the most enjoyable and rewarding experiences I have ever had. Starting with Joshua Logan, and running through the entire company, there was a love for the project that one finds very rarely in the theatre or motion pictures. A case in point is Richard Harris, who simply called up and insisted on playing the part. And, from a writing point of view, there is nothing like getting a second chance.

"I genuinely believe that *Camelot* realises what all of us set out to do. I do not believe you can just take a Broadway production and film it. It must be recreated for the motion picture screen. Perhaps *Camelot* is better suited for the media of film than for the stage. And it helps considerably when you are lucky enough to be surrounded by the kind of artistry that is at the fingertips of Vanessa Redgrave, Richard Harris, Franco Nero, David Hemmings, Alfred Newman, Ken Darby [the musical directors – Newman conducted] and the others. I am grateful to them all."

Joshua Logan outlined his approach to his task: "On film," he said, "we have treated it not as an operetta, but as a straight dramatic story with certain scenes assuming musical form." On that basis, the film was a triumph.

Chapter 9

Carmen Jones

The French composer George Bizet (1837-1875) was born in Paris into a musical family, and learned music almost as soon as he could read. His tragically brief life was a mixture of success and failure; from 1870 onwards his muse appears to have settled and much of his best work was written after that time, culminating in his masterpiece and crowning glory, the opera-comique *Carmen*.

This opera was finally staged on March 3, 1875 – and although everyone expected it to be a success, for some reason its premiere was very coolly received. Bizet was deeply distressed at the apparent failure of a work into which he had poured his finest efforts, whose worth he knew only too well.

The failure of *Carmen* may have had a psychosomatic effect upon his health: at any rate, following two heart attacks, he died less than three months later on June 2, never living to see the world take *Carmen* to its heart.

To call a work 'opera-comique' does not imply that it is a 'comic opera'; indeed, *Carmen* is a deeply tragic story. The French term was used to differentiate between those types of opera which were continuously sung, 'grand opera', and those which contained speech between numbers –

between the arias, duets, choruses and so on. Those which contained speech were called 'opera-comique'.

Carmen is arguably the most popular opera ever written, and so it was something of a courageous step on Oscar Hammerstein II's part to write a modern story, based loosely on the original, with completely new lyrics, to Bizet's music. Hammerstein himself, in collaborating with a number of distinguished musical composers, had furnished lyrics in the three general ways by which such lyrics are written: providing finished lyrics for composers to set; collaborating at all stages of the song with the composer, or by setting words to existing music.

In the case of *Carmen*, Hammerstein had no choice, for the music was already in existence. As he himself said, "*Carmen Jones* is not in any way an opera, but is, in fact, a musical play based on an opera. The score of Bizet's original music has not been altered in any way, not has the traditional tempo been varied."

The plot, provided by Hammerstein, is set at a US Army base during World War II. It was succinctly outlined by the great American character actor Mervyn Douglas – perhaps best remembered himself for appearances in

Harry Belafonte and Olga James in the 20th Century-Fox Cinemascope release, *Carmen Jones*.

Ninotchka and *Mr Blandings Builds His Dream House*: "The story begins when Joe, an Army corporal stationed in Jacksonville, is about to enter Flying School and a party is given in his honour by workers of the nearby parachute factory. Among them is his sweetheart Cindy Lou, for whose attentions Sgt Brown is a rival. During the course of the celebrations, Carmen Jones swaggers in and attempts to use her feminine wiles on Joe, who is not at all interested.

"Joe at that time is seeking permission from his commanding officer to marry Cindy Lou when Carmen chooses to pick a fight with another employee. Sgt Brown maliciously puts her in Joe's custody to take her to Jacksonville jail, and suggests to Cindy Lou that Joe has volunteered to be responsible for Carmen.

"Carmen continues to lure, and her attempts are eventually successful. Meanwhile they stop at a shanty town where she proudly shows off her Joe – all the time promising him that they will soon be aboard the train for Jacksonville and the jail. Carmen's grandmother, who is a fortune-teller, predicts evil things for the couple, which so much upsets the superstitious Carmen that she runs away.

"Joe is imprisoned for his neglect of duty, and during his imprisonment he is so devoured by his passion for Carmen that he cannot face Cindy Lou when she visits him. The only reliefs in his imprisonment are letters and promises from Carmen, with a gift of a rose.

"Carmen, meanwhile, settles down at BIlly Pastor's night-club to wait for Joe. Husky Miller, a heavyweight champ, wants her as his girl-friend, but Carmen will have none of it, despite the coaxing of her old friend, Frankie, whose job comes to depend on arranging things for Husky.

"Joe is released, and joy reigns until Carmen realises he still plans to go into flying school. She wants him to forget the army and go off to Chicago with her. He fights the temptation, but Sgt Brown overhearing the scene, intrudes sneeringly and is knocked out by Joe, who, knowing now that the alternative is prison, hides the unconscious sergeant and agrees to Carmen's plan.

"In Chicago they must evade military policemen and go into hiding. When their money has gone, Carmen goes to Husky for more. Frankie urges Carmen to be nice to the fighter, but Carmen swears she is no two-timer. When Carmen returns to Joe, who complains to her for being away so long, he is suspicious as to the source of the money provided for food. This drives Carmen back to Husky's where, at a party, she reads her own cards, forecasting death.

"Joe follows Carmen, eluding the military policemen, while Cindy Lou arrives in pursuit of Joe. All meet at Husky's training quarters where Carmen tells Joe it is all over between them, but helps him to escape. Cindy Lou departs in tears knowing that she has lost her Joe.

"At the championship fight, the crowd acclaiming Husky's triumph, Joe confronts Carmen, again pleading with her. When she refuses his love, he kills her. As the mob swarms out of the door screaming for their hero, the heartsick Joe weeps for the dead Carmen and voices his hope that they will soon 'hang him on the highest tree', so that he might join his beloved."

One of the most remarkable aspects to Oscar Hammerstein II's new lyrics is the way in which they fit Bizet's music like a glove: 'There's A Cafe On The Corner', 'Beat Out That Rhythm On A Drum', and 'Stand Up And Fight' are so absolutely right in every respect that even those who know the opera well have to stop and think for a moment as to what the original words were.

Another exceptional aspect to *Carmen Jones* is that the cast is all-black. In this instance, we find a show which is virtually contemporary with Gershwin's *Porgy And Bess*, and with Vernon Duke's *Cabin In The Sky* (now remembered principally for the fine song, 'Taking A Chance On Love') so *Carmen Jones* cannot be claimed to be a first; but, nonetheless, the concept was so wholly unusual as to constitute another noteworthy feature.

A corollary of this is that the show did a deal of good in promoting a greater racial acceptance of blacks in the USA. We should not forget the background to this: America was at war, and conscription meant the induction of blacks alongside whites – for many conscripts, this was their first experience of living alongside each other in close proximity. An entire show, in which virtually all of the soldiers, non-commissioned officers as well as other ranks, were black, was itself quite exceptional. *Porgy And Bess* had shown the blacks of Charleston in poor circumstances: *Carmen Jones* showed them to be the equal of their white counterparts.

Carmen Jones opened on Broadway on December 2, 1943. It caused something of a sensation, for not only was the concept utterly original but it had been carried off with conspicuous skill. What was somewhat unusual was that Hammerstein, who had conceived the entire project, did not direct the show himself, given his earlier successes in this aspect of the musical theatre.

The film dates from 1954. Shot in Cinemascope, and directed by Otto Preminger, the difficulties were compounded by having some leading roles not sung by the actors and actresses concerned, with them having to mime to pre-existing tapes. Faced with such vicissitudes, it is surprising the film comes off at all – once more, of course, an all-black cast was necessary, which in turn caused some studio worries in the era before desegregation at the time of the early days of the rise of black consciousness in the USA.

The leading roles were taken by Dorothy Dandridge and Harry Belafonte, with Olga James as Cindy Lou, the legendary Pearl Bailey brilliantly cast as Frankie, Diahann Carroll as Myrt, Joe Adams as Husky, and Broc Peters as Sgt Brown. The singing voices were principally Marilyn Horne and LaVern Hutcherson as Carmen and Joe respectively; a special interest was aroused by the young Marilyn Horne. At the time she was only 16 years old, yet already the possessor of a fine mezzo-soprano voice. Herschel Burke Gilbert, who conducted the score for the film, recalled that when the young Marilyn Horne came for the audition, he was convinced that she would be entirely unsuitable: "But when she began to sing, I realised that she was ideal for the part." It so happened that Marilyn Horne was to develop into one of the world's leading classical mezzo-soprano voices, and essayed the role of Carmen in Bizet's opera many times on stage, making a fine complete recording with the New York Metropolitan Opera for DGG, conducted by Leonard Bernstein – which recording marked Bernstein's debut on the DGG label. Incidentally, Miss Horne was to marry the black conductor Henry Lewis, who directed *Carmen Jones* at its successful London Old Vic revival in 1991. Herschel Burke Gilbert also later achieved fame for providing the music for the 1960s television detective series *Burke's Law*.

Chapter 10

Carousel

The extraordinary success of *Oklahoma!* in 1943 – the first collaboration between Richard Rodgers, Oscar Hammerstein II and the Theatre Guild – naturally led to discussions for a successor. The Theatre Guild itself had built up an enviable reputation as being one of the most innovative and successful of all theatre companies in the USA, and, as *Oklahoma!* had been based upon a play previously produced by the Guild, earlier productions were considered for a new musical adaptation.

One stood out above all others – *Liliom*, by Ferenc (Frederick) Molnar. This delightful play ("a fantasy of imaginative invention," as Alan Jay Lerner called it) had been a notable success when the Theatre Guild first produced it in 1921, in which Eva La Gallienne and Joseph Schildkraut played the leading roles. In 1932, the play was revived – with the same stars recreating their characters – and enjoyed another long run. In 1940, the Theatre Guild revived the play for a second time, but with a completely new production which starred Ingrid Bergman and Burgess Meredith. This, again, enjoyed no little success; and so, when trawling through earlier productions by the Theatre Guild for a new

vehicle for musical adaptation, *Liliom* was an almost universal choice.

It needed several changes, however. The play was originally set in Budapest, but Hammerstein cleverly relocated it – backwards in time – to New England, Maine, in 1873. Liliom, the title-role of the play, became Billy Bigelow, a handsome and proud barker for the carousel at the local amusement park. His girl, Julie, retained her first name, becoming now Julie Jordan – a lovely youthful innocent who works in a small factory.

In 1943, Oscar Hammerstein II had worked the most remarkable of all of his changes of locale, by turning Bizet's opera-comique *Carmen* into the Broadway musical show *Carmen Jones*. So complete was his achievement in that instance that the change of Budapest to New England would seem, in comparison, a mere bagatelle. However, such was Hammerstein's genius in choosing the right setting for an American musical audience that the relocation for *Carousel* appears to be the most natural and appropriate of surroundings for the touching and magical story.

The tale is essentially homespun to begin with, but ends in an unusual fantasy; the young couple fall in love but their attraction costs both of them their jobs. In Billy's case, the owner of the

20th Century-Fox production of *Carousel*, 1956.

carousel, Mrs Mullin, is herself in love with him, and the townspeople warn Julie of a liaison with an itinerant young man.

They marry, however, but without a steady job, and, knowing that he is to become a father, Billy is tempted into crime. He takes up with a ne'er-do-well, Jigger Craigen, and joins him in a hold-up. But the robbery goes terribly wrong: Billy, in trying to flee the scene, turns and falls on his own knife and is killed.

It is 15 years later, and Billy, now looking down from the gates of Heaven, is disturbed to see that all is not well with his 15-year-old daughter. She has been rejected by her youthful beau, and, granted dispensation by the Starkeeper, Billy is permitted to return to earth for one day, so that he can redeem himself by performing one good deed. He takes a star as a gift, but he is still the same gauche and awkward Billy as he always was. His daughter, naturally suspicious of the stranger and his strange gift, refuses his offer; angered, Billy slaps her – but she is not hurt by this. As she later tells her mother, his slap felt as though it were a kiss.

They realise that, with Billy's fatherly advice, the girl is now rid of her previous unhappiness, and Julie acknowledges that, in loving and marrying Billy in defiance of the advice she was given, in the end she has done the right thing.

Billy, in turn, knowing that he has accomplished the good deed he was sent to do, returns to Heaven, which he enters, free from all doubt.

If the newness of the conception and staging of *Oklahoma!* in 1943 marked a breakthrough in the Broadway musical – it began with a solo song, instead of the customary chorus, to take but one example – then *Carousel* carried that newness a stage further. The newness of *Carousel* lies in the strange and beautiful love story, the enchantment of Billy's redemption and the triumph of love, but perhaps most of all in the depiction of the working-class as being capable of mystery and tenderness.

If these aspects are unusual, the fact remains that the success or failure of any musical lies in the appropriateness and quality of the music. Once again, Richard Rodgers produced a score of astonishing originality, inspiration and timelessness.

Songs such as 'If I Loved You', 'When The Children Are Asleep', and 'When I Marry Mr Snow' are melting in their melodic contours; equally memorable, but very different, music is to be found in the brilliant 'June Is Bustin' Out All Over'. The concluding 'You'll Never Walk Alone' has become, for a variety of very different reasons, frankly inspirational to future generations.

It is also true to say that, in the famous 'Soliloquy' at the end of Act I, the music takes wing in truly convincing operatic fashion.

By any standards, the musical score for *Carousel* is an amazing achievement, and remains its most enduring feature. In fact, Richard Rodgers himself always cited this score as his personal favourite from all of those that he wrote. No wonder that the show, after opening at the Majestic Theatre on Broadway, on April 19, 1945, was another smash hit for this remarkable creative team.

Once again, Rouben Mamoulian was the producer, and Agnes de Mille's choreography was said to have surpassed anything she had previously accomplished in that field. The press was ecstatic: for example, the *New York Daily News* critic, the respected John Chapman, wrote that *Carousel* was "...one of the finest musical plays I have ever seen and I shall remember it always. It has everything the professional theatre can give it and something else besides; heart, integrity and an inner glow....[In] Rodgers and Hammerstein... the musical theatre does not have two finer creative artists."

We have noted the originality and unique freshness of both *Oklahoma!* and *Carousel,* qualities that were best summed up by Alan Jay Lerner:

"In style, both *Oklahoma!* and *Carousel* could musically be classified as modern operetta. But the legitimacy of the books, the dramatic use of lyrics and the wedding of choreographic movement to the story produced a new form of musical theatre, which very properly was called musical play. The total emotional impact of *Carousel* could not have better suited the times and for all time. There is no doubt that Rodgers and Hammerstein deserved the acclaim they received. Part of that acclaim was the Award for Best Musical of 1944-45, given by the newly-formed New York Drama Critics' Circle."

This Award, coming after the Pulitzer Prize for *Oklahoma!*, must have surely put the final seal of approval on the combined genius of this astonishing new music-theatre partnership.

The Theatre Guild cast assembled for the first production does not contain names that leap from the page, but the original cast recording, which was initially issued on a 78rpm set, has been preserved and we can hear that the members were individually very gifted, particularly John Raitt, who played Billy Bigelow, Jan Clayton as the homespun Julie Jordan, and Murvyn Vye as Jigger Craigen; other artists who participated were Jean Darling, Christine Johnson, Eric Mattson and Connie Baxter. The musical director was Joseph Littau.

Carousel opened in London, five years later, at the Drury Lane Theatre; on that occasion the leading roles were taken by Stephen Douglass and Margot Moser, and Eric Mattson journeyed to London to recreate on the West End stage the part he had brought into being on Broadway. Once more, the magnificence of a Richard Rodgers score had captured the entertainment capitals of the world, and songs from *Carousel* were on everyone's lips.

The film version was made by 20th Century-Fox in 1956, eleven years after the show first opened on Broadway. It was originally planned that Frank Sinatra was to play the part of Billy Bigelow, and Sinatra, contracted to the part, turned up for the shooting on August 20, which was to take place on location at Booth Bay, Maine. But he discovered, to his astonishment, that *Carousel* was to be filmed both in Cinemascope as well as in the Todd-AO system. Sinatra refused to go before the movie cameras, claiming, with some justification, that quite apart from the extra time taken in changing the cameras, he – and everyone else – would have to play each finished take at least twice.

One of Sinatra's points was encapsulated in his comment that "I have only one good take in me", as he argued his position with the film's producer Henry Ephron and director Henry King for two days, during which the the entire production company was idle. He expounded later on his reservations to a friend: "When musicians play on a sound-stage for a movie, you can't use their work on records without paying them again. Why should an actor make two films for the price of one? [Sinatra was scheduled to earn $150,000 for ten weeks' work] I'm not talking about the use of two cameras. They can shoot any scene with as many cameras as they want – and they do. I'm talking about playing the same scene twice."

Nine days after arriving at Booth Bay, Sinatra had walked (he had actually been flown) off the

20th Century-Fox production of *Carousel*, 1956.

location and was in New York City. There, he was served with a breach of contract by 20th Century-Fox for $1,000,000. This claimed that different types of cameras in film-making was not unprecedented, that only some scenes – not all – would have to be shot twice, and that a large cast and crew had been left stranded by Sinatra's walk-out.

Two days later, Sinatra was in California, by which time he had been replaced as Billy Bigelow by Gordon MacRae. Sinatra commented that "Gordon's a good man and should do fine". The two men retained their friendship; Sinatra would introduce MacRae to friends as the man who "does all my outside work".

So Frank Sinatra was out of *Carousel*, but he was soon proved to have been in the right when, on September 19, 20th Century-Fox issued a statement to the press that *Carousel* "would be filmed only in 55mm". Gordon MacRae went on to give a fine performance in the film, as Sinatra had hoped he would, but there remains an intriguing souvenir of the Sinatra episode: for Columbia Records; Sinatra had already recorded an outstanding version of the 'Soliloquy' from *Carousel* on both sides of a 12" 78rpm disc.

Chapter 11

Company And Other Aspects Of Stephen Sondheim – The Unfilmable Musicals

ompany was the seventh musical in which Stephen Sondheim had been involved as lyricist, but only the third for which he provided both words and music, after *A Funny Thing Happened On The Way To The Forum* of 1962 and *Anyone Can Whistle* of two years later.

It was, however, the first musical that Sondheim had written in collaboration with the the brilliant stage producer and director Harold Prince, and it is the change of direction – or, rather, an extension of the direction in which Sondheim had been heading – that *Company* marked that places it at the beginning of this part of our observations.

The collaboration between Sondheim and Prince was to last for a little over ten years and produced six extraordinary works of the greatest range and variety. These included, in the early part of their collaboration, *Follies* and *A Little Night Music*, and later such extraordinary extensions of the genre as *Pacific Overtures*, *Sweeney Todd, The Demon Barber Of Fleet Street* (the long title is necessary to differentiate it from an earlier musical, *Sweeney Todd*, by which was first produced in London in1960), *Merrily We Roll Along* and *Sunday In The Park With George*.

Sondheim's impact as a single creative artist – always bearing in mind that his musicals, as with all such works, come to their first night as a result of his collaboration with a number of others – on the Broadway musical stage has been huge. More than any other American composer of his generation, he has been responsible for pushing back the confining boundaries of the musical theatre to create, deliberately, in one sense, a medium of essentially popular entertainment which is also capable of handling serious subjects in depth and with an insight which raises the level of these works to that of a modern-day opera-comique and even containing elements of grand opera.

There is a very strong case to be made out for claiming that, when the history of opera in the last quarter of the 20th-century comes to be written – in, say, 50 years' time – it will be the works of Stephen Sondheim from this era that will be revived in new productions by the world's leading opera houses far more frequently, and with far greater appreciation of their qualities as coherent works of art than the hundreds of musically worthless 'operas' that have appeared and sunk again without trace during this period.

For Sondheim realised, probably when he was

still a teenager, that it ought to be possible to express new things, and to do existing things in a new way, within the 'musical comedy' field than had been done before. Stephen Sondheim is a quiet and gentle man, but one whose inner driving creativity has given him a strength of purpose which has helped to steer him through these previously uncharted waters with a certainty that we can only admire in an artist. This is not to say that everything he has done since 1970 has been flawless – far from it, and he might be the first to agree – but his work has, more often than not, been enchantingly original, provocative in the best sense, fluid and flexible in approach to every aspect of the job in hand, and – here is the most important factor – so utterly, completely theatrical in essence that, for once, we encounter a successful and original creator of works for the musical theatre whose 'musicals', to use the term in its broadest sense, cannot be translated into another medium. These musicals are unfilmable: they are theatre pieces, solely and utterly.

This is not to say that these works cannot be filmed successfully at some time: after all, anything is possible in art, given two criteria – imagination and ability. The point is, not only have these works resisted such filming thus far –

in the case of *A Little Night Music* (which we shall encounter later) even with the active participation of Sondheim and Prince – but that their subject-matter and theatrical treatment have not appealed to film-makers up to now.

And so we have a number of quite outstanding musical shows that have been enormously successful with public and critics – the Broadway notices for *Company* read like a literary roll of drums – and which have, in the process, expanded the genre to previously unimagined levels, yet which can only be appreciated *at all* in the theatre.

If they present challenges in terms of theatrical production, how much more would they challenge the film-maker? It is a case of 'wait and see', but until the next film-maker of genius arrives who takes up the challenge of being told that some things 'cannot be done', we can only imagine at how the magnificence of *Pacific Overtures*, the exploration of evil in *Sweeney Todd*, or the deeply gentle sophistication (in the best sense) of *Sunday In The Park With George*, perhaps the most essentially operatic in terms of musical composition of all of Sondheim's works, with its overtones of both French Impressionism and the mid-19th-century Russian pastoral school, might translate into film.

Chapter 12

Fiddler On The Roof

As we have had more than one occasion to remark upon in the course of this survey, one of the more interesting sidelights on the provenance of many American composers of popular music in the 20th-century is the extraordinary number of them who were either born in what western Europeans later in the century tended to call Russia, recognising the spread of the USSR, or who were first-generation Americans born of Russian families. This is not perhaps the place to relist those composers, suffice to note the large number of them, and the common heritage they shared, which – it was perhaps only to be expected – would itself be celebrated in the later stages of the evolved verismo Broadway musicals.

In 1859, in the Ukrainian town of Pereyaslev, Solomon Rabinowitz was born, the son of Russian-Jewish shopkeepers. For much of his youth he lived in and around the town of Voronkov. He became a rabbi, and some years later devoted his life to the chronicle of Yiddish life and culture by writing for notable Yiddish-language publications. He adopted the pen-name of Sholom Aleichem, and began to write a series of stories of Russian-Jewish life, set in the mythical town of Krasilevke (which was closely based on the town of Voronkov).

In 1893 he moved to the Ukrainian capital, Kiev, but that was soon after new diktats, amongst the last that Tsar Alexander III was to enact, had come into force. Following the assassination of his father in 1881, Alexander III ended liberal reform and reformed the powerful secret police which hunted down anyone with revolutionary sympathies. In 1882, he compelled Jews to confine themselves to 15 selected provinces, and the anti-Jewish legislation became onerous, reflected in the setting up of the Anti-Semitic League in Prussia at the same time.

In 1890-91, European Russia, especially the Ukraine, faced a full-scale famine as the crop failed disastrously. Many Jews, singly or in families, dispossessed by anti-Jewish legislation and denied what – 100 years later – would be termed their civil rights, and now facing full-scale famine in an inhospitable land, left Russia and emigrated to the United States. The Kiev in which Aleichem now lived was very different from that about which he had heard in his youth; after the abortive Revolution in Russia in January 1905, further anti-Jewish pogroms were set in train by a beleaguered government and absolute monarch. This was too much for Aleichem, who decided to try his lot in

A scene from the 1971 United Artists film version of *Fiddler On The Roof*.

America also, where in New York he wrote for the flourishing Yiddish Theatre there. Some years later, he had travelled across America and widely in Europe, and lived intermittently in Italy from 1908 to 1914, when he returned finally to New York City, where he died in 1916. His stories, in the Yiddish language, evoke with endearing enchantment life in pre-Revolutionary pastoral Russia, where in the little town called Anatevka, old traditions and patterns of living have been established for centuries.

After his death, nearly all of Aleichem's work was translated into English, and his writing came to the attention of a wider public, entranced by his vivid, humorous and sympathetic portrayal of Jewish family life. In 1943 Maurice Samuel's *The World Of Sholom Aleichem* was published, which in international terms was the breakthrough. For the first time, many thousands came to love this writer's work, including the writer Joseph Stein, who made a play from Aleichem's story *Teyve And His Daughters*.

Teyve and Golde are a long-married couple, living in Anatevka, a little backwater town of not much charm, steeped in traditions that have not changed for centuries. They have three daughters, Tzeitel, Hodel and Chava, and Teyve and Golde are looking for suitable husbands for each of them. Yente, the town matchmaker, lets it be known that Lazar Wolf, the rather elderly and somewhat lecherous butcher, is willing to take Tzeitel's hand in marriage. Golde is very pleased, for she realises that Wolf can improve their lot, certainly so far as good food is concerned.

But Tzeitel will have none of it. She wants to marry for love, and for nothing else, and she has found her beau in Motel, the shy but poor tailor. At first, Teyve is shocked at the news but he soon relents as he realises his daughter's happiness is more important than anything else – but such worthy thoughts are soon troubled by the fact that Teyve will have to convince Golde.

His way of doing this is to prey on her love of superstition: he pretends to have a dream in which Golde's grandmother, who has long been dead, appeared to him saying that Tzeitel should marry the tailor. Not wishing to go against her grandmother's wishes, Golde agrees to the match.

Having safely accommodated his eldest daughter's wishes, Teyve is approached by an earnest young man, Perchik, who offers to give lessons to the daughters in return for bed and board. Teyve accepts the deal, pleased that his offspring will now receive a decent education, and it is not long before his second daughter, Hodel, falls for Perchik, and is able to convince her father that the match – to the man she loves – is a good one.

The preparations are set in hand for Tzeitel's wedding to Motel but the day is ruined when the police arrive, on one of the regular Jewish pogroms, and wreck the presents and the Jews' homes, an extraordinary event in a musical, but nonetheless an everyday occurrence at the time that *Fiddler On The Roof* is set. Despite these vicissitudes, Tzeitel and Motel begin their married life with optimism. However, Perchik's social conscience will not let the matter rest there: he wants to marry Hodel but feels he has to join the anarchists; Teyve, seeing the depths of the emotion his second daughter feels for her lover, begins to wonder if the love between him and Golde is as strong. Perchik leaves Anatevka, but news comes of his arrest in Kiev and Hodel hurries to join him in exile in Siberia, sadly bidding her family goodbye.

Teyve's third daughter, Chava, is the last remaining. She has fallen in love, too, but her lover, Freydka, is a gentile. Teyve is deeply offended that she has chosen a non-Jew and will not budge from his implacable opposition – so far as he is concerned, Chava is no longer his daughter.

However, outside events conspire to bring more unhappiness as the Tsars order the evacuation of all Jews from the region. Freyda and Chava return to Anatevka to say that as they cannot continue to live under such a regime, they will also leave Russia. This gesture convinces Teyve of Freyda's inherent qualities, and he accepts that men of different faiths can also sympathise with the sufferings of others. With this in mind, he accepts Freyda and Chava back into his family.

Teyva now prepares to leave Anatevka, with his and Golde's belongings bundled into a handcart, to find a new life in America.

It must be clear that such a story was one with which many Russian-Jewish American families, and those in other lands too, would empathise. For some of them, it was the story of their own family – for Irving Berlin, it was his own story.

One of the great qualities of this show is that, although inherently Jewish of course, it eventually reveals such an ecumenical view of life from this wholly human and believable character as to have an appeal which ranges far wider than that of solely Jewish audiences. For Teyve's troubles, and his adventures, are those that beset many a man, Jew or gentile, and are expressed in such a way as to reinforce their universal relevance.

This is a quality of Sholom Aleichem's writing, but it is one that could easily have been diluted in a stage adaptation; it is also a measure of Joseph Stein's dramatisation that this inherent quality remains – to provide one of the reasons for the lasting success of the show. Another, of course, is the musical content.

Jerry Bock was born in New Haven Connecticut in November 1928 and after the war studied music at the University of Wisconsin. Around 1950, he moved to New York City and contributed music to various theatrical and television shows and elsewhere. His first major success for a complete score was with *Mr Wonderful* – which contained the hit song 'Too Close For Comfort' alongside the title number – to lyrics by various writers, followed in 1959 by *Fiorello!*, with lyrics by Sheldon Harnick, which won a Pulitzer Prize for drama.

Bock and Harnick were now very much a writing team, producing *Tenderloin* and *She Loves Me* before their masterly *Fiddler On The Roof* which opened at the Imperial Theatre, New York, on September 22, 1964 to universal acclaim. This remarkable show, which in the opinion of some authorities is arguably the finest musical comedy ever written, ran for 3,242 performances on Broadway, boasting a magnificent cast: Zero Mostel was Teyve, Maria Karnilova as Golde, and Joanna Martin, Julia Migenes and Beatrice Arthur as the daughters. The choreography was by Jerome Robbins.

The United Artists film of *Fiddler On The Roof* was released in 1971. The producer and director was Norman Jewison, and the photography was by Oswald Morris – which won him an Academy Award for reasons which remain obscure, as his work in this movie, although good, rarely rises above the serviceable. John Williams (as musical director) also won an Oscar, and the film also received four other Oscar nominations – Best Picture; Director; Best Actor and Best Supporting Actor: these last two categories were for the work of Topol as Teyve and Leonard Frey as Motel the tailor. Both deserved the nominations, particularly Topol, who had enjoyed a major international hit with the song 'If I Were A Rich Man' in 1967, and whose characterisation in the film was exceptionally outstanding, as was that of Norma Crane who played Golde.

20th Century-Fox production of *Carousel*, 1956.

With a fine adaptation, an excellent cast and technicians, and a gifted producer/director, the result should have been a memorable film. It is – up to a point – but at that point it becomes memorable for not always the best of reasons. The problem with the film is its length: three hours to the minute. It is far too long, and neither the drawn-out story nor the music is able to sustain this basically simple yet universal story for such an inordinate time. Self-indulgent and self-conscious, the 'universality' of the story and the magnificently well-structured and satisfying treatment it received in the original theatrical version are here swamped, irredeemably.

Chapter 13

Flower Drum Song

Considerable anticipation surrounded the arrival of *Flower Drum Song* – the first Rodgers and Hammerstein musical for eight years, since *The King And I* of 1951, and the longest period to have elapsed in their careers during which no new show appeared. If the public was keen to see the new offering by this team, they were neither disappointed nor rewarded with a masterpiece, but *Flower Drum Song* remains something of a curious work in their canon.

It was certainly something new. The story is based upon a novel by Chin Y Lee, and is concerned with the interaction between ethnic Chinese, Americans and Chinese-Americans, a subject which is treated with a charming lightness of touch but which remains one which would seem to have very little appeal in Europe – certainly with regard to reaching a popular audience.

Nor, it has to be said, would it seem to have such a vast appeal in the USA. Whilst the mixture of European/American and Oriental leading characters has always contained within it the kernel of dramatic juxtaposition, one which worked brilliantly in Puccini's *Madam Butterfly* and in Rodgers and Hammerstein's previous show, *The King And I*, in *Flower Drum Song* there was no real leading European role with which the majority of the creators' audience could empathise.

The story begins in San Francisco, where Mr Wang Chi Yang is presiding over his family with some concern. He is a Chinese gentleman of the old school, but his sons are each, to a greater or lesser degree, Americanised. His sister-in-law, Madam Liang, is keen to become an American citizen.

Mr Wang's elder son is looking for a wife, and tells his aunt – Madam Liang – that he wishes to make his own choice. A friend of the family, Sammy Fong, a local bar owner, comes in and tells them that he has sent off for a bride from a mail-order catalogue, and that she has arrived from China. In the meantime, that is between ordering the new wife and her arrival, Sammy has fallen in love with someone else, so to save face all round he is able to sell the bridal contract to old Mr Wang.

The bride, Mei Li, arrives with her father, and Mr Wang's eldest song, Wang Ta, has gone to see his girlfriend, Linda Low, to whom he proposes. She accepts him, but when Wang Ta returns home he finds Mei Li expecting to marry him

A scene from Universal's screen version of Rodger and Hammerstein's Flower Drum Song, starring Nancy Kwan, James Shigeta, Juanita Hall and Miyoshi Umeki.

under the contract his father has bought; to make matters worse, she is much taken with her proposed husband.

That same evening, Madam Liang is preparing for her American citizenship class; although Wang Ta finds himself drawn more and more to Mei Li, he cannot be unfaithful to Linda; his aunt, and his younger brother Wang San (who is wholly Americanised), at her graduation tell of the joys of America and its cultural melting-pot.

Linda now arrives, and, emboldened, Wang Ta informs his father of his engagement to her. This decision comes as much of a shock to Mei Li as it does to old Mr Wang.

But the plot is complicated when Sammy Fong arrives and it transpires that the girl he abandoned his mail-order wife for, was none other than Linda. He invites the Wang family to his bar, where Linda is a singer, believing that when his intentions are revealed the proposed marriage will not take place. Linda is enjoying herself at the party, and, unaware of Sammy's plan, she returns to the bar where she tells Sammy she is to marry Wang Ta. A further twist is that Linda's seamstress Helen has been secretly enamoured of Wang Ta, and when the Wangs arrive at the bar they are treated to a selection of low-life songs and a Linda strip-tease – all normal entertainment at the place.

As Sammy hoped, confusion reigns; the Wangs leave in some disgust and Wang Ta cannot decide between Linda and Mei Li, and seeks solace in Helen's attentions. Mr Wang and Madam Liang berate the younger generation as Mei Li and her father leave the home, determined to enforce the original contract with Sammy. The agreement is held to be binding, and as Mei Li and her father move in with Sammy, Wang Ta realises that it is Mei Li whom he loves after all.

Young Wang San and his contemporaries are amazed at this tangle, and it is only through the clever inventiveness of Mei Li that honour is satisfied all round, and the two sets of lovers are finally allowed to follow their hearts, to the pleasure and contentment of all.

Such a story would seem to lend itself particularly well to musical treatment, yet a problem in *Flower Drum Song* remained. This was not so much in the casting, which was generally excellent, nor in the direction, which was by the magnificent Gene Kelly making his Broadway debut. It was a more fundamental problem – that of the general inability of the audience to empathise with the characters.

The music is good, and naturally runs the gamut from pastiche Chinoiserie to mainstream Rodgers and Hammerstein Broadway material. The score contains some excellent numbers – most notably 'I Enjoy Being A Girl' (which proved to be a hit – of sorts – in 1960 for Pat Suzuki, who created the role of Linda Low) and 'Love, Look Away', but overall *Flower Drum Song* lacks the sheer sustained melodic invention and memorability of this duo's finest creations, and at times it is difficult to tell the difference between the Siamese music of *The King And I* and the American-Chinese music of this show. On the other hand, this team was to return to their top-drawer standard one more time in *The Sound Of Music* the following year.

Flower Drum Song opened on its out-of-town run at the Shubert Theatre in Boston on October 27, 1958, and at the St James Theatre on lower West 44th Street on December 1. The book was by Oscar Hammerstein II and Joseph Fields (this was the first time these gentlemen had worked together) and the choreography was not by Gene Kelly but credited to Carol Haney. Oliver Smith had designed the scenery, and Irene Sharaff the costumes. The show was respectfully received rather than totally enthusiastically.

Three years later, Universal-International released their movie of the show, which – being a faithful representation of the original – seemed to fall between several stools. In the early 1960s, the essential nature of the original story seemed dated and somewhat irrelevant to a younger generation that was beginning to make itself heard.

The treatment of this particular American ethnic minority appeared even insulting to them, and although it was beautifully wrapped up in a charming, somewhat passé manner, Leslie Halliwell's description of the film as being "remorselessly cute" seems tellingly apt. Some of the cast was retained, notably Miyoshi Umeki and Juanita Hall, and Nancy Kwan as Linda Low was outstanding, but the world's cinema audiences found it difficult to become involved in the comings and goings of the Wang family. The film is not a bad one – far from it – but it remains something of a curiosity, albeit a valuable document as revivals of the original stage show are exceptionally rare.

Chapter 14

Gentlemen Prefer Blondes

In 1948, just one year before she appeared to stunning public and critical acclaim in *Gentlemen Prefer Blondes*, Carol Channing, who had recently graduated from Bennington College in Vermont, had found it impossible to obtain a theatrical job in any capacity on Broadway, and had decided to try her luck in Hollywood. Just at that point, she was attracted by advertisements announcing an audition for a new revue *Lend An Ear*, to be produced by a young and talented husband-and-wife theatrical team, Marjorie and Gower Champion.

This was Gower Champion's first major theatrical assignment, and as he said, "The moment I saw Carol Channing, I knew she was it". *Lend An Ear* opened on Broadway on December 16, 1948, with Carol Channing, William Eythe and Yvonne Adair as her co-stars, and undoubtedly declared in Carol Channing that a new female star had arrived.

One of the first to see Miss Channing in *Lend An Ear* was Jule Styne, who returned the next night to the theatre with Anita Loos, keen that she should see her. Loos was working on an adaptation of her novel with Joseph Fields for a new show to be called *Gentlemen Prefer Blondes*, and she was soon persuaded that Carol Channing should star in it, along with – as it transpired – Yvonne Adair.

This was the novel's second adaptation: a film had already been made based upon the comedy of two girls in Paris on the lookout for rich husbands. If it seemed to Styne and Anita Loos that they may just have found their two leading ladies in one visit the other collaborators were not so sure.

Another problem was raising the money; the shrewd lawyer Herman Levin had decided some years earlier that his heart lay really on Broadway – and he was triumphantly to achieve his heart's desire in *My Fair Lady*, alongside other successes – and he, with his partner Oliver Smith, was keen to present a musical version of Anita Loos's charming story. Not all the backers who were approached were interested, for although Styne had by then a fine track record as a composer, and had collaborated with Sammy Cahn on a successful musical, *High Button Shoes*, this was a new, untried partnership. Although the raising of money for shows does not really form part of this book, any more than do the negotiations in finding a suitable theatre for their staging, it is certainly worth mentioning that four backers who were convinced as to the viability of this musical treatment of *Gentlemen Prefer Blondes* were Richard Rodgers, Oscar Hammerstein II, Leland Hayward and Joshua Logan – and four more experienced people in their respective fields would have been impossible to find. With their backing, other money was not difficult to find.

Jule Styne himself was a Londoner. Born in the working class East End, in a little house in Ducal Street, a tiny street hidden between Bethnal Green and Shoreditch, his family were immigrants of Russian-Jewish stock. Theodore Taylor's excellent biography of Jule Styne quotes from an 1898 book, *Curiosities Of London*, by John Timbs, that the area's "...outward moral degradation is at once apparent to anyone who passes that way". The Steins – as their name was spelled – had a small butter-and-egg shop, and young Jule recalled how, aged four, he would sit outside selling eggs. Fifty years later, he returned to Ducal Street, and found an elderly corner-shop owner who at last remembered the Stein family before they emigrated to the USA when Jule was about seven years old.

As so often with musicians, Jule's talent emerged early, and on leaving school at the age of 16, he formed a band which included for a while Benny Goodman in its ranks. His first hit as a song-writer was 'Sunday', written at the age of 21 to words by Ned Miller. Changing the spelling of his name to 'Styne', to avoid confusion with another musician, Julius Stein, like most popular song composers of his generation Jule travelled to Hollywood in the 1930s, where he wrote songs and background music for various movies. As a good example of Jule Styne's all-round compositional skills, the Scherzo for Orchestra, which is incorporated in the score of *Gentlemen Prefer Blondes* gives a good idea of his talent in this direction.

In 1942, he joined forces with the lyricist Sammy Cahn, which was to prove the most fruitful partnership of his career up to that time, and they wrote songs for various musical films, including several for Frank Sinatra. But Styne's heart lay in the theatre: in 1947 they collaborated on a stage musical, *High Button Shoes* which enjoyed a successful Broadway run of almost 750 performances following the show's opening on October 9, 1947. A contributory factor in the success was the choreography of Jerome Robbins, to some exceptionally fine ballet music by Styne. It is a pity that this ballet music has not enjoyed a separate life, for it certainly would seem to deserve revival. Harold Barnes, in *The New York Herald Tribune,* said, "The ballet is a classic, and Jule Styne has written a glittering score"; Milton Rosenstock, the musical director of both *High Button Shoes* and *Gentlemen Prefer Blondes*, said that the "ballet music by Jule is not merely good music, it is fine music".

Another star of the show should be mentioned: Phil Silvers.

Frank Sinatra attended the opening night party, thinking that "my team" as he praised them, would remain with him, but Sammy Cahn's contribution to the show was not praised as highly as was Styne's and the lyricist took the press criticisms personally.

He went back to Hollywood, but with his first Broadway success as a composer, Jule Styne remained in New York, hoping to capitalise on his personal ascending star.

He was right to do so, for as the inevitable trials and tribulations that attend all theatrical productions in rehearsal were encountered and overcome, it became clear to those taking part, and to those interested outsiders, that here was a hit vehicle in the making. The production was staged by John C Wilson, and other members of the original cast were Jack McCauley, Eric Brotherton and George S Irving.

The period of *Gentlemen Prefer Blondes* is set in the mid-1920s and the story opens as the transatlantic liner Ile de France sets sail for Europe. On board are Lorelei Lee and her friend Dorothy; Lorelei is sad at leaving her fiancé, Gus Esmond, but Dorothy, disenchanted by Prohibition, is looking forward to Paris and improving herself. At sea, Lorelei decides that she needs a new benefactor, and urges Dorothy to do likewise. Lorelei chances upon a suitable passenger on board, a rich bachelor, Henry Spofford, who is encumbered by his mother, and brings Dorothy and the bachelor together. In the mean time, Lorelei has borrowed $5,000 from a rich Englishman, Sir Francis Beekman, to buy a diamond tiara from his wife, Lady Beekman, Lorelei explaining that the nice thing about diamonds is that they always look new.

In Paris, Dorothy and Henry realise that they are in love, and Lorelei finds a suitable new benefactor in Josephus Gage. But Lady Beekman, on discovering from whom Lorelei obtained the money for the tiara, sets a firm of French lawyers on her. Gus Esmond is informed and arrives, to find Lorelei with Josephus Gage. Lorelei now sings the most famous song in the show, 'Diamonds Are A Girl's Best Friend' as Gus arranges for the debut of a dancer at a local night-club, which

turns out to be very successful. Lorelei makes her peace with Gus, and arranges to pay back Sir Francis, as both girls, with their boy-friends and Mrs Spofford, experience pangs of homesickness for New York. Back in the USA, Lorelei and Gus are to be married, and Dorothy takes charge of the big party which ends with happiness all round.

This was the fourth version of the story – a book, a play, a film, a musical – and now there was to be a fifth. This was the film of the musical, which was made in 1953 by 20th Century-Fox, and starred – as was so often the case – neither Carol Channing nor Yvonne Adair, but Marilyn Monroe and Jane Russell.

Film of the musical it may have been, but the music was barely recognisable. The story remained basically the same, but only three out of the original 13 songs in the show were kept in the film version. These were: 'Diamonds Are A Girl's Best Friend', 'Two Little Girls From Little Rock' (originally, in the show, it was a solo number for Lorelei, with the title 'A Little Girl From Little Rock'), and ''Bye Bye Baby'. Replacement material was by Hoagy Carmichael and Harold Adamson in the shape of two new songs: 'Ain't There Anyone Here For Love?' and 'When Love Goes Wrong'.

The cast was particularly strong: in addition to the female leads, there were Charles Coburn (one of his best performances), Tommy Noonan, Norma Varden, Elliott Reid, George Winslow and George Chakiris. The choreography was by Jack Cole, the musical direction was by Lionel Newman, and Howard Hawks was the director. The result is a stunningly successful recreation of a Broadway show in filmic terms, one of the best transitions from one art-form to another in the history of the genre – the film not seeking to ape a stagy production, but having fresh values wholly germane to the new idiom. The star of the film, as in each of her manifestations, was Lorelei Lee herself.

Chapter 15

Guys And Dolls

The American author Damon Runyon was born in Manhattan, Kansas – not New York City – in 1884. Like many 20th-century American authors, he was also a man of some energy, for by the age of 14, by lying about his age, he had already seen action in the Spanish-American war of 1898, before becoming a journalist. In 1911 he joined the *New York American* concentrating mainly upon sports journalism. The same year he published the first of several volumes of verse, and the entry of America into World War I in 1917 found Runyon as a war correspondent. After the war and back in Manhattan – New York City – he began also writing the short stories for which he is best remembered.

Runyon's stories of relative low life in New York, especially on Broadway, were characterised by a vivid, somewhat racy style, and were written almost always in the present tense. They were coloured by contemporary slang and struck a responsive chord for millions of readers.

One of the best collections of his short stories was published in 1931 and called *Guys And Dolls*; these stories became enormously popular – no less than 16 of them were filmed and one of them in particular, *The Idyll Of Miss Sarah Brown* was to form the basis for a musical adaptation in 1950

as the show *Guys And Dolls* – subtitled *A Musical Fable Of Broadway* – with music and lyrics by Frank Loesser, the theatrical book by Jo Swerling and Abe Burrows (the provision of which, in Burrows' case, was one of the most remarkable 'first-time' efforts in the history of the musical theatre) and directed by George S Kaufman. The settings and lighting were by Jo Mielziner, the dances and musical numbers were staged by Michael Kidd, and the costumes were by Alvin Colt. The orchestrations were by George Bassman and Ted Royal; the vocal arrangements and direction were by Herbert Greene and the musical director was Irving Actman. With this vastly experienced and gifted production team, the show could hardly have had finer creative backing; we shall return to the leading players later.

Runyon's stories made him, as Louis Untermeyer said, "the laureate of the illiterate. His heroes were the safe-blowers, hard-boiled (but sentimental) sports, beer barons, crap-shooters, horse-players, gangsters and slangsters of Manhattan-on-the-subway".

The material was ripe for Broadway treatment, and the team assembled for such a work-over could hardly have been improved upon, given the nature of the original material.

Marlon Brando, Jean Simmons, Frank Sinatra and Vivian Blaine in 1955 production of *Guys And Dolls*, produced by Samuel Goldwyn.

Frank himself had been born in New York in 1910 into a musical family – his father Henry was a fine pianist and his older half-brother Arthur, became a noted classical pianist and writer on music. Curiously, Frank refused to take music lessons, and in this subject he was entirely self-taught. He was a journalist, like Runyon, and also was a sometime night-club pianist until he went to Hollywood in 1936 to work for Universal Pictures, principally as a lyricist, in which field he collaborated most successfully with Hoagy Carmichael on *Two Sleepy People* in 1938.

During the war Loesser began to write music, and had a major hit with 'Praise The Lord And Pass The Ammunition', but when the war was over, he returned to New York and scored an astonishing success with *Where's Charley?* a brilliant adaptation of the English Victorian farce *Charley's Aunt*. This show, co-produced by Cy Feuer and Ernest Martin, ran for more than two years, during which time the team were at work on *Guys And Dolls*.

Runyon had died in 1946, from cancer, and his son scattered his ashes – as requested by his father – over Times Square from a chartered plane. The adaptation would surely have appealed to the writer: the plot of the show, *Guys And Dolls*, whilst based on the Sarah Brown story, includes other Runyonesque characters, typical of his Broadway yarns – Nathan Detroit, Sky Masterson, Big Jule, Benny Southstreet, Harry the Horse, Nicely–Nicely Johnson and others. They are all gamblers, to a degree, and we are soon embroiled in the combination of rolled dice and sentimentality – the trouble with their girls.

The show is about two love stories: in one, Nathan Detroit, a small-time (but hot-shot) operator, whose proud boast is that he runs 'The Oldest Established Permanent Floating Crap Game in New York'; some idea of Loesser's

suitability as composer of this score is that Detroit's boast is also the title of one of the show's songs. Detroit's girl is Miss Adelaide, a night-club singer of some talent, but Detroit is unwilling, or unable to tie the knot: they have been engaged for 14 years, the constant postponement of their wedding being largely due to Detroit's habit of having either to visit the Saratoga race track for every one of the season's eight major races, or take charge of an important crap game. Adelaide bears all of this uncertainty with a reasonable grace.

The second love story is centred upon Sky Masterson – a night-person in every respect, whose air of freedom extends to all areas of his life; he knows his attitude leaves something to be desired on the moral front, for he is attracted to Miss Sarah Brown. She is a Salvation Army girl who runs the local run-down Save-a-Soul Mission. In the end, all's well that ends well, and we end up with more than a sneaking regard for the inherent decency – in their own terms – of these vivid characters and their friends.

The book of *Guys And Dolls* is considered to be of outstanding quality – it has been said that it could quite easily be performed as a dramatic play as it stands. But the addition of Loesser's score gave the concept a layer of brilliant and fully integrated music in which the composer's ability to marry colloquial speech with entirely suitable melodies produced songs that were both germane to the dramatic and musical argument as well as being quite able to stand alone by themselves.

Guys And Dolls opened on Broadway at the 46th Street Theatre on November 24, 1950. Robert Alda (who had played George Gershwin in the film biography of the composer in 1946, and was the father of Alan) played Sky Masterson; Vivian Blaine was Miss Adelaide, and Sam Leven played Nathan Detroit. Isabel Bigley was Sarah Brown, and other members of the cast included Pat Rooney, Sr, BS Pully, Stubby Kaye, Tom Pedi, Johnny Silver, Paul Reed and Netta Packer.

The show was a famous hit. Such songs as 'A Bushel And A Peck', 'I've Never Been In Love Before', 'Luck Be A Lady Tonight' and 'Sit Down, You're Rockin' The Boat' enjoyed spectacular success outside of the show, and *Guys And Dolls*, when it opened in London on May 28, 1953 – five days before the Coronation of Queen Elizabeth II – surprisingly proved just as successful. The surprise was felt by some because the inherent 'New York low life' nature of the material might not be so readily appreciated by a British audience: but the widespread influence of American movies and popular music in post-war Britain made audiences as well-informed of such matters as any audience in Seattle or Galveston.

The two main cast changes in the London Coliseum production were Jerry Wayne as Sky Masterson and Lizbeth Webb as Sarah Brown: the production itself, and all other main characters, were the same as the original Broadway production of two-and-a-half years previously. *Guys And Dolls* ran in London for almost two years.

The movie followed in 1955. Produced by Samuel Goldwyn, who reportedly paid a million dollars for the film rights, he had signed an unusual collection of outstanding stars to appear in it: Frank Sinatra, Jean Simmons, Marlon Brando and Vivian Blaine were the four main leads, and were brilliantly supported by some of those who had created the roles on Broadway including Stubby Kaye, BS Pully and Johnny Silver. Michael Kidd was again responsible for the choreography, and the photography, in Eastmancolor and in Cinemascope, was by Harry Stradling. The musical direction was in the hands of Cyril Mockridge and Jay Blackton (these last three gentlemen each received Academy Award nominations for their work on the movie).

The script was by Joseph L Mankiewicz, and kept close to the original; Mankiewicz also directed the movie, but the music was changed by Loesser in such a way as to constitute almost a master-class in how such changes should be made for film versions. Goldwyn was adamant that the main leads should all sing their songs, and none of them should mime. This was fair enough, in a musical film, but the obvious question immediately posed itself: how would Brando cope with singing? What sort of a voice did he have?

Well, not much of a one, as it transpired, but his light baritone was not unpleasant at all, considered purely as timbre. What Brando really lacked was a trained voice, and natural musical intelligence – thankfully, Loesser realised this himself, and altered his score accordingly.

Guys and Dolls began filming at the Goldwyn Studios in March 1955, with Frank Sinatra playing the part of Nathan Detroit. It is no secret that he really hankered after the part that was given to Brando – Sky Masterson – because Sinatra rightly felt that that role was the real romantic lead, and in addition, Sky Masterson had all the solo romantic ballads. Nathan Detroit was, at heart, a comedy role – not at all beyond Sinatra's abilities – who only had one good song himself. Sinatra knew perfectly well that Brando was not a singer, but so did Loesser, who was mortified when Brando freely admitted that the song 'I've Never Been In Love Before' was quite beyond him. This great number, which had already been a hit song, was therefore dropped from the movie. Loesser wrote a new song for Sinatra – 'Adelaide' – and for Brando, a much easier song to sing, 'A Woman In Love'. In the duets with Jean Simmons, Brando

Marlon Brando in the 1955 production of *Guys And Dolls*.

was more than passable, as he was in the other ensemble numbers, but by himself he was not as good. Nor was Sinatra a fan of Brando for other reasons – he claimed that he had been promised the part Brando played in *On The Waterfront* in 1954, and successfully sued the film-makers, and he was not a fan of the so-called 'method' acting: "I don't buy this take and re-take jazz; the key to good acting on the screen is spontaneity – and that's something you lose a little with each take." He referred to Brando as 'Mumbles'.

There is a curious point concerning the sound-track recording of the film: Sinatra, under contract to another company, does not appear on the album, although he did later record Nathan Detroit's numbers for his own Reprise record company as part of an interesting series of show recordings by the Reprise Repertory Theatre.

The locale of the movie is decidedly studio-bound; some may have been disconcerted by this aspect of Hollywoodian fantasy, but Damon Runyon's stories were fantasy – an aspect of Runyonesque film-making that was copied in Howard Brookner's 1988 movie *Bloodhounds Of Broadway* and Warren Beatty's 1990 smash-hit *Dick Tracy* – both of which starred Madonna.

When one considers that at 140 minutes, this film of *Guys And Dolls* is somewhat long for the essential material – not for the only time in Mankiewicz's career – and Goldwyn's film of *Porgy And Bess* of 1959 came in ten minutes less (the original *Porgy And Bess* is at least an hour more), then some idea of the relative imbalance of structure in the movie can be gauged. This, however, is purely relative within the film itself, which has rightly garnered the reputation of being a cult movie. Its qualities far outweigh its drawbacks, and it remains an excellent version of a musical, the revivals of which by all kinds of theatre companies have shown it to possess outstanding, and lasting, musical, literary and dramatic merits.

Chapter 16

Gypsy

With the world-wide success of *West Side Story* assured, it was perhaps only natural that its four creators should look to repeat their success with a new show. However, it did not quite turn out in the way such a reasonable statement might infer. The two newcomers to Broadway, which *West Side Story* had introduced – Arthur Laurents and Stephen Sondheim – had shown they could do it, and with Jerome Robbins eager to get into a new project, the final member of the quartet was Leonard Bernstein. We have elsewhere outlined much of Bernstein's varied gifts, of which the principal – so far as the general musical public was concerned – was as a symphonic conductor.

Since the opening of *West Side Story* in 1957, much had happened to Bernstein to further that aspect of his career, the most important being his appointment in 1958 as music director of the Philharmonic-Symphony Orchestra of New York, one of America's greatest orchestras and one of the oldest in the world – it is six months older than the Vienna Philharmonic. Such a prestigious appointment would demand virtually all of Bernstein's time, and therefore he was not in a position to devote any time to the composition of a major new Broadway score.

Gypsy Rose Lee was the most famous, if not the most notorious, strip-tease artiste in the United States in the first half of the 20th-century. Although by all accounts a brilliant stripper, her speciality was in the tease – "once you've seen one, you've seen 'em all" – in not revealing absolutely everything. In 1954, she had written her autobiography, entitled *Gypsy*, and David Merrick had bought the rights to turn it into a musical, which was to star Ethel Merman. He approached Jule Styne and suggested he consider doing it with Betty Comden and Adolph Green. Styne read the book and was enthralled at the possibilities; he told Merrick that he was up for it, that he was dying to write for Ethel Merman and he, Betty and Adolph began work on an adaptation.

However, their work had not gone too far before certain problems arose with regard to the right way to treat certain characters. The story of Gypsy Rose Lee's life is that she was one of two daughters of Rose Hovick, a domineering, theatrical mother hell-bent on making at least one of her daughters a star. In real life, they both did; daughter June became the screen actress June Havoc. But the journey to stardom was not that which Rose imagined.

Rosalind Russell and Diane Pace in Mervyn LeRoy's production of _Gypsy_ for Warners, 1962.

And so, for a while at least, the project was shelved; Styne, Green and Comden moved on to other things, and it was not until some years later that Merrick, assured that Green and Comden wished to have nothing more to do with the project, approached Arthur Laurents and Jerome Robbins. They suggested he engage Stephen Sondheim to provide the lyrics and the music, but after Merrick went to Ethel Merman to seek her advice as to the composer with whom she would most like to work, she suggested Styne, amongst others, a name that had also been put forward by Jerome Robbins, perhaps remembering Styne's ballet music in *Gentlemen Prefer Blondes*. Styne had been waiting for Merrick's call. (Incidentally, the ballet music in *Gypsy* was to be arranged by John Kander, who, within several years, became one of Broadway's most successful original composers for the musical theatre.)

At first, Sondheim was a little put out; he felt the deal to write both words and music was firm, and he thought of withdrawing, but before deciding he sought the advice of his mentor, Oscar Hammerstein II, who counselled him that the chance of writing for a big star like Ethel Merman was not one that came along every day, and it would be priceless experience for him – from which he would learn a great deal. Sondheim consoled himself with the thought that there would be plenty of opportunities in the future to write music for the theatre as well as words, and Hammerstein was right – this *was* a great opportunity. Once Sondheim had met Styne, and persuaded him to write the score in a new way – basically following Arthur Laurents's lead as to what was needed dramatically at whatever point, and to compose the music chronologically – he realised that Styne could be an ideal collaborator for this project. But Arthur Laurents was not so **sure.** He thought Styne's music was a little dated,

but met the composer at his apartment with the others and was astonished at Styne's range and musical strength: "So then I readily accepted Jule Styne as the composer."

David Merrick had asked Styne originally, and he was delighted when he was prepared to work afresh on the story. Styne had not previously worked with Merrick, but the latter's Broadway credentials were excellent, and he was at that time one of the most successful and talked about directors in the American theatre. The project had finally got under way.

The curious dichotomy of the story was that although the title of the show would lead one to expect a musical based on the life of Gypsy Rose Lee, as outlined in her autobiography, the central character in the show was Rose's mother. It needed the hands of several masters to make this work: it is a tribute to the combined theatrical skills of the participating creators of the show that it worked so brilliantly, and their willingness to make compromise, even if in the making a few feathers were temporarily ruffled.

What was also interesting is the input that Ethel Merman had – not much in terms of quantity, but such an experienced performer as she was undoubtedly listened to with respect. When she had decided the show was complete, she called Irving Berlin and introduced herself as "Mrs Birdseye. The show's frozen." By 'frozen' she meant no more additions or excisions.

The story of *Gypsy* opens in the early 1920s, in Seattle. Two sisters (Baby Lousie and Baby June), under their mother's ever-watchful gaze, are appearing in a kiddie show in a vaudeville house. Rose, the mother, will stop at nothing to ensure the success of her daughters, and cannot understand why everyone else does not share her opinion of their talents.

In another town, Rose adds some boys to the

act and the girls are relaunched as Baby June and Her Newsboys. On this tour, Rose meets Herbie, and persuades him to become the girls' manager. A few years later, and although the girls are clearly older, Rose lies about their ages as they still tour with the same act. Herbie has fallen for Rose, and wants to quite touring and set up home with her, but she still wishes to see at least one of her daughters make it as a star. Despite several tempting offers, Rose turns them all down and in so doing further alienates the girls. Tulsa, a boy in the act, shows Louise a new routine he is working on; she joins in, hoping to be his partner, but soon afterwards Tulsa and June elope together.

Rose has no choice but to concentrate on Louise; by mistake, Herbie books Louise and boys into a low burlesque (strip-tease) joint, and while she is shocked at first – as is Rose – Louise, mindful of their parlous financial state, decides to fulfil the engagement – and seeks advice from other strip girls who work there. Louise gets her break when the top girl is arrested, and Rose pushes her daughter forward to take the spot, to Herbie's disgust, whereupon he quits.

Louise goes through with the strip-tease, carefully avoiding baring all, and it is immediately apparent that she has a gift for this form of entertainment. We now see her as Gypsy Rose Lee, her new stage name, and the toast of the circuit and topping the bill at Minsky's Club. But Rose still attempts to dominate everyone; alone in the theatre, she muses over her fate in life and what has befallen her. Gypsy hears her mother pouring her heart out for the first time, and, realising her mother's inherent vulnerability, she rejoins her on stage, and they now both realise that their future relationship will be based on understanding, trust and consideration for each other – even though Rose has the last song,

'Rose's Turn': part parody of her daughter's success, part reprise of Rose's big solo number, 'Everything's Coming Up Roses', and part pure belter for Ethel Merman's wide vibrato, for whom the role was designed from the start.

The adaptation had worked, brilliantly, and evinced a full realisation of the rather difficult relationships between the main characters. The show was an undoubted hit, but it seemed so essentially a home-grown piece – what with Broadway, tours across the USA and Canada, other American tours (most notably with Ann Sothern) that it was thought it might not travel too well. In 1962, the show was released on film.

The movie of *Gypsy* was Warners; directed by Mervyn Le Roy, its length – at 150 minutes – sprawled somewhat, and although the outstanding cinematography in Technirama by Harry Stradling earned him an Academy Award nomination, as the musical direction by Frank Perkins did for him, the casting was not the film's strong point. It starred Rosalind Russell in the part written for Ethel Merman, and whilst Miss Russell was a big star in her own right, the part was so much Ethel Merman's that no amount of shoe-horning could entirely convince that her alternative view was equally valid.

Nor was Natalie Wood well cast as Rose; as in *West Side Story*, her singing voice had to be dubbed (by the same singer, Marni Nixon), and her *persona* hardly fitted that of a great strip-tease artist: she was too nice, yet it all did seem to work against the odds. The only really good casting was Karl Malden as Herbie, taking the part that Jack Klugman had created on stage, and the best scene in the film was that of the three strippers enjoining Rose in 'You Gotta Have A Gimmick' – a great moment in film musicals from Roxanne Arlen, Faith Dane and Betty Bruce.

Chapter 17

Three Ivor Novello Musicals

Glamorous Night; The Dancing Years; King's Rhapsody

If one takes the title of this book literally, then strictly speaking, no Ivor Novello musical show should appear in it, for none was a significant Broadway hit, and the movies that were made of three of them were all, in essence, British – not Hollywood – productions. But if – as stated elsewhere – we interpret 'Broadway' to mean the English-speaking (and musical) stage, and 'Hollywood' as English-language films intended for a world audience, the fact remains that Ivor Novello bestrode London's West End musical stage, in the years from the first appearance of *Glamorous Night* (1935) to his final appearance in his own *King's Rhapsody* in 1951, like the colossus of the genre that he was – 'the Richard Rodgers of the British musical' as he has been aptly called.

Ivor Novello was more than that: he was an exceptionally gifted actor as well as being an immortal composer and author, and a fine theatrical producer as well. His influence on the musical stage was considerable, and later generations of British composers of musicals, whose work has appeared with great success on Broadway, have acknowledged their debt to him.

Sadly, the films that were made of his three greatest musicals were all less than satisfactory, so we do not have a suitable permanent record of the work of this theatrical genius on film. We do have some recordings made by Novello in three roles: as singer, pianist and conductor, and these are indeed precious, but the absence of a fine film version of even one of his best musicals is a standing reproach to the film industry of the time.

To be fair, it was not entirely the industry's fault, for Novello's career in one sense came at the wrong time: his run of West End musicals was interrupted, badly, by World War II, and he died aged only 58, a mere six years after that war had come to an end, when he was himself appearing on stage, taking the lead in *King's Rhapsody*. He died before the 'original cast recording' concept had been established in Britain, and before the notion of Hollywood-style films of musical stage successes could be made in the UK.

Quite apart from anything else, the subject-matter of Novello's shows was, at heart, backward-looking – set in far off Ruritanian kingdoms and principalities – and, with Novello himself having made the male leads in his own shows very much his own, there was no comparable performer of stature to take on those parts and reinterpret them for the cinema. As a consequence, these fine shows have remained almost unknown to a wider cinema audience.

But the attempt, however unsuccessful in realisation, was made. In fact, as we have mentioned, three attempts to film Novello musicals came to the screen. The first was *Glamorous Night* – which came about in an extraordinary manner. Indeed, the provenance of this show would itself make a fine subject for a musical. It arose in the following way.

Towards the end of 1934, HM Tennent – who was then manager of the Drury Lane Theatre – sat facing a bleak future. Richard Tauber's sometimes prickly temperament had caused the recent production of Franz Lehar's *The Land Of Smiles*' to run into difficulties; a new musical by Jerome Kern, *The Three Sisters*, had flopped badly, and there did not seem to be anything – after the traditional run of the Christmas pantomime had ended – in the offing to prevent the theatre from going 'dark' until the following Christmas. Tennent took Ivor Novello to lunch and bemoaned his fate.

Novello had been born in Cardiff in 1893 as Ivor Davies and took the name Novello from his mother's family. She was a talented and practical musician, and at the age of ten he entered the Choir School of Magdalen College, Oxford. The family had moved to London, and realising the impossibility of preventing her son from pursuing a musical career, his mother engaged him as a rehearsal pianist. At the age of 21 he found overnight fame when his patriotic song 'Keep The Home Fires Burning' caught the public imagination shortly after the outbreak of World War I, and he was soon conscripted into the Royal Naval Air Service. He survived two air crashes, and he was transferred to the new Air Ministry in London's Whitehall. This brought him literally within walking distance of the West End, and he continued to compose in his free time. After the

War, he cemented his growing reputation and his talents found new outlets in acting and producing as well as in music. It is certainly true that Novello had much in common with another giant of the English theatre, Noel Coward – Novello even appeared in Coward's dramatic play, *The Vortex* in 1928 – and Coward's name was mentioned by Tennent during that lunch, but only to say that Coward was unable to have a new show ready in time, and in any event was taken up with other projects.

On the spur of the moment Novello exclaimed: "I've got the answer to all Drury Lane's problems!" and proceeded then and there to outline an improvised story. Tennent was sufficiently impressed to ask for a synopsis to be delivered the very next day, which it was, together with the title, *Glamorous Night*. The upshot was that Novello was given five months to complete the show and have it ready for the opening night, which was fixed for May 2nd, 1935.

Working at fever-pitch, Novello called upon a number of highly talented and faithful young friends, writing the score with specific performers in mind. The result was that *Glamorous Night* was a dazzling success by any standards. The lyrics were by the fastidious young actor-poet Christoper Hassall, who was at that time playing in Novello's play *Murder In Mayfair*, and, despite a threatened strike by the acting union Equity which threatened the show's future, the star cast included Novello himself in a non-singing role, Mary Ellis, Lyn Harding, Elisabeth Welch, Olive Gilbert, Barry Jones, Trefor Jones, Victor Bogetti and Peter Graves.

The plot is set in Ruritania, where a young, and glamorous, King is saved from the machinations of "his scheming prime minister... [by] an opera singer and her gypsy friends", as Leslie Halliwell succinctly put it. This is hardly a thrilling plot, but we should remember that the world was then barely coming out of a global depression, and Novello was transporting his public – if only for a few hours – to a far-off land of romance and beauty. The sets were by Oliver Messell, and Leontine Sagan was the dynamic producer.

The score is chock-full of superb songs, and within two years a film was planned and made. Only Mary Ellis and Trefor Jones from the original leading cast were in the black-and-white film, which starred Otto Kruger as the King and was directed by Brian Desmond Hurst. But the result was not inspiring, in spite of some occasional good moments; at least the film was not over-long.

Novello himself should have appeared in the movie, but by the time filming began he was working on his next show, *Careless Rapture* which was also for Drury Lane, and which proved to be another great triumph. The part he wrote for himself was superb, and he had another fine supporting cast, including the excellent Dorothy Dickson, Zena Dare, Olive Gilbert, Walter Crisham and Peter Graves once more. However, no film was made of this show, nor of its equally triumphant successor, *Crest Of The Wave*.

Novello was now at the height of his powers, and when his next show opened at Drury Lane on March 23, 1939 he had surely reached the summit of his fame. This was *The Dancing Years*, a story of Vienna – somewhat ominously and prophetically set in the city both in the days before World War II and around the time of the Anschluss in 1938. Indeed, it was the outbreak of World War II in September 1939 that temporarily ended the run of *The Dancing Years* before it returned to the West End (at the nearby Adelphi Theatre) in March 1942. The cast again included Novello himself, with Mary Ellis, Olive Gilbert,

Minnie Rayner and a young actress, Roma Beaumont.

It was therefore not until 1949 that a film was made of the show, but the result was poor. Starring Dennis Price and Gisèle Préville, and directed with a somewhat wooden hand by Harold French, the Technicolor staging could do little to recreate a city before both world wars – and it was difficult in 1949 to make Austria a sympathetic country. Perhaps it could have been done, but the film failed badly.

Once more, Novello could not have appeared in the film, for he was working on what was to be his last show in which he himself appeared, *King's Rhapsody*. This was arguably his masterpiece, but it was not heard at Drury Lane; it was produced at the Palace Theatre in Shaftesbury Avenue and opened there on September 15, 1949, where it ran for 839 performances – its run would undoubtedly have been longer were it not for Novello's untimely death from a sudden thrombosis on the night of March 5/6, 1951, "a few hours after making a speech in response to the plaudits of an excited and cheering audience", as his friend and colleague, the critic W Macqueen-Pope, recalled.

Novello's death was a sudden and tragic loss to the British theatre – during the run of *King's Rhapsody* he had written his last show, *Gay's The Word* which opened at the Saville Theatre starring Cecily Courtnedge a few weeks before Novello died.

The film of *King's Rhapsody* came four years later, a Herbert Wilcox production which starred his wife, Dame Anna Neagle, as one of the only two leading people in the movie who were aptly cast. Errol Flynn took Novello's role and although the script was a good one, adapted for the screen by Pamela Bower, Christopher Hassall and AP Herbert, and the Cinemascope colour photography by Max Greene was intermittently outstanding, Errol Flynn was disastrously miscast, and Wilcox's direction lacked his customary sureness of touch.

The fact remains that Novello's shows are the work of genius in this field, and we may hope that at some point in the future they may be rediscovered for new audiences and, hopefully, turned into equally outstanding films which sympathetically treat and reinterpret them.

Chapter 18

Kismet

The great 19th-century Russian composer Alexander Borodin led a particularly colourful and fulfilling life; he began as the illegitimate son of Prince Gedeanoff, who ensured that his offspring had a fine education. But young Alexander showed a great interest in music, a profession which in mid-19th century Russia was looked down upon by the nobility.

Borodin was trained as a chemist, in which discipline he achieved distinction – indeed, a statue erected in his memory in Russia after his death commemorated his achievements as a scientist, not as a composer. But Borodin was able to write music in his spare time; not so much in quantity, it is true, for he was also only 53 when he died, but of a melodic memorability that has made him one of the best-loved of all Russian composers.

Such is the quality of his melodies that they achieved a circulation outside of the concert works in which they first appeared; in 1953 Robert Wright and George Forrest sought to emulate their 1944 success in *Song Of Norway* (a musical based upon the life and music of the 19th-century Norwegian composer Edvard Grieg). Wright and Forrest made very successful careers in using existing **classical music** as the basis for their shows; their **two musicals on** the story of Anastasia (*Anya*, **1964 and** *The Anastasia Affair* 1991) **use themes** by Rachmaninoff; *Dumas And Son* (1967) **is based** on music by Saint-Saëns.

By 1953 Wright and **Forrest had completed** their use of the music of Alexander Borodin as the basis for a musical adaptation, **with the** book written by Charles Lederer and Luther Davis, of a play dating from 1911, *Kismet*, written by Edward Knoblock.

This very successful drama **had opened on** Christmas Day, 1911, in New York City, starring Otis Skinner. The play was actually filmed three times; a silent adaptation from 1920 was followed by the first talkie version, in 1930, in the Vitascope process in black-and-white – notable for also starring Otis Skinner, recreating his stage role, and Loretta Young – and in 1944 the second talkie version, in Technicolor for MGM, with Ronald Colman and Marlene Dietrich.

1944 was therefore the year of *Song Of Norway* and of the third filmed version of the play *Kismet*: it was also the year in which two rather unsuccessful musicals by the Russian-

MGM's 1955 production of *Kismet*.

born composer Vernon Duke (he retained his real name, Vladimir Dukelsky, for his concert music) with books by Howard Dietz, opened in New York. The first was *Jackpot*, including words by Guy Bolton, and the second, marginally more successful, *Sadie Thompson*, based of course upon the novella *Rain* by Somerset Maugham. 1944 was also the year in which the notion of a musical version of *Kismet* was first mooted by Edwin Lester, but it was almost a decade before *Kismet* finally came to fruition on Broadway. Prior to its opening in New York – appropriately enough, also during the Christmas season, on December 3 – in 1953 the show had earlier been tried out in Hollywood, at the Los Angeles Philharmonic Auditorium, when it was presented by the Los Angeles Civic Light Opera Association. The problem with this try-out was that it could hardly be termed a success. It has been suggested that the serious nature of the original music may have lent the score a salubrious air, but this was not the first time that Wright and Forrest had created such a theatre piece, and there are indeed few musical shows which have not required some pre-opening night changes. It seems, however, that in the case of *Kismet,* these changes were reasonably substantial.

Once again, it was the finished result that counted, and whilst a number of classical music purists would no doubt have balked at what was perceived as the 'plundering' of 'art' music, there is equally no doubt that Forrest and Wright, who adapted the music as well as writing the lyrics, did an outstanding job: quite a lot of the music they used by Borodin was unknown, even in classical music circles, and the resultant score (which in the piano reduction runs to 172 pages) is wholly a music-theatre piece, by no means a rough paste-and-

scissors job. The use of pre-existing music is by no means a 20th-century phenomenon in the musical theatre – it has its basis in theatrical antiquity – and the only criterion which has to be applied is: does it work? In the case of *Kismet* – as we shall see – it most assuredly did.

The distinguished American stage producer Edwin Lester had worked with some success with Robert Wright and George Forrest in the late 1930s and early 1940s, principally in their successful adaptations of music by earlier composers to make new shows. It was Lester's idea to do something similar along the lines of an Arabian nights story. He suggested, it appears, that Wright and Forrest consider using music by Tchaikovsky or Rimsky-Korsakov, but they pointed out that they had already used music by both composers in earlier adaptations of theirs, so to look again at their music would inevitably result in choosing 'second-best' material for such a purpose. Edwin Lester now turned to his friend, Vernon Duke, and asked him for ideas; Duke suggested the music of Borodin, no doubt owing to the mildly oriental flavour of some of the Russian composer's works – *In The Steppes Of Central Asia* and his opera *Prince Igor*, for examples.

The themes having been taken from Borodin, they were then fashioned into the songs and ensemble numbers that make up the musical's finished score. The book was another matter, for the existence of the play would seem to indicate that here was finished dialogue, with perhaps only several minor adjustments having to be made. But the text of the original play, it would appear, was very much a product of its time – a time in which things Eastern were enjoying something of a vogue in Europe – and the original dialogue was both somewhat stiff, and no less dated in itself, for audiences of the 1950s.

The play was given a lighter treatment, a little self-deprecating in parts, and the central part of Hajj was virtually entirely rewritten. Edwin Lester had originally had the operatic bass Ezio Pinza in mind for the role, but in 1949 he had accepted the part of Emile de Becque in Rodgers and Hammerstein's *South Pacific*, in which he had had an enormous success. By January 1953, we are told, the brilliant Alfred Drake was signed to do the part.

Such is the impact of the score that most classical music-lovers are ready to suspend their reservations and enjoy an extraordinary achievement. 'Nothing succeeds like success', as the saying goes, and, in terms of awards, *Kismet* garnered a whole clutch of the most prestigious of them during its Broadway run, helped by – amongst other things – the stylish choreography of Jack Cole. These included a (naturally) posthumous award for Borodin as Best Composer (!) in the 1953-4 Tony Awards, amongst other Tonys that went to the show for Best Musical, Best Authors, Best (male) Performance In Musical and Best Musical Direction. These last two awards went to the great Alfred Drake (A Public Poet, later called Hajj) and to Louis Adrian respectively. Drake won two further awards for his portrayal of this role: a Donaldson Award for Best Performance In A Musical (male) and the Variety Drama Critics' Poll for Best Male Performance in 1953-54.

Kismet could have come from *Tales Of The Arabian Nights*; it is concerned with the fable of Hajj, a poet-beggar who, during the course of a single magic day, finds himself elevated to Emir of Baghdad; this occurs as a result of several 'wondrous happenings' – aided and abetted by his own machinations – when he obtains wealth, love, rights wrongs, triumphs over evil, "and rises to a place of true eminence in the fabled city".

However, the secondary dramatic theme tells of Hajj's daughter, Marsinah, and her love for the Caliph. In turn, the Caliph is temporarily disguised as a gardener. After several adventures and vicissitudes, Hajj triumphs over all, eloping to an oasis with the widow of the Wazir of Police, after Marsinah has married her Caliph. All ends happily, and this imaginative treatment of a most imaginative play wafts its mystery into the distance, as though borne on a magic carpet.

Kismet ran for 16 months on Broadway, finally closing just three days after the London production opened at the Stoll Theatre on April 20, 1955. In the cast were Alfred Drake and Doretta Morrow, repeating their Broadway successes; the Wazir of Police was played by Paul Whitsun-Jones, and it is interesting to note that in the dancers was the young Juliet Prowse.

In London, the Caliph was played by Peter Grant, and Lalume by Joan Diener, and another interesting fact regarding the London run of *Kismet* is that it ran longer in the British capital than it did on Broadway; produced by the legendary Jack Hylton, it ran for 676 performances, compared with the 583 it notched up at New York's Ziegfeld Theatre. Almost 23 years later, during a rather fashionable era which saw the revival of older musicals, *Kismet* was brilliantly revived at London's Shaftesbury Theatre, opening there on March 21, 1978.

'Kismet' means 'fate', and, despite the long gestation period which attended the birth of this show, it seems to have been fated to be a hit. Yet another curious fact is that the New York opening of *Kismet* coincided with a newspaper strike, so no reviews could appear in the press; although the response of the audience was highly favourable, it was partly due to an early use of the potential pulling-power of television that word of the quality of the show got around. A television programme about the show, with numbers sung live on camera and various respected stars and theatrical luminaries giving their thumbs up to the production did the trick. This was just as well, for the critics were not too impressed with the opening night – as Martin Sutton, who has chronicled the fascinating story of *Kismet*'s early adventures, said: "By the time such bad press as there was hit the streets, it was too late." The show was already a success.

An early admirer of *Kismet* was Cole Porter; as we have learned, Porter himself was a classically-trained musician, and he was so impressed with the result of the work of Wright and Forrest that soon after the show opened, he threw a big party at his home to present the music of *Kismet* to those who matter in Hollywood.

The result was that an option to film *Kismet* was taken by MGM; the movie was made in 1955 and proved to be – as could readily have been safely predicted – a very successful film musical. Once again, however, this was not merely a film of a show. The score had to be looked at again, and it was felt that a new song should be provided. This was 'Bored' – which, it has to be said, added much to the overall concept, but which unfortunately has had little independent later life.

Once again, however, the luckless Alfred Drake was not selected to recreate on film the part he so brilliantly made his own on the stage; in *Kiss Me, Kate* his part was taken on film by Howard Keel, and in the filmed version of *Kismet* it was Howard Keel once more who replaced Drake. Thankfully, the original cast album preserves Drake's performance, but there is equally no doubt that Keel's assumption of the role of Hajj was superb. Drake once ruefully mused over the similarities in the titles of *Kiss Me, Kate* and *Kismet* – and how fate prevented him from duplicating his stage successes in both shows on film.

The demands of Hollywood are different from those of Broadway – as we have noted before – and Keel was an established star in the film music genre, but added to his excellence were the appealing Ann Blyth as Marsinah and Dolores Gray, who took the part of Lalume. Vic Damone (as Frank Sinatra called him, "the best pair of Italian tubes in the business") assumed the role of the Caliph, and although the film version has had its detractors over the years – Leslie Halliwell described it as "unlucky" – it remains more than a worthy version of the show.

The director was Vincente Minnelli – no stranger to directing musical films – and the photography, by Joseph Ruttenberg, made full use of the new Cinemascope system. Perhaps it was the use of Eastmancolor – which does not always lend itself well to musicals – that contributed to the disenchantment of some critics, but with such an array of talent, including new orchestrations by André Previn, and at 113 minutes running not a second over-long, the film certainly has some outstanding moments. Keel himself can be heard to be in outstanding voice. Nonetheless, it does seem to be one of those musicals that does not entirely transfer well to the screen – and this may be down to the central role itself, Hajj, who, in the staged version, has to spark off the other characters in a way which does not pit him against a female lead in what might be called the usual manner.

What might make good theatre does not always make good cinema – a truism which can be applied with some justification in this instance.

Chapter 19

Kiss Me, Kate

The musical, Kiss Me, Kate is Cole Porter's masterpiece. It is as well to begin with this assertion, for it can surely be without contention that this work for the musical stage is one of the greatest scores ever written for that medium. Moreover, the lyrics were by Porter as well.

Cole Porter died in California in 1964 at the age of 73; he was born in June 1891 into a wealthy family – Alan Jay Lerner, describing Porter's family circumstances, said: "He was born... with a platinum spoon encrusted with diamonds in his mouth." As Cole Porter's mother was a talented pianist, music lessons were *de rigueur* within the household, and the young boy's natural gifts were soon in evidence.

His first instrument was the violin, and two years later at the age of eight he took up the piano – an unusual transition, the more so in view of his mother's own instrument. It may be that this also contributed to the chromaticism and innate singing quality of Cole Porter's melodic lines. From such a beginning, it was natural for a musical child to find his feet early on, and Cole Porter began to compose music before he was ten years old. Indeed, his first published composition, written in 1902 – 'The Bobolink Waltz' – was

written when he was eight. Later, at Yale, in New Haven, he wrote several songs which have passed into what might be called the standard repertoire of subsequent students – 'Bingo Eli Yale' and 'Bulldog'.

His father viewed his son's musical interests with good-natured puzzlement; the idea that his son should devote his life to writing popular music was definitely not to be encouraged, and Cole Porter was entered for the law. But a talent such as he possessed would not be gainsaid: he studied music at Harvard for a while, and then first visited Paris, which became a second home. After a while, Porter enrolled as a composition student at the Schola Cantorum, as a pupil of the great French composer and pedagogue Vincent d'Indy (whose most important work is the *Symphony On A French Mountaineer's Song* for piano and orchestra).

But Cole Porter could not join the class immediately. The reason for his Parisian sojourn was because he had been appointed to the American Aviation Headquarters in the French capital (America had entered the war in 1917). Following the Armistice he was able to undertake composition studies with d'Indy.

Porter's family wealth and social connections

Scenes from the MGM film of *Kiss Me Kate*, 1953, one of the finest ever made of a musical.

made it easy for him to move in high circles; urbane, witty and talented, he could so easily have become a dilettante, and for quite a few years he was so regarded. There were those who felt he could not be taken as a serious composer of popular music, simply because he did not have to do it. Furthermore, it seems that he did not use his influence and social position to further his own career as a songwriter. Finally, Cole Porter was a fastidious composer, by no means a prolific artist; in every sense, he could afford to wait and refine his art. In addition, his classical training (which was by no means unheard of for a popular composer, but was nevertheless sufficiently unusual for it to be noteworthy, particularly in the present context) caused him to be commissioned to write a ballet score for the Swedish Ballet Company. This was originally entitled *Within The Quota*, but was renamed *Times Past* for its revival in 1970. The orchestration was entirely Porter's own.

It is sometimes claimed that Porter also joined the French Foreign Legion for a while, but this story is now largely discredited: his trip to North Africa was for more personal reasons. However, he married, conveniently, a lady whose ancestry could be traced back to the Declaration of Independence, Linda Lee Thomas – who was herself from a wealthy family. She had been married before, the divorce settlement providing her with another small fortune; she was eight years Porter's senior.

For all this agreeable life-style, with plenty of time to do just what he wished, Porter was almost 40 years old before he wrote his first distinctive song: 'Let's Do It', from a largely forgotten show of 1928, *Paris*. This was followed, not by the proverbial 'string of hits', but by merely one or two major songs each year – such titles as 'What Is This Thing Called Love?' (1929), 'You Do

Something To Me' (also from 1929), 'Love For Sale; (1930), 'Night And Day' (from 1932). These standards were from various theatrical shows, so Porter's output was rather more prolific than a few titles would seem to suggest.

Nevertheless, Cole Porter was never a fast worker, but in 1934 came a truly major score, *Anything Goes*, which apart from the title song included 'I Get A Kick Out Of You' and 'You're The Top'. The following year, 1935, 'Begin The Beguine' and 'Just One of Those Things' appeared in his show *Jubilee*.

But in 1937 (the year in which died) Porter was seriously injured in a riding accident on Long Island. As a consequence, he lost the use of his legs at the age of 46 and was in constant pain for the rest of his life. He endured 36 operations on one leg that had been completely shattered, but eventually the condition of the limb became so degenerate that in 1957 it was amputated.

Such misfortune would have permanently discouraged many men; indeed, Porter was naturally despairing, but such was the man's courage that in 1939 he wrote one of the biggest hits of his life, the show *Du Barry Was A Lady* which opened on December 6, and which included 'Do I Love You?' and 'Friendship'. A succession of shows and films enabled Porter to keep working at what he did best. Constantly creating, therefore, and writing his own lyrics to an exceptionally high standard, he could hardly be said to be out of touch, but by 1947 he was 56 years old and not producing songs – still less a Broadway score – that really matched up to the best of his earlier output.

It was around 1945 that a young production assistant, Arnold Saint Subber, had the initial idea for the show that was to become *Kiss Me, Kate*. Saint Subber was backstage during a performance of Shakespeare's *The Taming Of The Shrew*, and at once conceived the idea of a musical, in which the cast of a performance of the play would mirror in their own lives the situations Shakespeare had created on the stage. Saint Subber found an enthusiastic co-producer in Lemuel Ayres, and together they persuaded Bella and Samuel Spewack to write the book for the show.

So who would write the music? Bella Spewack had no doubts – the show was absolutely right for Cole Porter, but she had the greatest difficulty on two fronts: Porter was not everyone's first choice, and his recent track record was unappealing. However, she succeeded in overcoming Porter's own resistance – he felt he was at one level being asked to take on Shakespeare – and the resistance of prospective backers. The show had been budgeted for $180,000 but raising the money was proving difficult. The eventual musical, *Kiss Me, Kate*, opened as try-outs in Philadelphia and by the time it reached New York City to open on December 30th 1948 at the New Century Theatre on Broadway it had become clear to all and sundry that a very great musical had been created. The first night was a sensation: glittering, literate and above all intensely musical, it lived up to the quip that was always applied to Cole Porter first nights, which claimed that such events "...brought out the finest autos in New York". The distinguished newspaper columnist John Chapman reported that "Mr Porter's opening night was so stylish it was attended by Mrs William K Vanderbilt, who usually confines her first-nighting to the opera".

Kiss Me, Kate ran at the New Century for 1,077 performances, the most brilliant success Porter had enjoyed up to that time. He later recalled that "Ever since my first whopping success, *Hitchy-Koo Of 1919*, it has gotten harder to and harder to write a good show. Why? Well, the standards today are so much higher. Rodgers and Hammerstein have lifted everything to such an incredible level that in order to compete you have to attain heights you never dreamed of before. In the past all you had to do was pull a drop down and sing a song in front of it, even if it had nothing to do with the plot. Nobody cared. But the integration of something like *South Pacific* is so complete that in today's musical everything has to be married to everything else."

Up to that time, 1949-50, *Kiss Me, Kate* became one of the few musicals to break 1,000 consecutive shows. The plot of *Kiss Me, Kate* concerns an actor-producer Fred Graham, who has engaged his temperamental ex-wife Lilli Vanessi to co-star with him in a musical version of *The Taming Of The Shrew*, together with his current girl-friend, Lois Lane. Fred is to play Petruchio, Lilli is Katherine, and Lois is Bianca. In turn, however, Lois is more interested at the present time in Bill Calhoun, a young actor who is to play Lucentio, who has been having a so-so relationship with Lois. The plot, therefore, is open to inevitable misunderstandings, which impart to the show its humour and charm. For all the interest of the story, and the undoubted quality of Porter's lyrics – he sometimes interpolates lines directly from Shakespeare into them, often so subtly that they pass by almost unnoticed, and always with such care that no stylistic dichotomy is created – the success or failure of a work of musical theatre rests primarily, as we have pointed out on other occasions, upon the music. Into this score Cole Porter put everything he had.

The music of *Kiss Me, Kate* is so consistently inspired, each song is so fully-formed within itself and yet fits the action so perfectly that one is hard-pressed to cite another show which is superior in this regard. The list of songs which have become 'standards' is remarkable for one score: 'Why Can't You Behave?', 'Wunderbar', 'So In Love' (perhaps the finest number in the entire show),

'Were Thine That Special Face', 'Another Op'nin', Another Show', 'Where Is The Life That Late I Led?'.

Perhaps the most amazing aspect of these songs is the variety they exhibit: 'Why Can't You Behave?' for example, has a melodic line that on paper looks almost unsingable for a musical actress – it would not be easy for any singer – but when heard in context of the underlying harmony, is eminently singable, the whole thing falling into place, making one of the most unforgettable and characteristic of Porter's melodic phrases. Nor is this all: as the song progresses, the intervals remain awkwardly uncertain – mirroring the words exactly. Only in the cadence of resignation, the final phrase of 'acceptance', demonstrates the love that Bianca has for her errant Lucentio.

'Wunderbar' is a splendid pastiche of a 19th-century Viennese waltz: beginning always on the second beat of the bar, and always falling directly on to the first beat of the succeeding bar (the whole being a balance of two-bar phrases, with the second bar being heard first), creates a tremendous sense of rhythmic elation, entirely within the waltz structure.

'So In Love' – as we have said earlier, possibly the finest song in the show – may well be the first popular song to begin in one key and end in another. As each climax in the song is reached, so the pivotal note rises, until it finally settles down to a warm, major key. When this finally arrives it comes as a shaft of sunlight. First sung in the show by Lilli Vanessi, it is recalled towards the end by Fred (Petruchio).

Other remarkable songs are 'Were Thine That Special Face?' (Petruchio), a powerful, tempestuous number with constant rising phrases and 'I Am Ashamed That Women Are So Simple', sung at the end of the play by Katherine. This is a complete setting of Shakespeare, with no changes to the Bard's original text at all, and is a song such as would grace any contralto recitalist's programme (the piano accompaniment in the piano score is particularly fine). Allied to these serious songs are the concerted numbers – 'Another Op'nin', Another Show', has particularly happy inspirations, and 'Brush Up Your Shakespeare' contains some outrageous rhymes.

Although Porter went on to have several more successful shows – *Can-Can* in 1953, and two films, *High Society* in 1956 and *Les Girls* from the following year – none surpasses *Kiss Me, Kate* for the sustained inspiration of the music. *Kiss Me, Kate* became the first American musical to be presented in Germany, Austria, Iceland, Yugoslavia, Italy, Belgium, Hungary, Switzerland, Poland and Czechoslovakia – all within 15 years of the show opening. At the Vienna Volksoper, where it opened in February, 1956, it became the most successful show ever to be mounted there (the theatre had opened in 1898).

The story of *Kiss Me, Kate*, as largely based on the outline by the late George B Dale, is as follows. As the show opens, the cast of the revival of a musical version of *The Taming Of The Shrew* is being assembled on stage for final instructions before the opening ('Another Op'nin', Another Show'). In the cast, with the central producer-actor Fred Graham, are his former wife Lilli Vanessi, Lois Lane – a singer in whom Fred is deeply interested – and Bill Calhoun, who is Lois's current primary interest. The irresponsible Bill informs Lois that he has signed Fred's name to a $10,000 IOU in "the most respectable floating crap game in town". Lois begs Bill to reform ('Why Can't You Behave'). Meanwhile, Fred and Lilli patch up their differences as they reminisce nostalgically about other shows in which they have appeared together, showing particular fondness for an old-fashioned operetta

('Wunderbar'), and when a bouquet which Fred has sent to Lois is delivered by mistake to Lilli, she is overcome with sentimental affections for her ex-husband ('So In Love').

On stage, *The Taming Of The Shrew* gets underway ('We Open In Venice') as Lois as Bianca and Bill as Lucentio discuss Bianca's inability to marry until her older sister (Katherine) has been betrothed ('Tom, Dick Or Harry'). Fred, as Petruchio, arrives in search of a rich wife ('I've Come To Wive It Wealthily In Padua') and although Katherine, played by Lilli, states her inalterable opposition to males ('I Hate Men'), Petruchio agrees to marry her, even though she is not the wife of whom he has dreamed ('Were Thine That Special Face'). Lilli discovers that her bouquet was originally intended for Lois, and threatens to leave the show. Her departure is prevented by two gangsters who have come to collect the IOU with Fred's signature, and as the curtain falls to end the first act, she is raging, both in character and in reality.

Later that same evening, Paul, Fred's dresser, passes time in the alley beside the theatre by commenting feelingly on the Baltimore weather ('Too Darn Hot'). As the revival continues on stage, Petruchio, although just married to Katherine and beginning his tempestuous wedded life, begins to yearn for his life as a single man ('Where Is The Life That Late I Led?'). Off stage, Bill discovers Lois flirting and reproaches her. Explaining her feelings ('Always True To You Darlin' In My Fashion'), Bill counters with a charming expression of affection for the character she plays in the revival ('Bianca'). Because of a sudden change in gang administration, the gangsters tear up the now-worthless IOU, and Lois prepares to walk out on the show as Fred muses on his love for her ('So In Love' – reprise). The gangsters pause to pay a decidedly unusual tribute

to Shakespeare ('Brush Up Your Shakespeare'), and – as the revival comes to a close – Lilli unexpectedly returns and, using Katherine's words, expresses her intention of returning to Fred ('I Am Ashamed That Women Are So Simple'). She and Fred are reunited, and Lois and Bill reach their own understanding in time for the finale.

In the spring of 1951, coinciding with the Festival of Britain, *Kiss Me, Kate* arrived in London for a spectacular run, presented by Jack Hylton, at the Coliseum Theatre. Patricia Morison repeated her Broadway triumph as Lilli Vanessi, and Bill John played Fred Graham. Walter Long played Bill Calhoun, and Julie Wilson was Lois Lane. Daniel Wherry played Harry Trevor, and the English actor Austin Trevor played Harrison Howell – a big businessman who is backing the show – and an old boy-friend of Lois Lane.

Two of the most enchanting smaller roles were taken by Sidney James as one of the hit-men and the legendary Adelaide Hall played Hattie, the dresser, who led the opening number, 'Another Op'nin', Another Show' with her customary style and verve. The London production was directed by Sam Spewack from the New York production of John C Wilson. The London production ran for almost two years.

As we have noted earlier, several of Cole Porter's stage shows had been filmed before *Kiss Me, Kate* appeared. But with the very great success of this particular musical, it was clear – when the decision to film it had been made – that a quite new approach would be appropriate.

At that time – 1953 – new approaches were very much in the offing so far as cinematography was concerned. The commercial threat posed to the cinema by the burgeoning rise of television in the USA was already leading to smaller audiences. It was clear that the cinema had to hit back in a

Kathryn Grayson, Howard Keel, Ann Miller and Tommy Rall in the 1953 MGM film of *Kiss Me Kate*, directed by George Sidney and prodced by Jack Cummings.

way with which television could not possibly compete. Cinemascope was then a practical possibility, as was VisaVision, and the idea of making technically feasible films in 3-D – three-dimensional films – had already come to fruition.

The MGM film of *Kiss Me, Kate* is one of the finest ever made of a musical. It is not entirely faithful to the original score in several respects: the song, 'Too Darn Hot', staggeringly well sung and danced by the breathtaking Ann Miller in the opening scene of the movie, actually opened the second act in the original show. An interesting point in this opening scene is that Cole Porter himself appears – played by Ron Randell, who 'ghosts' the piano part in the brilliant orchestration by André Previn.

Kathryn Grayson and Howard Keel take the roles originally created by Patricia Morison and Alfred Drake, and they are magnificent, as is every other part in the film. The splendid 'I Am Ashamed That Women Are So Simple' is dropped from the film, and the equally memorable 'From This Moment On' – a song from 1950, not written for any stage show – was added for yet another dazzling dance routine.

Indeed, the choreography of the film of *Kiss Me Kate* (for which cinematic manifestation MGM dropped the comma from the original title) is one of its greatest strengths, and in this regard, not only did it boast Ann Miller, but also Tommy Rall, Bobby Van and Bob Fosse – the last of whom went on to become a much admired choreographer and director in his own right.

Mention has already been made of André Previn's involvement in the movie; the musical direction was one of the greatest of this exceptionally gifted musician's early achievements in Hollywood – he was only 23 at the time, and was nominated for an Academy Award for his work on this film. A great movie, fully worthy of Cole Porter's masterpiece.

Finally, mention should be made of a recording of this score produced by Frank Sinatra for his own Reprise record label. Starring the Hi-Lo's, Jo Stafford, Frank Sinatra, Dean Martin, Sammy Davis Jr (for whom 'Too Darn Hot' might have been composed), Johnny Prophet, Phyllis McGuire, Lou Monte, Dinah Shore and Keely Smith, with Morris Stoloff conducting a somewhat reduced Los Angeles Philharmonic Orchestra (uncredited) in a variety of arrangements in the Reprise Musical Repertory Theatre series – another indication of the enduring superiority of this truly great musical.

Chapter 20

A Little Night Music

IN 1955, the 37-year-old Swedish-born film director Ingmar Bergman released a film that was to be his first international success. His father was a chaplain to the Swedish Royal Family and so young Ingmar soon came into contact with the upper classes and, later, with the moral choices that confront us all. Called (in English) *Smiles Of A Summer's Night* (*Sommarnattens Leend*), this comedy of manners, love and much else besides dealt with a group of genteel folk at the turn of the century enjoying a weekend in the country. The film – a masterly piece of work in its own right – inspired elements in Bergman's own *Wild Strawberries* (1957), and, more directly, Woody Allen's *A Midsummer Night's Sex Comedy* (1982), as well as a musical by Stephen Sondheim, *A Little Night Music* (1972) – the title of which translates Mozart's most famous serenade for strings, 'Eine Kleine Nachtmusik'.

The show opened at the Shubert Theatre on Broadway on February 25, 1973. The book, after the Bergman film, was by Hugh Wheeler, and the music and lyrics were by Sondheim. The work is a genuine masterpiece of the musical theatre, and was immediately recognised as such. In *The New York Times* Clive Barnes wrote enthusiastically:

"At last a new operetta!... heady, civilised, sophisticated and enchanting... It is a mixture of Cole Porter, Gustav Mahler, Antony Tudor and just a little of Ingmar Bergman... Mr Wheeler's book is uncommonly urbane and witty... Yet perhaps the real triumph belongs to Stephen Sondheim."

Other critics were equally ecstatic, and it seemed only a matter of time before this beguiling operetta would come to London. The show won six Tony Awards in 1973 and a Grammy the following year for the original cast album, and the song, 'Send In The Clowns' was set to become a big hit in the UK for Judy Collins. In fact, the Broadway run was nearing its two-year end when a London opening was announced, only to be postponed. In the end, the first night of the London production was set for April 15, 1975 at the Adelphi Theatre, produced by Harold Prince as it had been on Broadway and the show proved as important, as beguiling and as successful in the British capital as it had been in New York.

The show opens with an overture for five singers, sung virtually *a cappella* (unaccompanied); this leads dreamily to the 'Night Waltz', to which couples dance against the background of a woodland setting. A 'Prologue' follows, in which Madame Armfeldt speaks to her

Elizabeth Taylor and Len Cariou in the 1977 film version of *A Little Night Music.*

grand-daughter Fredrika of the smiles of the Summer Night – three smiles: the first to the young, who know nothing; the second to the fools who know a little, such as Desirée Armfeldt; finally, to the old who know too much, such as herself.

In the home of Fredrik Egerman and his wife, who are preparing for a visit to the theatre to see Desiree Armfeldt, Fredrik bemoans his fate at being married to Anne, who is still a virgin, "now"; but she chats away, oblivious to his frustration. Their maid, Petra, flirts with Henrik (Fredrik's son from his first marriage), but she leaves when Henrik gets too serious – "later" she says. Anne tells Fredrik that it is her intention to become a proper wife "soon", but he has dozed off.

In her dressing-room at the theatre Desirée, a past mistress of Fredrik, sings of the delights of an actress's life, and that evening she sees Fredrik and Anne in a box. Memories come flooding back for her and she runs from the stage, now upset by her past. After taking Anne home Fredrik goes for a late-night walk – straight to Desirée's apartment, where their love is rekindled.

Meanwhile, Madame Armfeldt complains of modern manners and ways of doing things, but Desirée and Fredrick are interrupted when her current lover arrives unexpectedly. They dream up an excuse for Fredrik's presence which does not prevent Carl-Magnus from sending Fredrik away minus his trousers. The next day, Carl-Magnus sends his wife to Anne to tell her of Fredrik and Desirée, who goes to her mother's country residence – having arranged for Fredrik and Anne to be invited for the weekend. At first, Anne is perplexed by the invitation, but decides to accept nevertheless. Carl-Magnus and his wife also plan to go, even though they have not been invited and sing of their looking forward to a week-end in the country.

The second act begins as the guests arrive: the quintet sets the scene once more, and as Fredrik bumps into Carl-Magnus they imagine how things could have been different. The guests now arrive for dinner which becomes a battle of words and ends with Henrik, deeply frustrated, smashing a glass and running out. Anne and Fredrika go to look for him, as Fredrik makes for Desirée's room – and tells Desirée he will not leave his wife for her. Desirée is left alone, and sings 'Send In The Clowns' – a highly poetical song of great beauty and depth of expression.

Anne comes across Henrik as he is about to kill himself: surprised by her own feelings, she realises that it is the son she loves, not his father, and they leave together. Petra, having indulged in a brief liaison with Madame Armfeldt's butler, sings of her hopes for the future. It is Charlotte, Carl-Magnus's wife, who consoles Fredrik over the loss of his wife and his son: as she embraces Fredrik sympathetically, Carl-Magnus is astonished to see them thus and challenges Fredrik to a duel.

A shot is heard as the duel takes place, and Carl-Magnus enters, carrying Fredrik's body. But he is not dead, merely wounded, and Carl-Magnus orders his wife to pack their bags, leaving Fredrik and Desirée alone together at last, when they realise that their destiny is to be together.

As the 'Night Waltz' returns and the lovers dance among the trees once more, Madame Armfeldt tells Fredrika that the night, having smiled twice already, will do so a third time for the old who know too much.

The score is a magnificent achievement, but it is not entirely in 3/4 time, as is often erroneously stated. Much of it is, which gives the music a delightful lilt in medium tempo, but Sondheim is not so hidebound as to restrict himself to one pulse only. In every respect, *A Little Night Music* is a masterpiece of musical theatre.

The film of the show, however, shot in Austria and west Germany in 1977, is quite another matter. The setting has been changed, the mystery and imaginative flair of the original are not recaptured here, and the show has been seriously miscast. Quite apart from these serious drawbacks, several of the songs have been seriously cut, and the entire result is a mutilation of a finely-judged and superb original, which adds nothing positive to the reputations of the director, Harold Prince, or the leading players – Elizabeth Taylor, Diana Rigg, Len Cariou and Lesley-Anne Down. Only Hermione Gingold (as Madame Armfeldt in the role she made her own on the stage) emerges with any credit from this affair.

Chapter 21

Mame

The American composer and lyricist, Jerry Herman, was born in New York on July 10th 1933, into a musical family – his mother was a music teacher. Curiously, although Jerry's early musical talents were not long in manifesting themselves, he did not study music until much later, preferring to play the piano entirely by ear. He studied drama at the University of Miami, and following graduation, he went to New York where he played the piano in various night-clubs and other venues.

He also wrote for television, and his first musical review *I Feel Wonderful* was presented off-Broadway in 1954, and was then followed by two others before his first Broadway musical *Milk And Honey* opened in 1961. This was set in Israel, and the most important song from the score, 'Shalom', was a hit for Eddie Fisher and won a Gaslight Award from station WPAT. Herman had also received a Tony Award as Best Lyricist and Composer for 1961 on the strength of the show.

Another show, *Madame Aphrodite*, failed to make the same commercial grade, but with *Hello, Dolly!* Herman had truly arrived as a major composer of Broadway musicals. This won no fewer than ten Tony Awards, and was followed by another fine musical about another strong female character, *Mame*.

This was in 1966, and the story, from the autobiographical novel *Auntie Mame* by Patrick Dennis, tells of an orphan, adopted by his rather hare-brained but wealthy aunt who decides to see to his education along very modern lines in permissive Europe during the 20s and 30s. The novel had already been translated into a play by Jerome Lawrence and Robert E Lee, and this in turn had been adapted into a film script in 1958 by Betty Comden and Adolph Green for Warner Brothers which starred Rosalind Russell, Forrest Tucker, Coral Browne and Fred Clark.

For the musical version, Jerome Lawrence and Robert E Lee readily reworked their play as the show's book, which beautifully dovetailed to Jerry Herman's score, for which Herman wrote both words and music. The cast was exceptionally well-chosen, and of myriad experience and discipline. Playing the larger-than-life character of Auntie Mame was the London-born Angela Lansbury, who had travelled to the USA and had appeared with acclaim in such films as *Gaslight*, *National Velvet* and *Samson And Delilah* before becoming an American citizen in 1951. Miss Lansbury had made her Broadway debut in Feydeau's *Hotel Pardiso* in 1957 and appeared starring with Lee Remick in

Stephen Sondheim's *Anyone Can Whistle* in 1964, which unusual and daring show – far in advance of its time – regrettably closed after only nine performances.

Frankie Michaels played the 10-year-old Patrick Dennis, and Beatrice Arthur was Mame's friend Vera Charles. Jane Connell took the part of Patrick's nanny, Agnes Gooch; Willard Waterman was the all-too-stuffy bank manager, desperately trying to keep Mame literally in check, Dwight Babcock. The smaller parts were filled with gusto and charm by a clutch of established and rising stars, and the dances and musical numbers were staged by Onna White, who had previously worked on such shows as *The Music Man*, *Irma La Douce* and *Half A Sixpence* – the Broadway production of this last show was directed by Gene Saks, and it was he who was chosen to direct *Mame*.

No fewer than four producers were responsible for bringing the show to Broadway, and the team – Sylvia and Joseph Harris, Robert Fryer and Lawrence Carr – had first come together to produce the highly successful *Sweet Charity* at the Palace Theatre in New York; *Mame* was the quartet's second corporate production, with sets by William and Jean Eckart, lighting by Tharon Musser and costumes by Robert Mackintosh, all of which brilliantly evoked the era with considerable skill and artistry.

Here was a rich mixture of theatrical talent, and it is undoubtedly the combination of the story – Lawrence and Lee's previous dramatic successes include the masterly *Inherit The Wind* – a dramatised account of the famous 1925 Scopes 'Monkey Trial' – with the direct appeal of Jerry Herman's score that made *Mame* such an extraordinary success, and, as with *Hello, Dolly!*, the show's title song is one of the great show-stoppers of all time.

Both on Broadway and in London, *Mame* was hit material; the movie came in 1974, from Warner-ABC and was directed again by Gene Saks; also from the original cast were Beatrice Arthur and Jane Connell. To play Mame, Lucille Ball was chosen. The movie is a faithful and occasionally brilliant version of the show, but it may be thought that Ball was not entirely at home in this role; something of the game was given away by Saks ensuring that every close-up of her was shot in soft-focus, but this adds to the camp unreality of the whole thing. It must surely be the case, however, that Ball's portrayal remains one of her most accomplished performances, and the movie has retained a coterie of admirers. All in all, a worthy film of the show.

Chapter 22

My Fair Lady

In 1913, a new romantic comedy by George Bernard Shaw, entitled *Pygmalion*, was first produced. For a play which centres so much on the English language, and which has come to represent one of the high-spots of English drama, it will no doubt come as some surprise to learn that this – of all plays – was first performed in German, in Vienna. The following year, the first production in English opened in London, with Mrs Patrick Campbell playing the part of Eliza Doolittle, for whom it had been written.

The play tells the story of a professor of phonetics, Henry Higgins – whose character was based upon a real such person, Professor Henry Sweet – who claims to his close friend, Colonel Pickering, that he could pass off a cockney girl as a duchess, by teaching her genteel manners and to speak well enough with a refined and educated accent. The Colonel bets Higgins otherwise. Together, Professor Higgins and the Colonel find such a girl by chance one evening in London. The girl is Eliza Doolittle, a flower-seller in Covent Garden, who, once the plan has been explained to her, is taken by the idea and readily agrees to become the Professor's guinea-pig.

During the course of the lessons she receives, Eliza is gradually transformed into – or, more properly, emerges as – a beautiful woman of grace and sensitivity. Higgins wins his bet, but in the original play Eliza finally rejects him and his values, asserting her own rights as an individual.

The play was an enormous success, and in 1938 the Romanian-born film director and producer Gabriel Pascal persuaded Shaw to grant permission to allow it to be filmed. It is unclear as to whether, in strict legal terms, Shaw could have prevented this happening in any event, as the ownership of the copyright in the play may not then have been within his gift. However, Shaw was much attracted by the idea, and agreed to change the ending of the play, so that Eliza and Higgins are reconciled at last.

The film was directed by Anthony Asquith and Leslie Howard, and starred Howard, with Wendy Hiller and Wilfred Lawson, and had music by the Swiss-born classical composer Arthur Honegger. The result was a masterpiece of British film-making of the late 1930s, and certainly one of the finest British films of its day, which – like the play from which it comes – has not dated at all.

Pascal, however, in obtaining the rights to film *Pygmalion*, also acquired the film rights to other Shaw plays and additional rights to the original

Audrey Hepburn in MGM's classic 1964 film production of *My Fair Lady*.

script of *Pygmalion*. Since wanting to make the film, Pascal had hankered after seeing a musical version of it come to fruition, a wish that he was now in a position to execute. If the idea was a good one, it proved a difficult – indeed, almost an intractable – proposition to fulfil for the succession of writers Pascal subsequently approached with his idea. At various times, Pascal suggested the project to Howard Dietz, Arthur Schwartz, Yip Harburg, Cole Porter and Noel Coward – and also to Richard Rodgers and Oscar Hammerstein II. Whilst each of these writers had shown varying degrees of interest – with Rodgers and Hammerstein later claiming to have worked on the project for more than a year – Pascal was unable to get his pet idea off the ground. It also seems that he had very strong ideas himself as to how the play was to be treated as a musical.

Pascal had settled in America several years after producing the film of *Pygmalion* and in 1951 he had decided to film another Shaw play, *Androcles And The Lion*, a rather whimsical allegorical comedy about a lion who, on having a thorn removed from his paw by a slave, refuses to eat him when they confront each other in the arena. Interestingly, Pascal's original intention was that the film was to have starred Harpo Marx and Rex Harrison. It had actually begun production when, for a variety of reasons, the project was abandoned.

However, in 1952 Pascal made a fresh attempt at filming the play. On this occasion he completed the project, which starred Alan Young, Jean Simmons, Robert Newton and Victor Mature. By this time, Shaw was dead, which may have been just as well, for Pascal's Androcles And The Lion, made in Hollywood by RKO, is not in the same class as *Pygmalion*. Be that as it may, during a break in the production, Pascal met up with Alan Jay Lerner, who was also in Hollywood at that time, adapting the musical *Brigadoon* for the screen.

Over lunch one day, Pascal mentioned to Lerner his long-term idea of turning *Pygmalion* into a musical. Lerner may indeed have earlier been aware of his concept – considering the theatrical writers he had already approached with it, it had certainly been 'going the rounds' – but he was thrilled to be asked to consider it along with his partner Frederick Loewe. It therefore transpired that, for six months or more, Lerner and Loewe worked at the project before they told Pascal that the idea was impossible.

Lerner himself later admitted that, "*Pygmalion* is a drawing-room comedy, and no matter how hard we tried we did not seem to be able to tear down the walls of the drawing room and allow the play to unfold in a setting and atmosphere that suggested music". In 1954, George Pascal died, his dream unfulfilled, and it may well have been his death that prompted Lerner and Loewe to take another look at the project. With their previous experience to go by, and without Pascal's well-meaning but inexperienced input as to how a musical should be written nagging at their creative shoulders, they "stayed with it to completion", as Lerner recalled.

It so happened that the combination of Lerner and Loewe was uniquely suited to undertake such a project. Lerner, who was a well-educated and literate American with a great love of the English language and of European art in all its forms, would treat Shaw's text with care and refinement; and Frederick Loewe, born in Berlin at the turn of the century, had shown himself in their earlier collaborations to be a master at conjuring up music of the appropriate period at the same time as making it contemporary in idiom – a great gift. The partners were, therefore, in essence Europeans who were proven masters of the

American musical theatre: surely, if any team could bring off such a project, it was Lerner and Loewe?

An early decision of Lerner's was to try to keep as much of Shaw's original dialogue as he could – the exigencies of the musical having always to come first. In this, Lerner was fortunate, for George Bernard Shaw himself had a great love and profound knowledge of music, and it has been said that much of his dialogue has a pulse not unlike that of a musical score. Not only would retaining as much of the original dialogue keep the essence of the play in the adaptation, but also it would make *My Fair Lady* (as it became) an exceptionally literate show, worlds away from the fantasy and Americana of much post-war Broadway musical subject-matter.

If Shaw would doubtless have applauded the "glow and grace and lilt", as George B Dale rightly commented upon regarding Alan Jay Lerner's lyrics, he would equally have felt the music by Frederick Loewe to have captured stylishly the character of London in 1912.

A subtle aspect regarding the music that would surely have delighted the musical playwright is that every one of the seven main songs in the score either begins with – or at crucial points otherwise contains – the same three notes. These are nothing more (or less) than the first three notes of the major scale – doh, re, mi – a small point, it is true, but an important one nonetheless, and one which gives to the entire show an underlying musical unity. What is remarkable about this aspect of Loewe's score is that this unity can be found in tunes as varied as the cockney songs for Eliza's father, Alfred P Doolittle – 'With A Little Bit Of Luck' and 'Get Me To The Church On Time', and the romantic songs – as, for example, the splendid 'On The Street Where You Live', sung by the character of Freddy Eynsford-Hill, an upper-crust suitor of the emergent Eliza Doolittle, and

Professor Higgins's 'I've Grown Accustomed To Her Face' – to say nothing of Eliza's dream-world opening number, 'Wouldn't It Be Loverly?'.

Loewe's score at these points – and at others – is quite clearly that of a master. As the late George B Dale commented: "So closely are the songs interwoven with the plot that even sketchy outline will serve to place the music in its context, tracing Eliza's development and her attitude toward Higgins. Each one seems exactly right when it appears so that it seems as if Shaw had been set to music, a high compliment to Mr Lerner."

This is a compliment, but nothing more than the plain truth. The show was to be produced by Herman Levin, who assembled a body of artists that was second to none. The staging was by Moss Hart, and the choreography – a difficult matter, this, in presenting a mixture of late Edwardian London high and low society to Cold War Broadway of the mid-1950s – was outstandingly well done by Hanya Holm. The stage designs were by Oliver Smith and the costumes – which had the audiences gasping in admiration – were by Sir Cecil Beaton, the famous British designer and photographer. The orchestrations and arrangements were by Robert Russell Bennett and Phil Lang.

If the staging was clearly amongst the finest that could possibly have been assembled at the time, the casting was equally inspired – for what had to be done was to find three English principal performers to take the main roles in a Broadway musical. This had never been done before, and it carried with it no little box office risk. Levin moved with a sure touch, for he persuaded Rex Harrison, "with fear and trepidation" on the actor's part, as Lerner later recalled, finally to appear in a musical. Lerner went on: "Every one of Higgins's songs was written expressly for him so that adjustments could be made to accommodate his non-singing

singing." Most composers will respond to a challenge, but it was a challenge way out of the ordinary to write solo songs for a leading character in a musical play for an actor who was a non-singer – and to succeed in such a way as to make a singing star out of the actor! This is another little-appreciated aspect of Loewe's compositional skill.

Levin, Lerner and Loewe were fortunate in the choice of actress to play the part of Eliza Doolittle. This was Julie Andrews. Miss Andrews had been born into a theatrical family – her parents, Ted and Barbara Andrews, were much-loved British entertainers – and made her television debut in Britain at the age of about 14 with her parents in a show presented by Henry Caldwell. There was no doubt as to the girl's star quality – even at that age, as your chronicler can vividly remember – for the purity and projection of her voice and the sheer integrity of her character made an immediate and lasting impact.

On October 13, 1953, the Players Theatre in London's Villiers Street began a six-week run of a musical show which had been expanded to a whole evening in length from a shorter production which had opened the previous April 14 – the success of which had surprised everyone, including its creator, Sandy Wilson. After various vicissitudes, *The Boy Friend* – an affectionate pastiche of shows of the 1920s – finally reached the West End at the personal invitation of Sir Bronson Albery, who offered Wyndham's Theatre for the production, which opened there on January 14, 1954.

This proved to be a remarkable success, and *The Boy Friend* opened on Broadway with a second cast later in 1954. As the show was still running successfully in London, with Anne Rogers playing the leading role of Polly Browne, the American producers picked Julie Andrews for the part.

This was a fateful step, for the show at once captivated New York audiences and brought Andrews virtual overnight stardom in America. At that time, Lerner and Loewe were working on *My Fair Lady*, and they naturally saw *The Boy Friend* on Broadway.

From the moment that Julie Andrews appeared on stage as Polly Browne, it seems, the part of Eliza Doolittle had found its personification.

For Alfred Doolittle, Stanley Holloway was chosen. This was also something of a risky proposition for Broadway, not because of any shortcomings in Mr Holloway's stage persona, but because he had only once before appeared on stage in the USA, in an Old Vic touring production as Bottom in Shakespeare's *A Midsummer Night's Dream*, and he was then 66 years of age.

But to those who remember Holloway, one of the more amazing things about him was his incredible energy and love of life. In his 60s he may have been, but he certainly did not look it, or act it – the part could have been, as it was for Rex Harrison, written for him.

Colonel Pickering was played by Robert Coote with enormous flair, and, with this cavalcade of major talent, the show opened in New York at the Mark Hellinger Theatre, 237 West 51st Street off Broadway, on March 15, 1956. It had previewed at the Shubert Theatre in New Haven on February 4, and in Philadelphia at the Erlanger Theatre on February 15.

The New York opening was a sensation. Brooks Atkinson, the most respected New York theatre critic of his day and himself a Pulitzer Prize-winner, called it "the greatest musical of the 20th-century", and later went on to write about the show as having "the uniformity of its skill: it brings as much enthusiasm to the intellectual elements of the story as it does to the characters". He continued: "The genius of *My Fair Lady* is even more elusive – a magic that distinguishes it from many other enjoyable musical works and that cannot be identified."

Such was the impact of the show that the music was banned from performance in Britain until after the West End opening; Liberace, then enjoying considerable fame in Britain owing to the screening of his popular weekly half-hour television programme on Sunday afternoons, had appeared in London just before the opening – his television appearance on *Sunday Night At The London Palladium* had the audience squealing with delight as he sang 'London Bridge Is Falling Down', which old ditty ends with the words, 'My Fair Lady' – the only words he could sing referring to the show at that time.

If the show was such a cast-iron success, it says something quite exceptional for the foresight and judgement of the greatest record man who has ever lived, Goddard Lieberson, who was at that time chief executive of Columbia Records in the USA, or CBS as it later came to be called world-wide as the name 'Columbia' was owned by EMI – a big rival of the parent American company – outside of the USA. Lieberson was a genius, a man of taste and refinement, but above all a musician of enormous talent and breadth of sympathy. He was the man who virtually created Columbia Records and had married the diseuse and dancer Vera Zorina; he had personally signed to Columbia Records artists as varied as the composer Igor Stravinsky, the cellist Pablo Casals, Leonard Bernstein, Vladimir Horowitz, Andy Williams, Mitch Miller and dozens of other great stars of popular and classical music. As a record producer, Goddard Lieberson tended, later in his career, to concentrate upon original cast recordings – a genre in which he excelled and which he raised to a very high level.

If the concept of three British stars – two of them barely known – in a musical set in London before World War I, based upon a very literate play by George Bernard Shaw, caused traditional backers of Broadway to have one or two reservations, Lieberson had none. In an unprecedented move, he committed Columbia Records money to the stage production – and secured the rights to an original cast recording. For a record company to back a musical was virtually unheard-of – certainly on this scale – but the result was an artistic and commercial triumph for Lieberson. Six months after the opening of *My Fair Lady* the Columbia original cast album was Number One in the American album charts, where it stayed for two years.

Not only had Lieberson produced one of the biggest-selling original cast albums of all time but he came to London in 1958 to see the triumphant success of the West End production open at the Drury Lane Theatre on April 30, – with Harrison, Andrews, Holloway and Coote recreating their roles for the London stage. Vic Damone's single of 'On The Street Where You Live' entered the British charts eight days later, and reached No 1, remaining in the Top 20 charts for 17 weeks; concurrently, the British singer David Whitfield – a week later – entered with his version of the same song, and Whitfield's disc stayed in the charts for 14 weeks.

With the commercial arrival of stereophonic records also in 1958, Lieberson returned to London and produced a second complete 'original cast' recording in the British capital in February of the following year, the show being then described as 'America's Greatest Musical'.

This means that, wholly exceptionally, two 'original cast' albums are in existence, the stereophonically recorded album having been made three years after the first, and in London,

Audrey Hepburn with co-star Rex Harrison in MGM's 1964 film production of *My Fair Lady*.

not in New York. The conductor of the London production was the brilliant Cyril Ornadel – himself a gifted composer of successful musicals and a famous conductor of shows for records.

Naturally, with the existence of these two recordings, a confusion exists in the minds of some record collectors. They are as two peas in a pod – with one exception. In the early days of stereophonic recordings the playing time for such long-playing records was less than that for monaural records, because the grooves were wider. It was a little while before the playing time became compatible. As a consequence, the early stereophonic recordings of the London cast omit the Finale, which can be heard on the Broadway cast album. Overall, however, with this one exception, the differences are slight, and any true lover of the musical stage ought to possess both versions. However, the situation is, to a degree, further complicated by the existence of the original soundtrack recording – also a CBS release – of the Warner Brothers film of *My Fair Lady*, in which two of the original stars – Rex Harrison and Stanley Holloway – appeared.

The Broadway production ran for six-and-a-half years – 2,717 performances – and the London production almost likewise, with 2,281 performances, or a little under six years – and so, as had become the custom, once the stage shows were drawing to a close in major cities, a film version was readied for production.

As we have noted, Rex Harrison and Stanley Holloway were signed for the film, but Julie Andrews was not. In screen terms, both English actors could point to long careers in successful movies, but Julie Andrews was not then considered to be 'bankable', as the phrase has it. The part went to Audrey Hepburn, who was not English, but of Belgian birth.

However, Audrey Hepburn had enjoyed a brilliantly successful career on screen, and had also made her stage debut on Broadway in 1951 in *Gigi* – not the musical version, which was done in 1958 by Lerner and Loewe for MGM, and in which Leslie Caron starred – and had appeared in a number of delightful movies of a light and charming character. She won an Academy Award in 1954 for *Roman Holiday* and in 1960 starred in one of her most famous roles in *Breakfast At Tiffany's*.

But Audrey Hepburn was not a singer – if she was to appear in the film, someone else would have to sing for her, and it is the singer's voice, not Miss Hepburn's which we hear on the soundtrack recording of the show. Julie Andrews was bitterly disappointed not to have been chosen by MGM, but her cloud at this time most certainly had a golden lining. Learning that she would not be recreating her role of Eliza Doolittle, Walt Disney signed Julie Andrews immediately for his forthcoming musical fantasy film – also set in Edwardian London! – *Mary Poppins*, the success of which was thought by some to have virtually eclipsed that of Miss Hepburn in the film of *My Fair Lady* – good though her assumption of the role was.

Hepburn's performance is quite astonishingly good, the only caveat being that occasionally her cockney accent causes a few problems. The director, George Cukor, recreated the area of the old Covent Garden fruit and vegetable (and flower) market surrounding the Opera House on the Warner lot in Hollywood with considerable skill and atmosphere, and the interiors of the film are quite brilliantly staged and lit – by an uncredited master of these disciplines, as well as others, Gene Allen, who had worked with Cukor for many years. Allen's work was uncredited as Beaton had been contracted as designer for the film, but his work was ultimately confined to the magnificent costumes. Another technical part of the film which has enjoyed a high reputation is the editing of William Ziegler, yet there are continuity lapses, at least in the restored version, which jar briefly from time to time for the attentive viewer.

Rex Harrison and Stanley Holloway recreated their roles of almost ten years previously with exemplary brilliance, and Wilfred Hyde White as Colonel Pickering was wholly exceptional; but technically, for all the magnificence of the costumes and sets (also by Sir Cecil Beaton), there are several continuity problems. These are relatively minor matters, but most people wished to compare Audrey Hepburn with Julie Andrews, and did so, it seems, mostly to Miss Hepburn's relative disadvantage.

It is impossible, however, not to be deeply impressed by the film; shot in 70mm SuperPanavision and restored today in digital sound, its qualities remain very considerable, in particular the captivating 'Ascot Gavotte' sequence with its astonishing costumes and stylised, almost slow-motion, choreography, surrounding the hilarious scene when Eliza, now speaking as a genteel young lady, meets Henry Higgins's mother (Dame Gladys Cooper) and her friends. The musical aspect could hardly have been improved upon. The music direction and supervision was under André Previn, who won his fourth Academy Award for his work on *My Fair Lady* in 1964, and his second such accolade for a Lerner and Loewe score, after *Gigi* in 1958 (it was also Previn's second consecutive Oscar, following *Irma La Douce* in 1963). The change to film also enabled the fantasy for 'Just You Wait, Henry Higgins' to reach imaginative heights with the appearance of King Edward VII in Eliza's daydream.

It also afforded Frederick Loewe the opportunity of adding more music to his original score, but it has to be said that the intervening period of almost ten years had led to a slight but noticeable change in his style. It is one thing to recapture a few bars of pre-existing music and run such a sequence to fit some new film business, but another to write fresh music in the same style. It can be argued that Loewe did not always succeed in this regard, that the original score was so good in itself that the filming of it tended to stretch the music beyond what, structurally, it could bear. On the other hand, such a comment would seem unnecessarily churlish, for there are very few stylistic shocks with regard to the music in the film. There were undoubted risks, for as we noted earlier, Audrey Hepburn was not a singer, and her singing role had to be dubbed by a trained singer. Exceptional for this difficult technique, Audrey Hepburn's miming was well-nigh flawless. The choice of singer fell on the 34-year-old California soprano Marni Nixon, who had earlier dubbed the singing voices of Deborah Kerr in *The King And I* in 1956 and Natalie Wood in both *West Side Story* in 1961 and *Gypsy* in 1962. Nixon was a wholly exceptional artist, who made a very successful career as an opera singer in 20th-century music as well as in more traditional operatic roles; she also pursued a successful television career, most notably in children's programmes, as well as appearing as a straight actress in various stage productions. It is Marni Nixon's voice, therefore, that we hear on the sound-track album; yet her name was nowhere to be found on the four sides of the record's gatefold LP cover – a great pity that this fine artist was thus publicly denied her due.

One result of the decision not to cast Julie Andrews as Eliza Doolittle was that – brilliant though Marni Nixon was at making herself sound for all the world like it was Audrey Hepburn singing – her voice was older and not so fresh as that of Julie Andrews. Eliza is, after all, meant to be a young girl of not more than 20, a characteristic of the role which Julie Andrews' voice realised to perfection. Audrey Hepburn/Marni Nixon's voice was clearly that of an older woman. A small point, maybe, but a not insignificant one.

Another aspect of the film of *My Fair Lady* is that the original SuperPanavision 70 print has been restored to extraordinary effect, a process of which was itself driven by the fabulous costumes and staging by Sir Cecil Beaton, notably the stylised 'Ascot Gavotte'.

If the three-hour film version of *My Fair Lady* was not quite the flawless masterpiece that the original staging undoubtedly was, it nonetheless won three more Oscars, additional to and more important than that already mentioned for André Previn, namely for Rex Harrison, George Cukor and Harry Stradling, for the photography. Notwithstanding any slight imperfections we may, at this distance of time, identify in the film of *My Fair Lady*, it remains a magnificent realisation of this great score – the more so in its restored version – and is undoubtedly definitive in the portrayals of Professor Higgins, Albert P Doolittle and Colonel Pickering; several smaller roles, as adopted by Dame Gladys Cooper, Jeremy Brett and Theodore Bikel, were equally outstanding. But, for all her doe-like charm and deserved success, Audrey Hepburn could not quite equal, much less surpass, the creation of Eliza Doolittle by Julie Andrews.

Chapter 23

Oklahoma!

The background to this show, one of the greatest, most significant and epoch-making in the history of the American Musical Theatre, was anything but certain. Indeed, as Louis Untermeyer recalled, "When the idea for *Oklahoma!* was first broached, no one was aware that an American classic was in the making."

Not that the omens were entirely unpropitious, but it was the first time that Richard Rodgers and Oscar Hammerstein II had collaborated on a show – in fact, it was often considered to be the first time they had collaborated on anything. In one respect, it was, but it so happened that the young Oscar Hammerstein II had provided lyrics for two tunes that the equally young Richard Rodgers had written in about 1916 – Hammerstein had been sent the tunes, and supplied the lyrics, without actually meeting the composer. In one way, therefore, *Oklahoma!* was their first real collaboration, although their paths had crossed from a distance many years before. Nonetheless, their mutual chemistry was, as yet, untried.

The book of the show was taken from the play by Lynn Riggs, *Green Grow The Lilacs*, which had been successfully produced by the Theatre Guild.

The play was written by Riggs in 1931, and was in a vein not unlike that which was beginning to assume theatrical importance the world over – the socially aware dramatists from Brecht in Germany to Maxwell Anderson and Clifford Odets in the USA. By 1942, Lynn Riggs was a sergeant in the US Army.

It was the Theatre Guild also which was to produce *Oklahoma!* – to far greater success than the original play on which it was based, for their production won the first ever special award of a Pulitzer Prize in the Drama Category in 1944. Perhaps significantly, also, the Drama award itself that year was not made by the prize committee.

Although this takes us a little further in our chronology than we are at present, it may be pertinent to note that the conditions of the Pulitzer Prize Award which have to be met in regard to the Drama section are that it is granted 'for an original American play which shall represent the educational value and power of the stage, preferably dealing with American life'. The previous year, Thornton Wilder had won it for *The Skin Of Our Teeth* and in 1945 Mary Chase won it for *Harvey*. The prestige of the award far outweighed its monetary value, which was $500.

One of the two producers of the original play,

'Laurie Makes Up Her Mind', in Rodger and Hammerstein's *Oklahoma!*
as directed by Fred Zinnemann in 1956

Theresa Helburn, is credited with having the idea of turning *Green Grow The Lilacs* into a musical. She later recalled: "I felt that *Green Grow The Lilacs*, like [Du Bose Heyward's] *Porgy*, which the Theatre Guild had put on, had a great native flavour, and a background rich in native music and dances. We wanted to keep the gaiety and freshness, the poetry and humour of the people in Lynn Riggs's play."

The play itself, set at the turn of the 20th-century, is basically concerned with the rivalry between farmers who wanted the land of the old territory to grow and harvest their crops and the ranchers who needed the land for their cattle to graze. This was one of the prime causes for friction in the mid-west in the latter part of the 19th-century, made more difficult by the coming of the railroad, the growth of the Union itself, and the residue of the Civil War. As a point of interest, the State of Oklahoma was only admitted to the Union as late as 1907 – the actual year in which Riggs had set his play.

The idea of making a musical out of such a subject was not wholly unusual: the text of the play incorporates folk-songs from time to time, and, in May, 1942, a ballad-opera by the temporary English immigrant Benjamin Britten on the American folk-character *Paul Bunyan*, with text by WH Auden, was first produced in New York. Wilfrid Mellers's apt description of the text of *Paul Bunyan* as being "not so much an opera libretto as a play for music" could equally apply to *Green Grow The Lilacs*.

Miss Helburn soon discussed her idea with her fellow-producer, Lawrence Langner, who suggested their mutual friend Richard Rodgers to write the music. Langner was Welsh, and it was he who insisted that the 'theatre' in Theatre Guild be spelled the British way, not the American 'Theater'. Both he and Theresa Helburn had

known Richard 'Dick' Rodgers for almost 20 years, since a show, *The Garrick Gaieties* – which included two immortal songs, 'Manhattan' and 'In A Mountain Greenery' – for which Rodgers had written the music to Lorenz Hart's lyrics, opened at the Gaiety Theatre in the spring of 1925. It was a great success, and, with the idea of a musical version of *Green Grow The Lilacs* now pushing itself forward as an ideal vehicle for collaboration, they put the idea to the composer.

But Lorenz Hart could no longer be seriously considered as a collaborator on this project. Alcoholism had taken hold of this sensitive and brilliant man; whilst he was able to maintain sobriety for a period, it was clear to his friends – including Rodgers – that it was unlikely he would be able to sustain his creativity at the level which a big musical show such as was envisaged would demand.

Not that Hart was entirely finished: he did manage to collaborate with Rodgers on one more production – a revival of their earlier *A Connecticut Yankee*, with new material. Within three days of the opening of this revival, in November 1943, Lorenz Hart had drunk himself to death.

If there was an initial degree of uncertainty as to the viability of a collaboration between Richard Rodgers and Oscar Hammerstein II, a curious coincidence which was later related by Hammerstein should have been reassuring. He had seen the play at the Theatre Guild himself, of course, and for the previous two years had been toying with the idea of doing a musical version of it.

Richard Rodgers himself, on speaking of the genesis of 'Oklahoma!', said that "the first thing we did, after agreeing on the play and tossing out the folk-songs in the original script, was to decide to do the whole thing over – to do it fresh, from start to finish. The next thing we did was to get hold of Oscar Hammerstein and ask if he would do the book and lyrics." At this point, Hammerstein revealed that he had been planning a musical treatment of the same play.

Richard Rodgers continued: "Then we decided together, Oscar and I, on the viewpoint – what kind of music, what kind of lyrics, what size orchestra – in other words, we tried to set the personality of the show we wanted to create.

"Then came the mechanical work: who would do what number and where, what the number should be like, and so on. Then I retired to get my ideas, and Oscar went to work on the book."

Luckily, as these experienced theatrical personages all realised, the original play lent itself admirably to this treatment. It has rightly been said that a great many 'musical comedies' up to this point had been hung around rather flimsy dramatic material – the plots, if such situations can be so described, of these shows were often transparently feeble.

Hammerstein possessed the considerable creative advantage of having thought about this project himself for some time; so he was able to put into immediate practice those aspects of his adaptation he had previously only mused over. "First, I cut the original script to make room for the music. Then I wrote in a sub-plot and added some characters. We put in Will, who was not in the original; we built up Ado Annie and the peddler. Curley and Laurey, the heroine, we left alone – they were perfect as they were. So was Aunt Eller. Then we had a first draft of the book, but no music and lyrics. Before I did anything else, I wrote the lyrics to the first song in the first act. That was for Dick and me – to set the mood of the show for us. And to set the mood for the audience, too. When Curly sings off-stage as the curtain goes up, and then wanders into the front

yard of Laurey's farmhouse singing, 'Oh! What A Beautiful Mornin'', you can feel the audience smile and relax and settle back. At least that's what we aimed for."

There is no doubt that they succeeded. From the first song, that first fruit of their adult collaboration, the combination of Richard Rodgers and Oscar Hammerstein had produced an immortal piece of musical theatre. The great conductor Arturo Toscanini, in 1944, as reported by Eugene Goossens, then conductor of the Cincinnati Symphony Orchestra and a friend of Richard Rodgers, "under the spell of *Oklahoma!*, sat down at the piano and played the opening of 'Oh! What A Beautiful Mornin'', raptly exclaiming the while, 'Che bella musica!'. I agreed," said Goossens.

This great song seemed to appear almost unbidden: for, when he received the text, Richard Rodgers continued, "I just put the lyrics on the piano and the music just wrote itself."

Everyone involved in the show up to that time would have been inspired by such an opening number: setting "the mood of the show for us" as Oscar Hammerstein said. What was really so interesting, as the genesis of the show developed, was the change in Rodgers' music compared with the songs and other scores he had composed up to that time. *Oklahoma!* was a very different proposition from anything he had attempted before – previously, his music had been amongst the most sophisticated and urbane yet written for the Broadway stage, matching perfectly the verbal idiosyncrasies and delight in language, almost for its own sake, which had tended to characterise the lyrics of Lorenz Hart. Now, with the equally – but differently – gifted Oscar Hammerstein II, Rodgers was presented with a much more direct style of utterance – no less subtle in its own way, but painted in broader, more vivid verbal colouring. The result was to draw from Rodgers a new type of show music, a type that mirrored Hammerstein's directness and brilliance in a particularly apt manner.

The producer chosen was Rouben Mamoulian – a very experienced and much respected man of the theatre who had directed the world premiere of Gershwin's *Porgy And Bess* and who, therefore, was completely at home with the integrated type of musical theatre – bordering on grand opera – which Gershwin's score, and later works like *Oklahoma!* came to typify. He outlined his view of his task by saying that "it has always been my conviction that the ideal theatre should combine drama and music interwoven to compose one rhythmic and dramatic pattern. That was the guiding principle which governed me in directing *Porgy And Bess* – the principle that the show itself is the star."

This was a new approach indeed. Such a view imposed a new perspective on other matters concerned with the production as well. And so, for the choreography, the 24-year-old Agnes de Mille (a niece of the great film director) was approached. Born in New York City, and trained in classical ballet, having appeared in London with the Ballet Rambert, she scored an instant success as a choreographer with *Three Virgins And A Devil* in 1941, before moving to Broadway. *Oklahoma!* was to be her first musical show, to which she brought her originality and natural enthusiasm – a gifted young 'outsider' to the Broadway scene was a particularly shrewd choice, for it had already been decided that *Oklahoma!* would not be produced along conventional lines. She recalled: "I got a group of girls and men who were all dance soloists in their own right, but who could also act. We did not want a 'chorus-line'. We wanted people – boys and girls you would remember when the show was over, friends you would hope to meet again sometime. We got them."

The sets and costumes were by Lemuel Ayres and Miles White – outstanding artists in their own fields – and a notable cast was assembled. Alfred Drake was Curly and Joan Roberts was Laurey. The latter choice was a compromise, but it worked splendidly. Theresa Helburn and Lawrence Langner wanted the 14-year-old Shirley Temple for the role, but Richard Rodgers thought that she was too young to sustain such a demanding part night after night; he would have preferred Mary Martin, who was then 29. In the event, Joan Roberts was chosen. The part of Ado Annie was played by Celeste Holm. Jud was portrayed by Howard da Silva – a gifted character actor, the range of whose voice was not above an octave. From this musical constraint, which most composers will admit to being a severe restriction, Rodgers composed a beautiful song, 'Lonely Room', which – as Jule Styne pertinently observed – is Rodgers' first approach to an operatic aria. This song did not appear on either the original cast recording or the film – its first appearance was on the Broadway cast album of the 1979 revival. The orchestrations were by Robert Russell Bennett and the orchestra was under the direction of Jay Blackton (who also conducted for the film and for the 1979 revival, 46 years later).

And so it was that *Oklahoma!* opened at St James Theatre, New York City on March 31, 1943. America was at war, and if allied successes at the battles of Stalingrad, El Alamein and especially Midway had begun to turn the tide against the Axis powers, the American people could more readily respond to a theatrical show that conjured up a nostalgic view of America in more innocent, more charming and poetical days. If they responded to such a show, they responded more fully to the outstanding musical score which

Richard Rodgers had written: from the 'bella musica' of the opening song, to the inspired waltz 'Out Of My Dreams', from the earthy, grey-black humour of 'Pore Jud Is Dead' (in which Rodgers creates a mock funeral-march with devastating effect) and 'Kansas City' to the delightful duet 'People Will Say We're In Love' – among others – the musical content of the show is on a consistently high level. *Oklahoma!* broke all Broadway box office records. It ran for 2,212 performances – far and away the longest run for any musical then in existence. In 1947 it opened in London, at the Theatre Royal, Drury Lane, where it ran for 1,548 performances; it can truly be said to have marked a new type of Broadway musical – of course, one can always find elements of such innovations in earlier shows, but how would it transfer to the screen, as it almost inevitably would have to?

The motion picture of *Oklahoma!* was released in 1956 – 13 years after the show had first opened. It is a measure of the timeless appeal of the story and of the music that the film, starring Gordon MacRae, Gloria Grahame, Gene Nelson, Charlotte Greenwood, James Whitmore, Shirley Jones, and Rod Steiger, was highly successful.

But, as we have noted before, the success of a Hollywood film of a Broadway show depends equally on how the film is made – not whether it remains true to the original production. Apart from having chosen an outstanding cast, no little credit for the film's success can be given to aspects of Fred Zinnemann's direction and the breathtaking – and breathless – choreography of Agnes de Mille.

From Gordon MacRae's opening scene, as he rides gently through the 'corn as high as an elephant's eye', to the delightful 'Surrey With The Fringe On Top', the combination of location shots and close-ups is particularly effective, and although some have criticised this film for its location work, it is difficult to see how such a subject could have otherwise been tackled.

Whilst it is true that the movie of *Oklahoma!* may not be the greatest film musical ever made, it remains a very good one, whose qualities, like those of the show it captures, seem to improve with the years – and not merely nostalgically.

Chapter 24

Oliver!

In the decade 1957-67 the West End musical stage was dominated by the output of one remarkably gifted creator – Lionel Bart. This exceptional young man – he had been born in 1930 – achieved a measure of success which redefined the British musical in a way rarely before seen.

More than that, the best of his shows transferred to Broadway and to films with equal success, and in so doing managed to reawaken a transcontinental interest in the British musical which had been absent for some time.

Born in London's East End, the youngest of twelve children, and the son of an immigrant tailor, Lionel Bart (as he became – after changing his surname to that of a famous London hospital) first studied art, after having won a scholarship to St Martin's School in London's Tottenham Court Road – in the heart of Theatreland. He was then obliged to do two years' National Service, which he spent in the Royal Air Force, and after demobilisation he joined a left-wing theatre club, Unity, in 1952.

He had a variety of tasks there – as one might expect – as scene painter, poster designer, occasional actor and understudy. Bart took part in several Unity productions, including a revue,

Peacemeal to which be contributed as a writer. His next project was entirely his, *Wally Pone*, a story of contemporary life set in the East End of London.

By this tine, the musical side of Bart's talent had emerged. In the vanguard of popular music, but not then so commercially popular as it was later to become, he had joined an early London skiffle group, The Cavemen, who played at small cafes and coffee-bars in Soho and nearby. Bart was one of three members of this band, whose music was part of a world-wide teenage reaction against the luscious orchestration and crooning style of more established – because it dated from war-time – singers. The other members were Mike Pratt and the Bermondsey-born Tommy Steele; Bart wrote much of the group's material, and their 1956 single, 'Rock With The Caveman' was not only Steele's first hit record but also the means by which Bart's song-writing gifts had emerged with no little success.

There was literally no looking back for Bart as a song-writer – for the next three years not a week passed without a song by Lionel Bart being in the British Top 20. At the same time, he won more Ivor Novello Awards than any previous songwriter. This was both a remarkable achievement in itself

Jack Wild and Ron Moody in Columbia's 1968 masterpiece, *Oliver!*.

but exceptionally so for a man who could neither read nor write music, nor play any musical instrument to any degree of facility.

Bart would pick out his songs on the piano keyboard with one finger or he would sing them into a tape recorder. On one occasion, visiting the British disc jockey David Jacobs at his home, Bart was able to pick out the tune of a song which had come to him on his journey on Jacobs' daughter's little toy piano.

His biggest hit song was not for Tommy Steele, however – although he continued to provide material for his fellow-Londoner – but for the other early British rock-and-roll idol, Cliff Richard. This was the million-selling 'Living Doll', a soft-rock number that, uniquely, also reached Number One in the charts 27 years later when Cliff Richard remade a 'fun' version with the anarchic comedy team The Young Ones (themselves named after a successful Richard musical film of the 1960s).

By this time, Bart had moved into writing music for films – one of his most under-rated scores being for the British Lion war-time comedy *Light Up The Sky*; others for which Bart provided music include *The Duke Wore Jeans* and *Tommy The Toreador*. However successful Bart was in providing popular hit material, his genius lay completely in the musical theatre. He had written some highly apt and original lyrics for a post-Restoration musical show, *Lock Up Your Daughters*, with music by Cyril Ornadel, based upon Henry Field's 1730 play *Rape Upon Rape* – this was written to open the Mermaid Theatre at Puddle Dock in London, a theatre for which the construction money was raised by selling individual bricks in the building to members of the public. The show has also been described as effectively ending the American domination of the London musical stage. *Lock Up Your Daughters* contains a witty 18th-century cha-cha-cha (!)

'There's A Plot Afoot', and, later in 1959, Lionel Bart's brilliant *Fings Ain't What They Used To Be*, for which he wrote book, music and lyrics, opened – a defining musical show of its time, as much as was Colin McInnes's novel *Absolute Beginners* in its field.

In 1960 came Bart's masterpiece, *Oliver!*. From the contemporary mid-20th-century London low-life of *Fings*, Bart turned to mid-19th-century London low life – as exemplified in Charles Dickens' novel *Oliver Twist*. This marked the high point of Bart's theatrical career, for, although he had two further marked stage successes – *Blitz!* (a musical on the rather unpromising story of civilians in London during war-time: note how London reappears again in his work) and *Maggie May* – both of these are really excellent pieces of musical theatre and are occasionally revived – he never quite reached the apogee of *Oliver!*.

Most of Dickens' novels are on a large scale – and *Oliver Twist* is no exception. For his musical adaptation, Bart concentrated upon Oliver's early years, claiming – with commendable justification and truthfulness – that he had 'freely adapted' the novel – or, rather, that portion of the novel (actually, less than half) that he used.

Oliver! was a project that had stalked Bart for some time; it became an obsession (as all good creative work should so become) with him, so that he had a vision in his mind's eye of precisely what he wanted to achieve – not that this is to assert that Bart himself knew, down to the last nail, how the stage sets should appear – a vision that he kept before him as the music poured out of his creative consciousness. And so it was that *Oliver!* was completed before Bart attempted to secure a producer. He managed to persuade Donald Albery of the score's worth, but it seems that – even if both men were convinced of the show's merits – the casting posed problems.

In the end, the part of Fagin went to the gifted (but as yet comparatively unknown) actor and singer Ron Moody. Then 36 years of age, Moody was catapulted by his portrayal of Fagin to overnight, and lasting, fame. A similar destiny befell the outstandingly talented singer Georgia Brown, who essayed the part of Nancy – her moving song 'As Long As He Needs Me' has taken its rightful place as one of the finest British standards of all time.

The cast that author, producer and director – the admirable Peter Coe – assembled for the opening night, June 30, 1960 at the New Theatre, London, was of wholly exceptional talent: Oliver Twist himself was played by the young Keith Hamshere; Mr Bumble, the officious beadle, by the commendable established character-actor Paul Whitsun-Jones, and the part of the undertaker, Mr Sowerberry, by the then-rising Australian star Barry Humphries. The part of evil Bill Sikes was brilliantly taken by Danny Sewell, and the rest of the large cast – 16 separate roles – was universally outstanding. Nor is this all; one of the other 'stars' of this initial production of *Oliver!* was the designer, Sean Kenny. His sets were of a character and technical excellence such as had not before been seen on the London stage; constructed so as to form and reform various settings of the dingy London streets of a century and more earlier, they proved to be one of the show's major talking-points.

Lionel Bart's music had been characterfully orchestrated by Eric Rogers, and the conductor, Marcus Dods, was one of the most versatile then before the public. He was a symphonic and operatic conductor – and, indeed, better known in those roles – as well as being one of the most experienced conductors for British films of his day. He had also conducted in the theatre, so his choice to conduct the score for *Oliver!* meant that

the musical realisation could not have been in better hands.

The book of Lionel Bart's *Oliver!* naturally follows Dickens' original; however, the synopsis is worth consideration, the better to appreciate Bart's mastery in encapsulating those elements he took from the novel from which to fashion such a great musical show.

As the distinguished musical theatre writer Rex Bunnett has well written of the synopsis: "*Oliver!* opens in one of the many charity workhouses of Victorian London. The orphan boys begin to fantasise about what food they could eat ('Overture' and 'Food, Glorious Food') just before their miserable, daily ration of gruel is served. Oliver dares to ask Mr Bumble, who runs the workhouse with the widow Corney, for more food, saying: 'Please sir, I want some more'. He is rebuked by Mr Bumble, Mrs Corney and the boys ('Oliver'). The workhouse is no place for a greedy boy and Oliver is taken off by Mr Bumble to be sold ('Boy for sale'). He is hauled through London's streets and is bought by the undertaker, Mr Sowerberry. Alone in the funeral parlour, he feels sorry for himself, and he daydreams of the mother he cannot remember ('Where Is Love?'). Bullied by another apprentice about his longing for a mother, Oliver hits out at him and as a punishment he is put in a coffin. He escapes and runs out into the streets.

"The Artful Dodger comes upon a tired Oliver. Always on the look-out for likely lads, he takes him to the thieves' kitchen where he is told to make himself at home ('Consider Yourself'). As the boys come into the kitchen, Oliver meets their leader Fagin and hears what he is expected to do if he wants to stay ('Pick A Pocket Or Two').

"Before long, Oliver has made a friend of Nancy, the girlfriend of the thief Bill Sikes. She tells him that a life of crime is fine as long as you look after yourself and your friends ('I'd Do Anything'). The next morning, Oliver is taken out by the Artful Dodger to learn how to pickpocket as Fagin entreats them to hurry home ('Be Back Soon'). Oliver is caught at his first attempt to steal and is taken away by the police.

"Meanwhile, Nancy is entertaining the locals in the Three Cripples pub ('Oom-Pah-Pah'). Her singing comes to an abrupt halt when Sikes appears and is told by the other boys of Oliver's capture. Worried that Oliver will tell the police about them, Sikes tells Nancy to get him back. Nancy feels guilty about the prospect of taking the boy away from his only hope of a home life, but she loves Sikes and will always do what he asks ('As Long As He Needs Me'). She goes to the home of Mr Brownlow, who has taken the orphan in, despite his attempt to rob him.

"Oliver is well looked after in Brownlow's spacious house. Early one morning he looks out and sees the street vendors selling their wares ('Who Will Buy?'). Oliver sets out on an errand but is captured by Nancy and Sikes. They take him back to Fagin's den where he is threatened by Sikes. Nancy steps in to save him from physical harm, so Sikes takes his money while Fagin strips him of his new clothes. Once everyone has calmed down, Fagin begins to reconsider a life which is filled with cruelty. He wonders whether the time has come to settle down ('Reviewing The Situation').

"Meanwhile, Mrs Bumble, formerly the Widow Corney, hears the deathbed confession of an old woman. It transpires that Oliver is the child of a wealthy woman who died in childbirth. Realising that she could be on to an easy fortune, Mrs Bumble determines to find the boy. Her husband goes to visit Brownlow, who is shown a locket stolen from the mother. The portrait inside reveals that she is Brownlow's daughter, who left home to bear her illegitimate child.

"Nancy proves a willing accomplice in Brownlow's plans to get Oliver back. They plan a rendezvous, but before she can hand the boy over, Sikes kills her in retaliation for her betrayal. He takes Oliver back to Fagin's den, with Bow Street Runners in pursuit. Sikes dies in the chase and Oliver is reunited with his grandfather. Fagin is nowhere to he found, but he eventually emerges from his hiding place to a strange new world. As the show closes, Oliver's happiness seems assured ('Finale')."

Oliver! is a masterpiece. Its most enduring element, as with all great musicals, is the music itself, which is where Bart's genius is most fully realised than at almost any time in his career. The songs themselves maintain a high level of melodic inspiration, and the lyrics not only fit the music like a glove but also have no little merit in themselves. No doubt Bart's personal Jewish background played its part in his musically formative years, but the Jewish inflexions of Fagin's two outstanding numbers, 'You've Got To Pick A Pocket Or Two' and 'Reviewing The Situation' are so endemic to the character and as such play the major element in the creation of this fully-rounded character.

This is, however, but a small part of the whole score; for many musicians the extraordinary tapestry of 'Who Will Buy?' – an amalgam of traditional London street cries, but welded together with haunting, consummate mastery – will remain one of the high-spots of the score. If it may remind some listeners of the 'Strawberry Woman's Call' in Gershwin's *Porgy And Bess*, there is no doubt that Bart has here created a far more involved and involving passage, entirely appropriate to his subject and, in turn, leading to an exciting choral treatment of the same material, before the early-morning street-sellers return to end the number as it began – as much a genuine picture of Victorian London as any reportage by Mayhew, the musical equivalent of a Turner-esque picture. That such a moving episode could have been conceived and realised by a man who does not read music at all is an extraordinary testament to his natural talent, which finds equal – but equally varied – expression in such songs as 'Food, Glorious Food' and 'As Long As He Needs Me'.

The film version, as almost always turns out to be the case, made several compromises with the original score. Three varied songs, which appeared in the show, were omitted from the film. These are: 'I Shall Scream' (Widow Corney and Mr Bumble); 'That's Your Funeral' (Mr Bumble and Mr and Mrs Sowerberry), and Bill Sikes's song ('My Name'). These can be heard not only on the Decca original cast recording but also on a little-known EMI recording of the entire score made in the presence of Lionel Bart. This version starred Stanley Holloway as Fagin, Alma Cogan (who at one time proposed live to Lionel Bart on television – which proposal Bart, very diplomatically and politely, turned down! – Miss Cogan, a very popular singer of the day, was to die tragically within a few years) as Nancy, Violet Carson as the Widow Corney and the young Dennis Waterman as Oliver. Tony Tanner was the Artful Dodger and Leslie Fyson Mr Bumble.

Oliver! ran for six years in London, and opened on Broadway at the Imperial Theatre on January 6, 1963. It subsequently moved to the famous Shubert Theatre where Oliver was played by Bruce Prochnik and the Artful Dodger by the young David Jones (later to achieve greater fame as the English boy in the television pop band The Monkees). Georgia Brown recreated her portrayal of Nancy, as did Danny Sewell as Bill Sikes, and the part of Fagin was taken by Clive Revill.

Overall, on Broadway, *Oliver!* ran for more than two years, by which time, when it closed, plans for the film version were advanced.

If the cast and production staff for the London premiere were brilliantly chosen, those assembled for the filmed version were no less distinguished. Sir Carol Reed, one of the finest of all English film directors, was responsible for the movie; his reputation was made internationally by his immediate post-war films – *The Fallen Idol* and *The Third Man* especially – notable for, among other things, their extraordinary sense of time and place. If the filming of *Oliver!* demanded a wholly convincing recreation of Dickens' London, then it could not have been in better or more experienced hands. With *Oliver!*, Sir Carol won his only Academy Award; other Oscars went to the musical director, John Green and to the film for Best Picture.

The cast included Ron Moody, brilliantly recreating on film the role he had created on the London stage – one of the few actors to transfer successfully from one medium to another in the same part – and the sultry Oliver Reed was exceptional as Bill Sikes. Young Mark Lester played Oliver to perfection, in a touching combination of vulnerability, inherent decency and inner strength. Sir Harry Secombe and Peggy Mount were Mr and Mrs Bumble, and Shani Wallis played Nancy. Jack Wild was the all-knowing Artful Dodger, and Vernon Harris's screenplay, together with John Box's outstanding cinematography, combined to make arguably the finest film ever made of a British musical.

Columbia Pictures knew a good investment when they saw one, in those days, and this is a great version of a great musical – both of which have stood the test of time.

Two days after *Oliver!* opened, Lionel Bart received a telephone call from New York.

"Is that Lionel Bart?" asked the clipped voice.

The orphan boys.

"Yes, it is," the composer replied.

"It's Noel here," the caller said.

"Noel who?"

"Noel Coward, you bloody fool."

"Oh, sorry."

"Look, I understand you have had a bit of a success with your new show *Oliver!*. I'd like to talk to you about it. Could you see me in New York at my apartment next Tuesday?"

"Yes, I suppose so."

"Good. Shall we say mid-day?"

"Yes."

"Right, that's settled, then."

The following Tuesday, Lionel Bart met with Noel Coward, who, after congratulating him, said: "I'm going to give you three pieces of advice. The first is, never put any of your own money into your own shows. The second is, if you have had a success, take a week's holiday and then start work on your next project. The third is, if you have had a failure, don't take the holiday but start work the following morning on your next project."

Chapter 25

Porgy And Bess

One evening in September 1926, unable to sleep, George Gershwin idly picked up a copy of a recently-published novel *Porgy* by Du Bose Heyward and began reading it. He was soon enthralled by the story and finished the book at one sitting, finally going to bed at four in the morning, and fired with the notion of turning it into an opera – the one genre in which he so much wanted to write.

In the event, Gershwin wrote three 'operas', of which *Porgy And Bess*, as it became, was his last. The first was *Blue Monday* a one-act opera contributed as part of George White's *Scandals Off 1922*. The opera was conceived and written within five days, which may account for its shortcomings – yet it remains rather more than a curiosity, although it was only given once in the parent show's run in 1922, and once more, in a new orchestration by Ferde Grofé, in a concert performance at Carnegie Hall in December 1925.

That same month saw the premiere of Gershwin's even less well-known second operatic work, *Song Of The Flame*, described as a 'romantic opera' when it opened on Broadway, two days after another Gershwin musical comedy *Tip Toes* opened at the Liberty Theatre. The score for *Song Of The Flame* is almost wholly by Gershwin,

although it incorporated other songs by Herbert Stothart; the book was by Oscar Hammerstein II and Otto Harbach.

The facts are, however, that both *Blue Monday* (which is also known as '135th Street') and *Song Of The Flame* were little more than attempts at a new type of musical show, and were not planned from the start as operatic pieces – although an interesting adjunct to *Blue Monday* is that it requires an all-black cast. From finishing Du Bose Heyward's novel, Gershwin was crystal clear in his own mind of how he wanted it to be treated – if he had anything to do with it.

He contacted Heyward and eventually obtained permission to use the novel as the basis for an opera. Perhaps it was this notion that was at the back of Gershwin's mind when he signed a contract with the Metropolitan Opera in 1930 wherein the organisation commissioned from him an opera for an unspecified date. But if it was, he realised that the demand the novel made on the casting – it was set in the working-class black community of Charleston, South Carolina, and would therefore demand a virtual all-black cast.

In 1933, events conspired to cause Gershwin to give the *Porgy* opera serious consideration. Early in that year, the Theatre Guild had approached Du

Brock Peters and Dorothy Dandridge starring in the 1959 Goldwyn film version of *Porgy And Bess*.

Bose Heyward to permit a musical version of the novel to be made into a vehicle for Al Jolson; Heyward, not forgetting Gershwin's earlier interest, informed Gershwin of the Guild's approach. Gershwin replied that Heyward should not forgo such an opportunity, but Heyward responded that he would prefer the piece to be fashioned into an opera, not a musical show. That virtually settled the matter: Gershwin could not refuse, and could no longer delay the writing of the work.

He finally realised that an opera of *Porgy* would go against the spirit of the Metropolitan Opera contract – and possibly against his own feelings concerning the kind of work he wanted to write. He was anxious that the work should reach a wider public than that which would have attended the (at most) half-dozen or so performances it would have received at the Opera House during a season. Furthermore, *Porgy And Bess* would necessarily demand an all-black cast, which would prove impractical for major opera houses. And so Gershwin signed a contract for an operatic version with the Theatre Guild in October 1933, and began work on the score.

It consumed him, utterly. The idea, which had been crawling around parts of his mind for years, now burst forth in a virtually unstoppable flood. It was an amazing outpouring, for over a period of just over 18 months, from August 1933 to April 1935, the resultant score – if played complete – would last for four-and-a-half-hours, without a break. *Porgy And Bess* is a long opera, but its length is not the result of loquaciousness, rather the result of Gershwin's teeming imagination being given full rein at last.

The work has never been performed complete as first written. Nor should we fear that this meant an irredeemable loss to the world. As originally completed, no operatic composer – no experienced man of the theatre, as Gershwin was –

would have countenanced a work which in continuity plays for such Wagnerian length. It had to be pruned; but with so much music the task was both easy and difficult. Gershwin's dilemma was that when he was presented, in the cold light of day, with the results of his work, he had to decide whether to treat *Porgy And Bess* as grand opera – which it undoubtedly is – and yet permit it to be produced not by an opera company, or as a musical theatre piece – with the fact that in the latter event, the production company's experience in such matters, and therefore their approach, would be very different from that of an established opera company.

The work therefore posed problems in casting and production: rehearsals were long and occasionally proved quite difficult; it was an expensive undertaking, and – to make the point again – *Porgy And Bess* was not to be performed in an opera house. Described as *An American Folk Opera*, a not misleading title, it was perhaps only to be expected that some people would be perplexed by the composition. But, as with all musical works of art, it had to stand or fall through its musical impact, and – given its unusual, unique qualities – one has to count the first production as a major success.

The trials and tribulations in finding a suitable all-black cast were finally overcome, and the production, prior to opening in New York, was first seen on September 30, 1935 at the Colonial Theatre in Boston. A week previously, a concert version of the complete score was given at Carnegie Hall, New York City, before an invited audience.

The first night in Boston was a triumph, as was that two weeks later in New York at the Alvin Theatre at 250 West 52nd Street. A stage photograph, showing Gershwin taking a curtain call on that opening night with members of the cast and the opera director Rouben Mamoulian, is dominated by the composer, centre front. The look of elation on his face, a combination perhaps of triumph and exhaustion, is surely unique in photographs of him. From this one shot alone, it is not too fanciful to see that he knew he had not only succeeded in his task, but his music had also won the hearts and minds of the overwhelming majority of his audience. An operatic composer – any composer, in fact – can wish for no more than that.

Porgy And Bess ran consecutively in New York for more than three months: but, apart from its own artistic success in operatic terms (for a run of three months is, in terms of performances, unheard of in even the most successful of operas), financially the work lost money as a stage production. Within two years, Gershwin was dead.

The fate of this opera has been remarkable. It has often been stated that the critical reaction was generally unfavourable, but this was not, in fact, the case. By far the majority of critics praised the work, and whilst some found the work difficult to take – they were unsure whether it was an opera or an operetta or a 'musical' (given the tragic nature of the story, it could hardly be termed a 'musical comedy'), and it was this hybrid aspect to some which gave rise to their reservations.

It was revived several times soon after Gershwin's death, and it returned to Broadway in 1942, where it enjoyed a run greater than that of any revival in New York City's musical theatre history. The New York Music Critics' Circle awarded *Porgy And Bess* a special commendation.

The first performance in Europe took place under unusual circumstances. Germany had invaded Denmark on April 9/10, 1940, so by March 1943 the country had endured three years of Nazi occupation. It was in Copenhagen, on March 27, 1943 that the European premiere of *Porgy And Bess* occurred: this was a courageous act on the part of

the Danish Royal Opera company – an American work, and moreover a work by a Jewish American composer, the scheduled number of performances of *Porgy And Bess* was drastically curtailed. Plans for a Covent Garden production after the war were cancelled.

In 1952, an American company, following the first CBS almost complete recording of 1951, began a transcontinental tour of *Porgy And Bess*, which lasted several years and which saw performances in London (with Leontyne Price as Bess), Berlin, Vienna and other European cities, in Russia and at La Scala in Milan (the first American opera to be produced there) in February 1955. Five months later, the company began a South American tour.

If these performances brought the work for the first time to millions, it was still some many years before *Porgy And Bess* was finally accepted as a work suitable for staging in the world's leading opera houses. By 1990, it had been given at the (new) Metropolitan Opera House in New York (which was more than probably a dream of Gershwin's when he had finished the work – or, more properly, at the 'old' Metropolitan Opera House, which he knew), and – notably less successfully artistically – at the Glyndebourne Opera in England.

The story of *Porgy And Bess* tells of the inhabitants of Catfish Row, a black run-down tenement in Charleston, South Carolina. Clara is singing a lullaby to her baby, telling the child that it is Summertime, whilst watching a crap game taking place down below. The game is far from friendly: Crown quarrels with Robbins and kills him, and escapes before the police arrive. The drug dealer, Sportin' Life, who has fancied Crown's girl, Bess, for some time, sees – with Crown's escape – his chance.

But Bess has found refuge in the home of, and a newly growing love for, the cripple Porgy, who adores her. She has settled down with him and they share their new-found happiness in each other. When the inhabitants of Catfish Row stage a picnic on Kittiwah Island, with Bess having gone to join in the festivities, she is astonished to discover Crown has been hiding on the island. He emerges and confronts her; she succumbs to his blandishments and stays with him for several days on the island.

She returns to Catfish Row after this time, and Porgy finds her sick and delirious. He nurses her back to health when the other women on Catfish Row are perturbed as a hurricane blows up, for their menfolk have gone fishing. Clara's husband, Jake, is missing and suddenly Crown returns, offering to save him, and in so doing he derides Porgy's disability.

Crown saves Jake and returns to claim Bess once more; Porgy, however, fearful that he will lose Bess, fights Crown and fatally stabs him. The police arrive, but are unable to find sufficient evidence to charge anyone; they suspect Porgy, however, and take him to the police station. During his absence, Sportin' Life makes a new play for Bess, and at last persuades her, with some happy dust, to go with him to New York.

Porgy is released, owing to lack of evidence, and when he returns he finds Bess has gone. Hearing that she has gone to New York, he determines to follow her, and, with his few pitiful belongings in his little cart, he leaves Catfish Row.

As the role of Porgy is a cripple, the physical demands it makes upon a singer are considerable; today, however, with operatic producers keen to make singers perform from the most unsuitable and unmusical of positions, such demands are not as infrequently encountered now as they once were, which may be one reason why *Porgy And Bess* is no longer the impossible score to stage that was previously thought.

But in the mid-1950s, *Porgy And Bess* was yet to make its final transition to the repertoires of leading opera houses, and for several years the great motion picture producer Samuel Goldwyn had been keen to make a movie of the score. In the event, his negotiations with the copyright owners took ten years, and he paid $650,000 for the film rights, plus a percentage of the gross receipts. This was not such a vast sum as might at first appear, even accounting for the changing value of currency since those days, for there were several studios willing to put up a million dollars for those rights. Goldwyn was the only person who was found to be acceptable by both sets of trustees – for George Gershwin and for Ira's lyrics, and for Du Bose Heyward's book and for his contribution to the lyrics.

The film was to be Samuel Goldwyn's last as a movie producer and one of the most expensive then made as the production costs exceeded seven million dollars. The sets were designed by Oliver Smith, who was astounded to hear the news shortly before shooting began that the massive set of Catfish Row on Stage 5 of Goldwyn Studios had gone up in flames, with a loss of $300,000. Samuel Goldwyn had called him with the news and said, "I want the rebuilding of that set begun tomorrow." It was.

It was Goldwyn's first intention to have Rouben Mamoulian direct – this would have been particularly apt, as he was responsible for the staging of the world premiere production in 1935 – but this did not work out, and Otto Preminger was engaged instead.

Shooting of the film of *Porgy And Bess* – 33 years after the opera was first given – began in September 1958, on the 5,500 acre Venice Island (the Kittiwah Island scenes in the opera) in the San Joaquin River near Stockton, California. The cast and crew then transferred across the water to Tule Island where the picnic and fishfry scenes were shot. The location filming took approximately ten days, and then all transferred to the Goldwyn Studios in Hollywood, where, for the next ten weeks, the rest of the movie was shot.

As the film was that of an opera, the music had to be recorded first. André Previn was engaged as musical director, and Ken Darby as his assistant. Previn was an inspired choice, for he was on the verge of beginning a career as a symphonic conductor, but – amazingly – he was unaware that an original Gershwin orchestration of the score existed. The only music published at that time was the 1935 vocal piano score, which Previn and Darby entirely reorchestrated for the film. Although the film is the only time that Previn has recorded the complete score of this opera as a conductor, the orchestration used is not Gershwin's.

Interestingly, both Previn and Darby won Oscars for 'Scoring A Dramatic Picture', when in fact there was no need for them to have done so.

And so, in July 1958, using wholly new six-track stereophonic recording, the cast assembled to record the opera. In many cases, they were not the stars who appeared in the movie: Sidney Poitier was to play Porgy, but his voice was dubbed by Robert McFerrin, the first black singer ever to join the Metropolitan Opera Company – this was in 1954; Dorothy Dandridge was Bess, and her voice was dubbed by Adele Addison; Diahann Carroll played Clara (her voice was dubbed by Loulie Jean Norman) and Ruth Attaway was Serena (her voice was dubbed by Inez Matthews). Sammy Davis Jr was Sportin' Life, and did his own singing in the film – but not on the sound-track album! He was under contract to Decca Records at the time, so Cab Calloway (a legendary Sportin' Life) was engaged to record the part for the album. Pearl Bailey did her own singing and acting in the film as Maria, and she appears on the sound-track album –

the only performance thus contained by one player from start to finish.

The screenplay was by N Richard Nash, from the original novel, from Dorothy Heyward's 1927 play *Porgy* of her husband's novel and from the opera's libretto; the choreography was by Hermes Pan and the brilliant cinematography was by Leon Shamroy, who was nominated for an Academy Award – which he deserved to win, being filmed in Todd-AO and in Technicolor.

As we noted earlier in this chapter, *Porgy And Bess* runs for more than three hours; the film runs for a little over two hours, twenty minutes. So – the opera is cut, drastically; the orchestration is not that by the composer; four of the leading roles in the film were dubbed by other singers, which meant that – as we are dealing with an opera – virtually every time the leading characters open their mouths on screen they were obliged to mime.

The result was profoundly disappointing, as may have been expected. Some such view may be held by the estate of the creators, for this film of has not been screened, either in a movie theatre or on television, for many years, and a video version, almost a *sine qua non* for a major movie, has not been released as of this writing.

Quite apart from these shortcomings, since the film was made the opera has finally come into its own in the opera house. It is not a flawless masterpiece – of very few works by Gershwin can that claim be applied – but the strength of the inspiration and the appeal of the story are enough to have elbowed into the major repertoires of opera houses. It has thus been televised, and we can but hope that a new version, more suitably staged than the vast and eventually overpowering set that Preminger used, and utilising Gershwin's own orchestration, with singers that can act taking the roles on screen, will appear.

Chapter 26

Show Boat

"On Monday morning, November 5, 1945, an elegant gentleman of 60 years of age was browsing through the antique shops along East 57th Street in New York City. He reached the corner of 57th Street and Park Avenue, and while waiting for the light to change suddenly fell to the pavement unconscious." Thus Alan Jay Lerner began his tribute to the man he called 'The Master' – Jerome Kern.

Kern died five days later, leaving a legacy of popular music which had touched the hearts of millions of his contemporaries, music which has brought pleasure to millions more since his death.

'The Master': Jerome Kern was just that. Born in New York in 1885 into a wealthy family – in whose house the mother of Winston Churchill once lived – Kern was recognised as a gifted composer as a young man, and from his earliest years he produced a series of wonderful songs that showed he had few equals.

One of his early successes, 'They Didn't Believe Me', led inevitably to his masterpiece, *Show Boat* in 1927, which contains two of his finest songs, 'Can't Help Lovin' Dat Man' and 'Ol' Man River'. The following decade he wrote songs for movies – including 'The Way You Look Tonight'

and 'Smoke Gets In Your Eyes' – two of the immortal songs by the man who, almost single-handedly, created the 20th-century American musical theatre, and in so doing made it the musical personification of the hopes and aspirations of millions of music lovers the world over.

In 1942, the Academy Awards included a nomination for a song by Harry Warren and Mack Gordon, 'I Got A Girl In Kalamazoo', from the Glenn Miller movie *Orchestra Wives*. It might have been – but was not – about Edna Ferber, the greatly-admired American writer who had been in Kalamazoo, Michigan, in 1887, and who had endeared herself to millions of readers with her numerous novels and short stories, of which *So Big* won a Pulitzer Prize in 1924. Her next novel, *Show Boat*, appeared in 1926, and caused something of a sensation.

The novel was written from first-hand source material; Miss Ferber had herself become fascinated by this largely unsung slice of American folk-history and took an extended trip on 'John Adams Floating Theatre' boat on Pamilico River in North Carolina. She took down many of the old-timers' stories about life on the boats and the great rivers of the USA, some of which boats –

Ava Gardner in MGM's *Showboat*, 1951.

particularly on the Ohio River – still run today, even if essentially as tourist attractions.

For Americans in the mid-1920s, it was a part of their heritage that was fast disappearing; Edna Ferber's combination of original locale, nostalgia, her adept skill at creating rounded characters based on real-life events – all of these ingredients helped to make the book a major success. Indeed, so instantaneous a mark did *Show Boat* make that Jerome Kern immediately acquired the rights to make a dramatic musical version. He knew exactly the young man he had in mind to do the book and lyrics – Oscar Hammerstein II, then just 28 years old, but already a young master of the genre, as his collaboration with Sigmund Romberg in *The Desert Song*, which had opened in November 1926 to enormous acclaim, confirmed.

The great Florenz Ziegfeld was already in Kern's mind as the producer, but Miss Ferber doubted whether such a producer, who had made his name on girls and legs would be quite the right man for *Show Boat*. Ziegfeld felt the same way, but Kern knew what he was doing. He already envisaged a big production, and Ziegfeld was noted for not skimping on showmanship; with Kern's imprimatur, Miss Ferber agreed, but the enthusiasm both Kern and Hammerstein felt for the project was soon turned to anger when Ziegfeld suddenly told them that he wanted to wait another year before putting the show on. In the event, although neither of the creators thought so at the time, this was the best thing that could have happened, for as Hammerstein later recalled, the delay "made a much better play than it would have been had we produced its first draft" – it also gave Kern more time to mould his score into what was virtually an operatic composition.

But the year's delay brought extra problems, too. The show, as originally completed, was far too long – inordinately so, with over an hour-and-a-half having to be cut from it during its try-outs in order to make it acceptable as an evening's entertainment, and even then the resultant musical is a long one. A whole series of quite disheartening accidents and postponements followed – including the withdrawal of Paul Robeson from the cast, owing to prevarications on Ziegfeld's part regarding the opening date: Robeson could not afford to waste the time, or turn down other lucrative offers. Eventually, the world premiere of *Show Boat* took place at the National Theatre in Washington, DC, on November 15, 1927: it was an absolute sensation, but the cuts referred to above had to be made, including eight songs. That evening, the audience present were the only people ever to have heard the complete original score.

As if the cutting were not enough for the creators to contend with, a new song had to be added: it did not really have to be added, but one day during rehearsals Charles Winninger, who played Cap'n Andy, made the extraordinary comment to Kern that while he thought the music of the show was good, there were not really any 'hummable' songs in the score. Whereupon Kern dashed off a new tune, and sent it to Hammerstein for lyrics to be fitted. The result was 'Why Do I Love You?' which turned out to be one of the great hits of the show.

Another song added to the show, which also enjoyed considerable success by itself was 'Bill'. This actually dated from 1918, when Kern had written it for the musical *Oh, Lady! Lady!*, since when it had sunk without trace. The lyrics for this were by PG Wodehouse and Oscar Hammerstein II was insistent that the following be inserted in all programmes and other printed material connected with the show:

"I am particularly anxious to point out that the lyric for the song 'Bill' was written by PG

Wodehouse. Although he has always been given credit for it in the programme, it has frequently been assumed that since I wrote all the other lyrics for *Show Boat*, I also wrote this one, and I have had praise for it which belonged to another man."

Yet another 'addition' is the inclusion of a song, at Kern's insistence, by another composer – the famous 1892 melody, 'After The Ball', by Charles K Harris, to give a necessary period feel with which all listeners could empathise. Harris – then still alive (he died in 1930) – made himself a millionaire from his songs and his own publishing company, and he was more than happy to allow his music to be used in this way, with suitable payment, of course.

There were other additions, for subsequent productions, which we shall mention later, but to all intents and purposes, the format of *Show Boat* as given at the New York opening on December 27, 1927 at the Ziegfeld Theatre is that which we know today, one of the main differences being the addition of suitable period dance music in the 1946 revival – which Kern did not live to see. The show has been revived on quite a few occasions, but it is a curious fact that the longest run that *Show Boat* has enjoyed was in London, at the Adelphi Theatre, which opened in 1971 in Harold Fielding's production and starred the British star Cleo Laine. This revival ran for more than 900 performances.

Show Boat begins at the small city of Natchez, in the south west of the Mississippi river, some time in the 1880s. After work for the day, the stevedores and the other citizens are attracted by the arrival of the riverboat, the Cotton Blossom. The riverboat has a show company on board, who sing what is in effect a second overture – the opening chorus, which, in traditional guise opens the musical. Today, the original words of this chorus are changed, out of respect for black sensibilities; some of the words used have, in modern parlance, becomes terms of racial abuse.

After this, the entry of the infamous Gaylord Ravenal, a dashing, romantic figure who is a notorious gambler, introduces the leading male character: he sings of his essentially carefree life, but when the young Magnolia, who is the riverboat captain Andy Hawks's daughter, comes on board, it is a case of love at first sight for them both. The effect of her appearance causes Gaylord to begin wondering 'where's the mate for me?', and his song segues into one of Kern's most inspired melodies, 'Make Believe'. This song develops into a haunting duet for Gaylord and Magnolia.

Old black Joe, however, one of the traditional members of the riverboat's show company, has observed this wryly: So far as he is concerned, he has seen it all before, and in his magnificent 'Ol' Man River', he muses over the timelessness of the river itself, and of the timelessness of human nature. The leading lady of the company, Julie Laverne, has also seen this sudden romance, and attempts to warn Magnolia of the danger of getting involved with a man like Gaylord, but Magnolia replies that she 'Can't Help Lovin' Dat Man'.

The local sheriff now arrives, accusing Captain Andy of harbouring a black woman married to a white man – this was, in the 1920s, an offence under Mississippi state law. The couple in question are Steve Baker (the leading man of the show's company, who is white) and Julie (who is of mixed race). By a neat twist, Steve tells the sheriff that he has black blood in his veins – he has just sucked his wife's cut finger – but when the sheriff reluctantly lets them go, they decide they must leave the company.

Now Andy has to find, quickly, new male and

female leads for his show. Although her mother has misgivings, he decides that his daughter Magnolia would be suitable, and – with rather more misgivings all round – that Gaylord could be the male lead. There is a sub-romantic plot, in Frank and Ellie, an enamoured couple in the show's company; but during rehearsals it becomes clear that Gaylord and Magnolia are truly in love. Although Andy is happy to give their love his blessing, his wife, Parthy Ann will not; Andy wins the day for now, and leads the couple to church.

Some years have passed, and the setting is the Chicago World's Fair – Gaylord and Magnolia are still very much in love, but his way of life has brought them close to ruin; a few years later still, and Frank and Ellie come across Magnolia in a theatrical boarding house. She appears destitute, and although she assures them that all is well between her and Gaylord, a letter arrives from him, saying that he is ruined, and can she return to the Cotton Blossom. A few weeks later, and Julie – whom we learn has been deserted by Frank – is working as a singer at the Trocadero. Magnolia now enters, not knowing that Julie is there, to audition for a job; when Julie sees her, and realises the true position, she gives up her job in order that Magnolia can have it.

Andy comes to the Trocadero on New Year's Eve to see Magnolia perform; at first, she is nervous, but when he quietens the crowd, she gains in confidence, singing the old waltz 'After The Ball', to great acclaim. Her future is assured.

The show now moves to the present time: Magnolia has retired, and her daughter Kim has grown up to become a big show boat star in her own right. Andy, now a much older man of 82, sends his daughter a telegram asking her to come to Natchez, where Gaylord is now living. She leaves immediately, and when she arrives, Gaylord – unaware of her visit – gets up to go. But Magnolia rushes to stop him and they embrace at last. Kim, and the show's company, now sing a stupendous reprise, as Ol' Man River – who has seen it all – just keeps rolling along.

The success of *Show Boat* in the 1920s made it the longest running Broadway show of that decade: a film version was clearly called for, and since then no fewer than three versions have been made. The first, in 1929, was – given the nature of film technology in those days – a rather primitive effort, by all accounts: part talkie, part silent, and reputedly now lost. What is known is that Helen Morgan, who created the role of Julie on stage, repeated her part in this version – as she did in the second film of *Show Boat*, which was made in 1936. This splendid film, produced for Universal Pictures by Carl Laemmle Jr and directed by James Whale, was distinguished by many participants, including Kern and Hammerstein themselves: three new songs were added (most of the original score was retained), and Hammerstein rewrote the book to take account of the differing demands of a screen adaptation. The story keeps pretty much to the original, and the film is one of the finest in terms of photographic brilliance of its day: the photography was by John Mescall. One tiny caveat of this aspect of the movie is that it was shot in black-and-white, when the treatment would seem to demand colour. The film starred Irene Dunne as Magnolia, Allan Jones as Gaylord, Helen Morgan of course and Paul Robeson as Joe. Other parts – equally well-taken – were played by Charles Winninger (Captain Andy), Hattie McDaniel (Parthy), Donald Cook and Sammy White. The very fine choreography was by LeRoy Prinz. An interesting point is that Allan Jones was by no means first choice for the part of Gaylord; Walter Pidgeon, Robert Taylor, Fredric March and Nelson Eddy were all approached before Allan

FROM BROADWAY TO HOLLYWOOD

Jones was finally chosen. The result, however, was a performance from Jones which could hardly have been improved upon, and in which certain aspects of his portrayal may well have had some influence on Clark Gable as Rhett Butler in *Gone With The Wind*.

The third screen version of *Show Boat* came in 1951. It was made by MGM and produced by Arthur Freed. This is the version that most film-goers will remember, starring Kathryn Grayson, Howard Keel, Ava Gardner, Marge and Gower Champion, Joe E Brown as Captain Andy and William Warfield, the outstanding black bass singer, as Joe.

The musical direction was by the London-born Adolph Deutsch (who emigrated to the USA with his family in 1910 at the age of 13), and the choreography – a quite spectacular feature of the film – was by Robert Alton. Although Ava Gardner's name appears on the original sound-track MGM album as the singer of 'Can't Help Lovin' Dat Man', her voice was dubbed by Annette Warren, who was nowhere credited on the original disc.

A minor point is whether the title of the show is one word *Showboat*, or two *Show Boat* – both have been used in various productions, but it is clear that the two-word title is the original, and is surely therefore preferable.

There are some works whose inherent qualities are such as to shine through even the dullest production: *Show Boat* is one of these, and we must be thankful that we have – in the 1936 and 1951 cinema versions – two such outstanding and moving recreations of one of the genuine masterpieces of the American musical theatre.

Chapter 27

Silk Stockings

Following the superb flowering of his genius in the sensational *Kiss Me, Kate* in 1948, and his very successful show *Can-Can* together with the release of the outstanding film of *Kiss Me, Kate* five years later, Cole Porter's stock in the musical theatre in 1953 had never been higher.

The anticipation therefore for his next show, *Silk Stockings*, was equally high; it was based on a famous and brilliantly successful MGM film, *Ninotchka* – famous not only for being good in itself, but also for being the film in which the publicists could, for the first time, claim "Garbo laughs!" This was the slogan that MGM wanted to use for their enigmatic Swedish-born star Greta Garbo, and, over lunch one day in Hollywood nearing the end of l938, the Hungarian playwright Melchior Lengyel was asked if he had any ideas for the subject of a film which would star Garbo, in the comedy scenes of which she would laugh – her previous parts in movies had all been very serious dramatic roles.

Lengyel recalled the scrap of an idea he had had several years before, which he had jotted down in his notebook as, "Russian girl saturated with Bolshevist ideas goes to fearful, capitalistic, monopolistic Paris. She meets romance and has

an uproarious good time. Capitalism not so bad, after all."

The playwright met Garbo and read her the three sentences, on the side of a swimming pool: she laughed and said, "I like it. I will do it." And with that, she turned round and dived back into the pool and swam away. The 'story' was expanded by a trio of exceptionally gifted writers, namely Billy Wilder (no less), Charles Brackett and Walter Reisch, and starred Garbo with Melvyn Douglas, Stig Rumann and Alexander Granach, with Bela Lugosi playing a supporting role – another surprise, a comedy appearance for him. The director was Ernst Lubitsch, a past master of light comedy, and the film was a smash hit. The only element that perhaps was not quite up to the equal of the others was the rather mundane incidental music by Werner Heymann.

The film, described by *Variety* magazine as being "high calibre entertainment" and "a top attraction for the key deluxers", was a must-see Hollywood offering for 1939, and amongst the many who followed *Variety*'s advice were the Broadway producers Cy Feuer and Ernest Martin. They were both enchanted with the film, and thought there may be material there for a successful stage musical, but it needed a lot of

Fred Astaire and Cyd Charisse in MGM's 1957 film version of *Silk Stockings*.

work on the book, for the setting of Paris in the mid-1930s might not be suitable for the post-1945 world, with its Cold War, Korean War, and atomic threats a distinct possibility.

Over a decade was to elapse before Feuer and Martin's plan could come to fruition, towards the end of which time they had also collaborated successfully with Cole Porter on his show *Can-Can*.

Once this musical, coincidentally set in Paris, but in the 1890s, had been triumphantly launched, Feuer and Martin persuaded Porter to write the music and lyrics of *Silk Stockings*, as the new show was to be called. It was to be directed by George S Kaufman, who was also engaged to write the book with his wife, the actress Leueen MacGrath.

Robert Kimball has said that "the focus of *Silk Stockings*' gently satiric edge was on the crassness of Hollywood's lack of aesthetic sensibility as well as the Soviet Union's secret craving for the fruits of capitalism." The "key deluxers" who had been pinpointed by *Variety* in 1939 were to find their musical in *Silk Stockings* – at least, so far as the aim of the story was concerned, which opens with a leading Soviet composer, one Peter Ilych Boroff, being detained in Paris by a Hollywood musical agent, Steve Canfield. Canfield is keen to use Boroff's *Ode To A Tractor* for a movie which is to star Janice Dayton, and dangles the notion of western riches under the composer's nose.

The Russians, in their usual manner, send three undercover agents to Paris to take Boroff back to the USSR, but Canfield invents a French father for Boroff, claiming that he is in fact of French nationality rather than Russian. Whilst this has been going on, back in Moscow a new Commissar of Art has been appointed, who is ordered by the authorities to send Comrade ('Ninotchka') Nina Yaschenko to Paris to bring back Boroff and the three agents, who have also apparently succumbed to Parisian charms.

In Paris, Nina finds that Janice Clayton, the movie star, has made a pass at Boroff in an attempt to get him to agree to his music being used; in turn, Nina is gradually smitten with the charms of both Canfield and Paris. The three agents realise that they stand every chance of being received as heroes in Russia if they take Boroff back with them, and, with Canfield confessing that the story of Boroff's French father is a fabrication, he and Nina agree to marry.

But when Boroff hears Janice's westernised version of his *Ode* he is furious and all five Russians – he, the three agents and Nina – decide to return home, disenchanted with the West.

Canfield is desolate, for he has just bought Nina 365 pairs of Silk Stockings.

Back in Russia, Nina has a new job as superintendent of a building, and reserves room there for those Soviet artists who wish to experiment. Despite his initial annoyance at Janice's 'hot' version of his *Ode*, Boroff is taken with jazz, and organises a jam session. To everyone's surprise, Canfield arrives at the apartment building just before the new Commissar of Art also arrives; Canfield soon convinces the Commissar that there is money to be made in the USA if he writes his story – Canfield and Nina are reunited, and they all escape to the West.

Silk Stockings opened at the Shubert Theatre in Philadelphia on November 26, 1954; the previews were excellently received, but an unusual amount of rewriting was necessary. The revised musical opened once more, in Boston, to a mixed reception, and again, in Detroit, after further changes. All this must have seemed perplexing to a cast which included Don Ameche, Hildegarde Neff and Gretchen Wyler all making their Broadway debuts – at least, in major roles.

The final version of *Silk Stockings* at last opened at the Imperial Theatre on West 45th Street on February 24, 1955 where it ran for well over a year. It was successful, if not quite the outstanding success that had been hoped for, but it marked Cole Porter's swan-song on Broadway; he had not attended the opening night, for he had left for St Moritz, a weary man saddened by his ill-health, the death of his wife – a genuine companion – whilst he was working on *Silk Stockings* in 1954, and the uncertainty over his damaged leg, five days before the show opened.

Silk Stockings was not, however, Porter's last score; two more were to come, for films – the brilliant *High Society* in 1956, and *Les Girls* in 1957; his final score, for television, was *Aladdin* in 1958, the year in which his damaged leg was amputated. This effectively brought his career as a composer to an end.

If the score of *Silk Stockings* was Porter's last for Broadway, the MGM Cinemascope Metrocolor movie of the show, made in 1957, was effectively the 58-year-old Fred Astaire's last appearance in a film musical – except for in *Finian's Rainbow*, eleven years later, which left a great deal to be desired, and the MGM *That's Entertainment* compilation of 1974.

In the movie of *Silk Stockings* Astaire plays an American businessman, a change from the artists' agent of the original, and Cyd Charisse co-stars as Nina/Ninotchka. Charisse was clearly inspired by being reunited with Astaire, since *The Band Wagon* of 1953. Her brilliance is captured at its best in one scene, in which – alone in her hotel apartment – she first wears Parisian silk, and dances to the song 'Silk Stockings', which in the stage show was sung by Canfield. In the film, the song is not sung, but the tune is used as a ballet and for the film Porter added two new numbers – 'Fated To Be Mated' and 'The Ritz Roll-And-Rock'.

Some critics have felt that the film sags somewhat in places, but this is not a universal comment, and may be one brought about by the nature of the story itself – after all, two of the leading roles do not speak English as a first language, and the natural hesitation, assuming we can suspend our disbelief long enough, is a part of the overall characterisation. The director was Rouben Mamoulian, and André Previn was the musical director.

Chapter 28

South Pacific

Following the sensational successes of *Oklahoma!* and *Carousel*, it must have come as something of a shock to the award-winning team of Richard Rodgers and Oscar Hammerstein II to see their next show, *Allegro* flop badly – at least, by comparison. This is the one show about which the duo spoke the least in later years, although it remains a curiosity for the enthusiast of the musical theatre. After this setback, their next collaboration turned out to be one of their most enduring – in a joint career marked by enduring successes.

It arose in a somewhat extraordinary manner. The great operatic bass, Ezio Pinza, had, it appears, been engaged to appear in a Broadway musical, but the original producer could not find a suitable vehicle for him. Somewhat in desperation, he mentioned his plight to Richard Rodgers, who agreed to speak with Oscar Hammerstein II to see what could be done. In the event, they decided to write a new show specially for him.

The play of *South Pacific* was adapted from two stories, *Our Heroine* and *Fo'dolla* which appeared in James A Michener's *Tales Of The South Pacific*, a collection which won him a Pulitzer Prize in 1948. In order to provide a suitable plot, other characters were added from other stories in the collection.

The scene of *South Pacific* is located on two south-sea islands. It is the time of the war against Japan, and the action takes place during a lull in the fighting. The characters are therefore drawn from varied backgrounds – sailors, local inhabitants, marines and nurses; amongst the local inhabitants is a French immigrant planter, Emile de Becque, the character created for Ezio Pinza. One of the young nurses is a rather high-spirited girl, who hails from Little Rock, Arkansas. She is Ensign Nellie Forbush, who is much taken by the charm and experience of the older Frenchman. Here is an additional dramatic element, for their age difference is quite great – and forms an aspect to their story. For Nellie, after she and Emile fall in love, is saddened to learn of his previous marriage to a Polynesian woman, who died leaving him with several children in his care.

Emile realises the cause of her disenchantment, and decides to volunteer for a dangerous mission with Lieutenant Cable. In turn, the handsome young Lieutenant has fallen in love with a beautiful Tonkinese girl, Liat, whose mother, Bloody Mary, sees a fine catch in the

Rossano Brazzi as de Becque in South Pacific, 1958.

officer for her daughter.

However, the mission has its share of tragedy; Emile returns safely but the Lieutenant is killed. During Emile's absence, Nellie has grown very fond of his children, and, additionally admiring his courage, she realises that her future happiness lies with him and his young family.

There were, therefore – what by now was becoming a staple of the romantic interest in musical plays – a main romantic lead and a secondary one; in *South Pacific* the dramatic intensity of this quartet of lovers lies in their seeming incompatibility. The main lead is made up of a middle-aged Frenchman in love with a young American girl. The secondary romantic lead is between a young American soldier and a Tonkinese girl. The question of race is an element in the subplot, the secondary lead, and for a rather neat dramatic twist the death of Lieutenant Cable serves two purposes – our sympathy is engaged and the racial element is removed.

The setting, also, was something with which millions of ex-US soldiers and marines could empathise – up to a point, for this was a rose-tinted view of the south Pacific in time of war; the memory, here, has become bearable, without the realities of Iwo Jima or Midway. Hammerstein rightly saw the dangers in such a sanitised dramatisation; at the end of the show, the war intrudes to remind the protagonists of why they were there. This, also, was a touch of theatrical genius.

For *South Pacific* Oscar Hammerstein II had delivered a splendid scenario, together with a superb book in collaboration with Joshua Logan, who also directed the show, and a set of outstanding lyrics. Once again, he was matched by music from Richard Rodgers that in all makes *South Pacific* another of their great shows. The characterisation here, in music, is quite

outstanding: the bright, high-spirited Nellie Forbush is 'A Cock-Eyed Optimist', who tells us 'I'm Gonna Wash That Man Right Outa My Hair' before finding that she is in love with 'A Wonderful Guy'.

The experienced, more restrained Emile is entranced by 'Some Enchanted Evening', feeling later that 'This Nearly Was Mine' – both songs are amongst Rodgers and Hammerstein's greatest creations. The younger couple's innocent moments of happiness are caught in both the Lieutenant's outstanding 'Younger Than Springtime', and by Liat in her charming 'Happy Talk'. Allied to a set of other songs which in turn pinpoint both locale and character – most notably Bloody Mary's mysterious 'Bali Ha'i', in which she weaves a wondrous spell of native charm, and the troops' overtly masculine 'There Is Nothing Like A Dame' – the result was a score of incomparable quality.

Less than a week after it opened on Broadway, *South Pacific* was voted best musical of the New York Drama Critics' Circle; it went on to win the Tony Awards in every category for the 1949-50 season (the fact that it opened when it did meant that it cut across the two seasons covered by the different Awards) – in the Tony Awards, the musical won in every category for which it was entered. Most importantly of all, however, *South Pacific* won for its creators a second Pulitzer Prize for Drama.

The critics, as well they might have been, were ecstatic: *Variety* said: "It is one of the most enjoyable and satisfying musicals in theatre history." Richard Watts Jr, in the *New York Post*, expressed himself in almost identical words: "One of the greatest musical plays in the history of the American theatre." Brooks Atkinson, in the *New York Times*, declared that the show was "rhapsodically enjoyable, a tenderly beautiful idyll of genuine people". Of the two leads, *Life* magazine claimed that "Mary Martin, at her peak as singer, dancer and actress, becomes in *South Pacific* one of the stage's really great ladies", and of Ezio Pinza, the *New York Daily News* wrote that his performance demonstrated "the authority of a superb musician is at once apparent – and so is the authority of a big and handsome actor".

The daring of casting the queen of Broadway, Mary Martin, with one of the world's great opera singers – Ezio Pinza – had been triumphantly vindicated; but no less brilliant were the characterisations of the other members of the cast. In particular, William Tabbert as Lieutenant Joseph Cable was exceptional, as was Barbara Luna as Liat, the Tonkinese girl and her mother, played by Juanita Hall. Myron McCormick took the part of Luther Billis, a marine concerned with combined operations who also played "a wonderfully comic role in the amateur entertainment provided by the temporary residents of the island" – as Morris Hastings has described.

The stage success of *South Pacific*, therefore, was completely and deservedly assured. The film of the show came nine years later, during a period in which the making of such movies had become a regular event. But there was little in the film of that was predictable; it is a long movie – almost three hours, even if the CBS/Fox video running time is shorter – and was made by Magna Productions and SP Enterprises, not one of the big, traditional, musical-making studios. It was shot in Technicolor – no surprises there – and in the Todd-AO process, and the film's director was Joshua Logan, attempting to recreate on film the success he had so brilliantly steered on stage.

The first thing that catches the eye is the location chosen for the movie: here is no studio-bound piece of construction work but real locations shot on the Hawaiian island of Kauai,

which look terrific in themselves and whose beauty provide naturally attractive settings to enhance the story against which they are played. Another remarkable aspect of the photography is the use of various colour filters to point – and sometimes to over-emphasise – the music. The photographer, Leon Shamroy, was nominated for an Academy Award for his work on this picture, along with the musical directors Alfred Newman and Ken Darby.

Not everyone was entranced by the use of these colour filters; many felt that they were unnecessary in themselves, tending to detract from the dramatic point and – more importantly – from the music. Others felt that they were simply ugly, an experiment that did not work, a view Logan himself came to share, but the fact remains that the movie of *South Pacific* is the only one we have, and whatever faults we may subsequently come to find in it, the film does possess some considerable advantages.

Amongst these are the locations themselves and the casting of Mitzi Gaynor as Nellie Forbush and Rossano Brazzi as de Becque. Brazzi was no singer, and his voice was well dubbed by Georgio Tozzi, a noted American classical bass. By this time, 1958, this son of a Chicago day labourer had appeared at the Metropolitan Opera as well as at La Scala in Milan, and went on to enjoy an admirable career in international opera, in roles as varied as those by Mozart, Puccini and Wagner. Tozzi also did not shun singing in a television advertisement for the Fiat motor-car company; so dubbing for Brazzi in *South Pacific* was entirely in keeping for this lively and gifted singer.

The deliciously maternal Juanita Hall was retained from the stage production, to repeat her role as Bloody Mary, although her singing voice was not: this was dubbed by Muriel Smith, a change that seems unnecessarily extravagant

Director Joshua Logan attempted to recreate on film the success he had so brilliantly steered on stage.

when one listens to her Broadway cast recording of the role, which is more than adequate.

John Kerr as Lieutenant Cable and France Nuyen as Liat were perfectly matched, and Ray Walston was quite outstanding as Luther Billis, getting the film's ensemble scenes off to a cracking start with 'There Is Nothing Like A Dame'. An interesting point is that the movie contains one song, 'My Girl Back Home', which had been written for, but dropped from, the original Broadway show.

On balance, despite the drawbacks which are more technical than musical, and which do not encroach too greatly on our enjoyment, the movie is a success and a worthy version of this fine show. As a postscript, we may note that in the mid-1980s a fashion grew up amongst the classical departments of the world's major record companies to record quite a few of the great Broadway musical shows with semi-operatic casts – often with significant commercial success. In 1986, CBS/Sony issued such a recording of *South Pacific*, with Dame Kiri Te Kanawa and José Carreras as Nellie and Emile, with Sarah Vaughan and Mandy Patinkin and the London Symphony Orchestra under Jonathan Tunick. The result was a considerable success in terms of record sales, but an almost total disaster in terms of the musical score. As we have seen, the essence of the main romantic story of *South Pacific* is the love of an older man for a much younger girl, and the music – written for an operatic bass and a light soprano – reflects that.

Now, Richard Rodgers would probably have been the first to agree that his music was not Holy Writ, but in this version – quite apart from the fact that in real life Dame Kiri is several years older than her co-star, and manifestly does not sound 20 or so years younger – the music of the part of Emile de Becque was transposed upwards to accommodate the much lighter tenor voice of Carreras. The result removed the experienced gravitas from de Becque's role and severely damaged the inherent musicality of the score – what this version provided was not at all that which the show's creators went to such pains to give us. Had the part of de Becque been sung on this recording by, say, Sherrill Milnes – then we might have had something completely worthwhile.

Chapter 29

The Boy Friend

In discussing *My Fair Lady*, we mentioned this show, which came about, in the words of its creator, Sandy Wilson, "in the autumn of 1952 [when] the Players' Theatre Club asked me if I would be interested in writing a musical scene for their 'Late Joys' programme. They suggested that it should be a pastiche of the musical shows of the 1920s period and should not last more than an hour. The show was to be included in the bill for a run of three weeks as a change from the usual Victorian songs, and I do not think that any of us, at the time, imagined it would go further than that."

The show was duly written and produced, except that it lasted an hour-and-a-half, and owing to a very favourable reception from its opening on April 14, 1953, it was expanded into a whole evening's entertainment. After several vicissitudes en route, the final show *The Boy Friend* opened for its main West End run on January 14, 1954.

It was a very great success, and struck a responsive chord in post-war London audiences who were attracted by nostalgia for the 1920s, as Sandy Wilson also commented: "Both on the part of the older people who lived through that era and of the younger generation who have heard about it and found their own post-war period rather drab by comparison. That *The Boy Friend* tapped this spring of affection so tellingly is chiefly due to the manner in which it has been produced; and here I must acknowledge an undying debt of gratitude to my director, Vida Hope, whose unceasing care and vigilance made *The Boy Friend* such an authentic piece of a theatrical era."

The show also opened off-Broadway later in 1954 and proved to be a surprising success, without actually being a smash hit. This production marked the Broadway debut of the 28-year-old Julie Andrews. The story of *The Boy Friend* is set in a finishing school in the south of France, whose pupils are in a state of some excitement in their preparations for the forthcoming Carnival Ball. The drama is nicely pointed when the leading young lady's father, on a visit to the school, finds himself meeting up with an old flame, Madame Dubonnet.

The composer concluded: "The cast, too, none of whom was known to the public by name, have individually and as a whole achieved a perfection in their interpretation which could not be bettered." And there, one might reasonably have thought, as the show was not filmed at the time, *The Boy Friend* might have rested in some peace.

It undoubtedly would have so done had it not been for the efforts of the British film director Ken Russell who, in 1971 for MGM, filmed a version of the show which – so far as most people are concerned – is the only version they are likely to have seen in their lives. It effectively killed the piece.

By engaging a "non-star" (as Leslie Halliwell put it, referring to Twiggy) to play the lead, by changing the story and locale and just about everything else and using poor staging and other cinema-style disastrous tricks, a fragrant and unique period piece was turned into a major aesthetic manic-depressive disaster of no small consequence.

Even when Ken Russell is at his most self-indulgent, there will always be some fascinating piece of film-making *per se* to watch, and so it is here, but as a film of a musical that was not without significance itself, it is a disgrace.

Chapter 30

The King And I

Gertrude Lawrence was one of the great ladies of the theatre of the first half of the 20th-century. She was born into a far from prosperous family, of Danish extraction, as Gertrud Klasen in south London in July 1898. The name Lawrence came from her father, who was a minor music-hall artist, and whose alcoholic propensities led to a break-up of his marriage soon after Gertrud was born. He left his wife and daughter to their fate, but his wife – herself with no little experience of the theatre – soon realised the dramatic qualities of humour and mimicry that her daughter possessed, and trained her from a very early age, as a child star.

Gertrude (as she soon became) first appeared in public at the age of ten, and had a so-so career until, with the onset of puberty and the emergence of her own distinctive personality, her natural stage presence began to make itself felt. When she was 17, she obtained her first notable chance as understudy for the Canadian revue singer Beatrice Lillie (they were the same age) in one of André Charlot's 'intimate revues' – a Parisian entertainment which Charlot had brought to London from Paris soon after the outbreak of World War I (when the hostilities made such productions in the French capital impossible) and which enjoyed enormous success in the West End – as much for their unique qualities as for the natural desire of Londoners to support their Allied comrades.

This was in 1916, but Gertrude Lawrence's ebullient personality was not always to be subdued by mercurial producers; as with Beatrice Lillie, Gertrude Lawrence moved in aristocratic circles (Lillie became Lady Peel, wife of the fifth baronet, in 1920) and – with Gertrude's disastrous marriage to Frank Gordon-Howley having soon floundered (her classic search for an older father-figure was a disaster) – she embarked upon an affair with Philip Astley, a descendant of the 18th-century theatrical impresario. Gertrude had a daughter whose upbringing – owing to the peripatetic nature of Gertrude's profession – was placed largely in the hands of her mother.

By this time, Charlot had dismissed her, but he was obliged to re-engage her some years later as her growing reputation and her outstanding stage qualities could no longer be ignored. In 1924, she made her Broadway debut in one of Charlot's shows, along with Beatrice Lillie and Jack Buchanan, at a time when things English were something of the rage in America. The show, *André Charlot's London Revue* proved to be a

Yul Brynner and Deborah Kerr in the 20th Century-Fox film production of
***The King And I*, 1956.**

major success, and Gertrude Lawrence had conquered Broadway at the age of 26.

So great was her success that the Gershwins wrote one of their most ebullient shows especially for her, *Oh, Kay!*. Apart from the undoubted qualities of her singing and dancing, she was also a gifted straight actress, as she demonstrated time and again, most notably in dramatic roles by Noel Coward, with whose name she became theatrically almost inextricably linked in *Private Lives*, and the incredible series of nine unusually varied one-act plays *Tonight At 8.30*.

But her free spirit continued to bring personal troubles during the 1930s. It was not until her later successes in *Susan And God* and *Skylark*, and her second marriage in 1940, bringing with it the comparative stability of New England life, that the tempestuous side of her character appeared to have been brought under control. In 1941, her portrayal of the character of the *Lady In The Dark* – the Kurt Weill musical on the effects and revelations of psychoanalysis, a subject not a million miles from Lawrence's own character – caused a sensation, not least by her singing of the haunting song, 'My Ship' – and as the show drew to its close, she had already been appointed a Lieutenant in the Red Cross Motor Corps, a Colonel in the American Ambulance Corps and Vice-President of the American Theatre Wing. She also toured the Pacific, as well as France and Belgium, with her own USO Company as the war came to an end.

It was around this time that her agent Fanny Holtzmann sent her the novel *Anna And The King Of Siam* by Margaret Landon, which had appeared to great acclaim in 1944, with the suggestion that, if Gertrude agreed it might make a fine musical show, they might pursue the idea.

The story of the novel is based upon the true story of a young English widow, Anna Leonowens, who has been brought to the Oriental kingdom of Siam in 1862 in order to impart some Western culture to the King's court. After several early skirmishes with the King and his courtiers, Anna manages to educate the King's many wives and his even more numerous (in fact, 67) children.

However, her teaching abilities do not end there, for she manages to educate the King himself – to a degree. As it transpires, the essence of the drama of the story is the struggle of wills between the two protagonists: on the one hand the King, described as "a stubborn, half-tyrannical, half-childish, but surprising, charming and always fascinating, semi-barbaric, inflexible, but curiously 'scientific' monarch" and the prim and proper English Anna – "hoop-skirted, genteel, but firm-minded" individual.

One of the more fascinating aspects of this juxtaposition of the main characters is the unstated but growing affection which each feels for the other, played out also against the quasi-political nature of their occasionally conflicting cultures. These situations are often quite touching, if well played, as is the subsidiary and more straight-forward love story between the beautiful concubine Tuptim (whom the King naturally considers to be his property in every regard) and the Burmese emissary Lun Tha. It is the attempt by the King to thwart their love that proves to be the last straw for Anna – she prepares to leave, but events oblige her to stay.

The show exudes also a genuine vein of comedy with the actions of the King's various children, and one should not overlook the character of the King's head wife, Lady Thiang – she has a natural dignity which demonstrates that in the Orient there are qualities of human nature which exist even if the King appears not to possess them.

This, then, is the outline of the story that

eventually Oscar Hammerstein II was to turn into the book, and supply the lyrics, for the show that became *The King And I*. For in 1946 Gertrude Lawrence, agreeing with Fanny Holtzmann that it did indeed contain the kernel for an excellent musical adaptation, had approached Richard Rodgers and Oscar Hammerstein with the idea. At first, they were not entirely convinced, for their main hesitation was that they were being asked – for the first time in their careers – to write a show for a specific star.

The problem was they felt that, with a specific star in mind, they would be denied the creative freedom they had always previously enjoyed. They were, however, prepared to be persuaded, and a significant event in changing their minds was a private screening of *Anna And The King Of Siam* – a film made in 1946 of the novel starring Irene Dunne and Rex Harrison. This comparatively little-known film has its good moments and excellent cinematography, but is otherwise not wholly convincing; on the other hand, it treats the central story well, and it was this treatment that immediately convinced Rodgers and Hammerstein of the essential validity of the idea of turning it into a musical.

But at the time, Rodgers and Hammerstein were working on a show which would turn out to be their least successful – *Allegro* – which opened in October 1947 and was soon followed by the great *South Pacific*, which opened early in 1949. They could not even consider *The King And I* for at least two-and-a-half years, but when they began, Oscar Hammerstein II had the more difficult job, of translating the book for a Western musical treatment, and making the characters sympathetic. "I did not want to tread on any Oriental toes," he explained. "I had to be careful about gags, about the huge number of wives in the royal family."

He succeeded admirably, as did Richard Rodgers in composing the music, carefully avoiding the precious and all-too-easily pervasive Oriental sounds, at the same time as offering just the right amount of colour and thematic interest which would place the music in the correct locale without patronising, or offending, anyone. Indeed, in some instances he goes rather further than that: the little-known (because hardly ever recorded) music 'Children Sing, Priests Chant', is a fusion of musical styles of east and west, as, from one side of the stage, a line of chanting Oriental priests enter, to be contrasted with – entering from the other side of the stage – a line of the King's children, singing 'Home Sweet Home'. Their music fits together perfectly, personifying the unifying element that Mrs Leonowens has brought, and which her rather later song 'Getting To Know You', personifies to a greater degree. Incidentally, Richard Rodgers confessed that the music for this latter song came originally from a discarded number written for Lieutenant Cable in *South Pacific*.

Richard Rodgers also recalled that the aim of both creators was to create Oriental characters as human beings, with whom all could empathise, not as stereotypical caricatures. As the progress on *The King And I* developed, and they realised their initial fears in writing for Gertrude Lawrence were largely unfounded, Rodgers and Hammerstein had to find the right actor for the King. They wanted the great Alfred Drake very much, but he was already committed elsewhere and could not be released.

Whereupon, without more ado, after meeting with Drake and realising their first choice was unavailable, they hailed a cab and drove directly to the Majestic Theatre on West 44th Street to where their casting director, John Fearnley was holding auditions for the part of the King.

The first candidate they saw was a young man who had been seen by New York audiences in only one other production: the male lead in *Lute Song* starring opposite Mary Martin. He had been born 'in the Far East', probably in Vladivostock on a date and in a year which no-one knows for certain, and educated in France; leaving school in his early teens he became a night-club singer, accompanying himself on the guitar. He then became a circus acrobat and followed this by joining the famous French repertory company of Georges and Ludmilla Pitoëff, working both behind the scenes as well as taking roles on stage. He had also studied at the Sorbonne and held a Bachelor of Philosophy degree. He came to the United States just before the war and worked for the United States Government as an announcer and commentator before becoming a television pioneer and directing several important shows, including the drama series Studio One.

The young man's name was Yul Brynner. It meant nothing either to Richard Rodgers or to Oscar Hammerstein II as he strolled to the edge of the stage, scowled at these two Broadway luminaries and the casting director, sat cross-legged, and "howled" (as Richard Rodgers recalled) a song in a language that meant nothing to anyone. Above all, his stage presence exuded a savage, yet controlled, ferocity. Rodgers and Hammerstein looked at each other and nodded. They had their King.

The American soprano Dorothy Sarnoff, a regular at the New York Metropolitan Opera (who had recorded a scene from Halévy's *La Juive* with Jan Peerce), was cast as Lady Thiang, and the appealing Doretta Morrow was the slave Tuptim. Larry Douglas was Lun Tha. The musical director was Frederick Dvonch; the choreography was by Jerome Robbins.

The King And I opened at the St James Theatre on March 29, 1951, eight years almost to the day since *Oklahoma!* had opened at the same theatre. The unusual appeal of the story, the superb staging, the outstanding performances of Gertrude Lawrence and Yul Brynner – each of these ingredients contributed massively to the show. Yet it was the musical score, the range, richness, depth and memorability of its finest numbers, that catapulted *The King And I* to the stature of a masterpiece of the musical theatre.

Such songs as 'I Whistle A Happy Tune', 'Hello Young Lovers', 'Getting To Know You', 'We Kiss In A Shadow', 'Something Wonderful' and 'Shall We Dance' – to say nothing of the piquant 'March Of The Siamese Children' as the youngsters file on stage, sometimes one at a time, sometimes two by two – these were singly and together some of the finest songs ever heard on the Broadway stage. Here was a great show that appealed to all the family, and which ran for 1,246 performances – yet this had not been achieved without considerable rejigging. Indeed, at one point late in rehearsals it was seriously considered pulling the plug on the entire show. It was too long. There was something wrong with the structure, and no-one could put their finger on it. There were considerable disagreements between Yul Brynner and the director, John van Druten – and between Brynner and others engaged in the production – disagreements which some found distasteful, owing to Brynner's relative inexperience. There was also the barely-concealed problem of Gertrude Lawrence's love-hate relationship with alcohol and her fight against cancer.

But – to take the last problem first – this was the most expensive Rodgers and Hammerstein show ever mounted, and needed a big star to balance the inexperience of the unknown Brynner, and it had been written specifically for Gertrude Lawrence. But they needed a star who could still cut the mustard. By this time, all associated with the show were in it too far; as Fanny Holtzmann owned the musical rights to the book, and had bought them for the specific purpose of providing a vehicle for Gertrude Lawrence, without Lawrence there was no show. Richard Rodgers harboured some reservations about the state of Lawrence's voice, and got Doretta Morrow to sing the entire score for her before rehearsals began. Lawrence barely spoke to the composer again.

Brynner's disagreements may have been temporarily unpleasant, but it seems they were adopted more as a protection for Gertrude Lawrence's growing unreliability at rehearsals. In addition, for all his inexperience in the musical theatre, Brynner's myriad background stood him in the best possible stead: he was born in the Far East, he had a cosmopolitan upbringing, he was a trained acrobat and had directed casts on the legitimate stage as well as on television and he had appeared on Broadway as the male lead opposite Mary Martin. His ideas, no matter how forcibly expressed they may have been, were almost always excellent ones, and were largely adopted – towards the end of rehearsals – without demur. Several members of the cast felt that Brynner should have been credited with being co-director.

The remedying of the length of the show, and the tightening of its structure, owed not a little to Gertrude Lawrence; it was she who suggested dropping one song from Act I and adding a lighter one – which turned out to be 'Getting To Know You'. In the event, as the *New York Post* reported on the opening night, the musical was "a show of a thousand delights with the magic of Gertrude Lawrence and a remarkably believable performance by Yul Brynner". It was a palpable hit.

Yet the run was not without additional problems; 17 months – and less than 600 performances, not half-way through the Broadway run – later, Gertrude Lawrence died, on September 6, 1952 from liver failure, a combination of cancer and her growing alcohol dependency. In her final months, her problems had grown to the point where she left the cast for some time; her singing voice, already no longer what it was – as parts of the original Broadway cast album confirm – had deteriorated further, and her decision to return to the role, in the event, probably hastened her end.

The King And I opened in London at the Theatre Royal, Drury Lane, early in October 1953 and ran for more than 900 performances, with Valerie Hobson as Anna (Miss Hobson married the British politician John Profumo during the following year) and Herbert Lom as the King. It proved almost as big a hit with British audiences as it had on Broadway.

In 1956 came the film version. Had Gertrude Lawrence lived, it is unlikely that she would have been chosen for the film – her stage presence was, by all accounts, utterly magnetic, but it was one of those rare natural talents that did not transfer to film; her few film roles reveal a competent actress, nothing more – those who knew her as a stage artiste all confirm that her films fail to do her justice. It was not insignificant that the film of *Lady In The Dark* – Gertrude Lawrence's previous major hit – was made without her in the cast (she was replaced by Ginger Rogers); significantly, also, but for puzzling reasons, is the fact that the one outstanding song in *Lady In The Dark* – which Lawrence sang to perfection – was dropped from the movie *My Ship*.

The 20th Century-Fox movie of *The King And I*, released in 1956, was the third Rodgers and Hammerstein musical to be filmed within a year,

Yul Brynner's stage presence – young and inexperienced as he was – exuded a savage, yet controlled, ferocity.

following *Carousel* and *Oklahoma!*. Unlike the other two, *The King And I* did not star Gordon MacRae and Shirley Jones, and indeed was something of a gamble in so far as the casting of Yul Brynner was concerned. It was a gamble that paid off brilliantly. This was his first starring role, and in it he won the Academy Award as Best Actor. Deborah Kerr was Anna, and her songs were dubbed by Marni Nixon (who was later to perform similar services for Audrey Hepburn and Natalie Wood).

Rita Moreno was Tuptim and Terry Saunders played Lady Thiang. Lun Tha was played by Carlos Rivas.

The film broadly follows the show's scenario, but – like the pre-Broadway show's failings – it runs too long, at around 135 minutes, and would certainly have benefited from being no longer than 115-120 minutes, with perhaps most of this somewhat redundant time coming from the secondary love story. But what *The King And I* has in all of its manifestations – novel, dramatic film, stage musical and musical film – is a strongly dramatic narrative, and Walter Lang's production, brilliantly realised through the photography of Leon Shamroy, successfully plumbs the depths of this narrative.

On balance, this was the best of the three films of Rodgers and Hammerstein musicals of 1955/56, fully deserving the Oscar nominations for Best Picture, Director, Photography and Best Actress (Deborah Kerr) as well as the two it did win: Yul Brynner for Best Actor and Alfred Newman and Ken Darby for their Musical Direction.

Chapter 31

The Pajama Game

Richard Adler was born in New York City on August 3, 1921 into a very musical and musically well-connected family. His father had actually given piano lessons for a while to George Gershwin, and young Richard's own burgeoning musicality was encouraged at home. Following military service, Adler returned to New York where he was determined to pursue a career as a composer in popular music.

He had written a song, 'Rags To Riches', which he had taken to Mitch Miller, who had a few years previously been appointed by Goddard Lieberson as head of pop artists and repertoire (A&R) of Columbia Records (CBS). Miller was looking for a new song for Tony Bennett (who was five years to the day Adler's junior), and told Adler that if this difficult song was recorded by Bennett Adler would have to promote it himself. That is precisely what happened. For weeks, Adler toured radio stations throughout the north-east USA with copies of the disc, and, virtually through his own efforts, managed to break the song into the pop charts. This brought him into contact with Jerry Ross, a young lyricist, and Adler recalled that meeting Ross "was like meeting the other half of myself".

As a creative team, they worked as one. Almost immediately, they had conceived the idea of writing a musical show together, and, very unpredictably, they were approached by Richard Bissell and George Abott to see if they would consider writing the songs for a musical treatment of a popular novel, *Seven-And-A-Half Cents*, which Bissell had written. The plot of the novel was another unpredictable part of the story, which the late Leslie Halliwell summarised succinctly as "workers in a pajama factory demand a pay rise, but their lady negotiator falls for the new boss".

The ingredients of *The Pajama Game* came together remarkably swiftly, and gelled admirably, for most of the participants were new to the musical theatre, including the choreographer, Bob Fosse – then virtually unknown as a choreographer although earlier that same year he had appeared in the film version of *Kiss Me, Kate* (his third or fourth film appearance as a dancer). Fosse's later spectacular career can be said to have begun with his work on *The Pajama Game*. By the end of 1953, the entire team was ready to go into rehearsal, with the main characters taken by John Raitt, Janis Paige and Eddie Foy Jr, and amongst the notable supporting roles included those played by the brilliant Carol Haney – whose

Doris Day and John Raitt in *The Pajama Game*, 1957.

premature death some years later was a very great loss to both stage and screen – and Peter Gennaro.

The following is a more detailed scenario of the plot: The Sleep-Tite Pajama Factory in Iowa has engaged a new superintendent Sid Sorokin to keep up production quotas. He is new to town, and, like most newcomers, is a little unsure of how he will be accepted. At the factory, he soon comes up against a female member of the union's Grievance Committee, Babe Williams – and almost immediately falls in love with her. She denies having similar feelings towards him.

The secondary love interest is provided by a time-and-motion study official, Vernon Hines, known as 'Hinsey', and Gladys, the secretary of the President of the pajama company. Another secretary begins to tease the time-and-motion study man regarding Gladys, but he does not fall for this provocation. The production superintendent, Sid, equally, is now hopelessly in love with Babe, and – particularly interestingly – "dictates some advice to himself on a dictaphone" in an absolutely inspired song, 'Hey There, (You With Stars In Your Eyes)'. He then joins the staff on a company picnic, where the union President makes a play for Gladys. At the height of the picnic, with everyone in a good mood, superintendent Sid finally manages to kiss his girl Babe. From that moment on, their love blossoms rapidly, and back at her home she finally realises that he is the man for her.

However, the union negotiations regarding a rise of seven-and-a-half cents an hour have stalled; the Sleep-Tite factory is the only one in the trade not to have received it, so a strike is called, which immediately opens up a rift between the lovers.

At a union meeting, it is Gladys who opens proceedings with one of the most remarkable theatrical songs of the age – 'Steam Heat' – the composition of which declares Richard Adler's

knowledge of contemporary music. Both sets of lovers are separated by the strike, and Sid, realising that Gladys holds the key to the President's secret papers, determines to get it from her if he can, at a dive in town, Hernando's Hideaway, to where he takes her. But both Babe and Hinsey are also, separately, there – and they each see their partners – but with the wrong partner.

The union plans a big rally to press their claim, but the company President is confronted with the fact that the raise had already been built into the pajama factory's costs, so the profits were already covering the money, and no reason could now be given for withholding paying it. The company President capitulates, the couples are reunited, the workers get their extra money and everyone goes to Hernando's Hideaway to celebrate, ending with a parade of the latest pajama fashions.

Around this somewhat unpromising story the music and lyrics of Richard Adler and Jerry Ross weaved a genuinely amusing and whimsical show of much charm and no little power. What is so remarkable about this score is the way in which Adler was able to use all kinds of modern dance idioms alongside more traditional, lyrical romantic ballad styles and create a masterly piece of integrated musical theatre. Perhaps it is the surprising quality of integration that has ensured the continuing success of *The Pajama Game*, for it is a quality that had been brought to the Broadway stage many years before but raised by Richard Rodgers and Oscar Hammerstein II to the level of art in their ground-breaking shows of the mid-1940s and onwards. With their examples, the climate was right for new writers and composers to take a more serious approach with their creations – even if the subject-matter and treatment were essentially those of light-hearted entertainment.

To take but one example: the song, 'Hey There' would have been a hit at almost any time. The dreamy melody winds around the central note, and the song begins with a memorable hook that is surely inspired. However, what really raises the song way above the merely tuneful is the extraordinary harmonies underneath. They not only support the melody, but punctuate it emotionally, and in so doing bring new perspectives to the song giving it added depth and richness. The fact also that it ends with a plaintive question adds to its charm, as does the technical aspect in the show that the singer comes to duet with himself as he plays back his musings into the dictaphone machine. It is such subtleties as these that have ensured the continuing life of the show. No wonder no fewer than four separate hit versions of this song were in the charts at the same time in 1955 – by Rosemary Clooney, Sammy Davis Jr, Johnnie Ray and Lita Roza.

Another contributory factor to the success of *The Pajama Game* is its very unlikeliness: a musical show, set around the happenings in a pajama factory, immediately puts the audience in a pleasant frame of mind – for whatever happens during the course of the evening, they are not going to be emotionally challenged. In short, what public and critics alike responded to in *The Pajama Game* was its sheer entertainment. It is fun.

But what also contributed to its success was that it was about modern business methods – with which many of the men in the audience could sympathise in their daily lives. Having spent a demanding day 'in the office' the show they took their wives to in the evening took a light-hearted look at the kind of things they had been tearing their hair out over during the day. This was new, also.

The shaft of fresh air that these young talents brought to the Broadway musical garnered a host of awards in the 1954-55 season, and *The Pajama Game* became only the eighth musical in Broadway history to enjoy more than 1,000 consecutive performances during its first run – for, wholly exceptionally, after the two-and-a-half year run at the St James Theatre at 246 West 44th Street, it was successfully revived less than six months later at the City Centre, starring Paul Hartman, Jane Jean, Larry Douglas and Pat Stanley. It has been revived many times since – a further tribute to its timeless contemporaneity.

A show that had run for over 1,000 performances and had also produced at least three hit songs – 'Hey There', 'Hernando's Hideaway', and 'Steam Heat' – was a natural for the screen, and in this adaptation the writers were again exceptionally fortunate.

The rights had been acquired by Warner Brothers and the brilliantly gifted Stanley Donen was chosen as director. The exceptional nature of the good fortune was two-fold: the film kept very close to the original piece and – with one important change – it was shot with the original cast.

The one important change was the casting of Doris Day as Babe. This proved to be an inspired choice, for there can be no doubt that in this role Miss Day gave one of the best performances of her career.

Being based so closely on the original stage production, the film moves at a cracking pace, and only seriously departs from the original – to very good effect, it must be said – when the firm's annual picnic is an extended sequence. The high-spot of this film is the brilliant dancing and singing of Carol Haney during the 'Once-A-Year-Day' location shots. Carol Haney was equally outstanding in the factory 'Steam Heat' sequence, and the use of lighted matches during the

Doris Day outshone her co-stars, conveying the depth of artistry in the original score.

'Hernando's Hideaway' number is another imaginative touch.

Bob Fosse was entrusted with the choreography, as indeed he should have been, and excelled in this task. But it is Doris Day who outshines them all here; her recapitulation of 'Hey There' is not only a beautifully touching piece of singing in its own right, but also briefly reveals the depths of artistry which went into the original score as conveyed by the excellence of the film itself. Many people regard the film of *The Pajama Game* to be superior to the original production – a rare consensus, but one which would appear to be not so far from the truth.

Chapter 32

The Sound Of Music

The Sound Of Music was the last work by Richard Rodgers and Oscar Hammerstein II. Less than ten months after the show's opening at the Lunt-Fontaine Theatre at 205 W 46th Street on November 16, 1959, Oscar Hammerstein was dead at the age of 65; but he had lived long enough to see his final creation achieve the success it undoubtedly deserved, to crown his life's work in a remarkable way and to bring it to an end in a positive and optimistic manner.

Rodgers and Hammerstein's previous musical show, *Flower Drum Song*, had certainly been a success, but not an absolute smash-hit, even though it contained one song – 'I Enjoy Being A Girl' – which was fully up to their previous highest standards. Nonetheless, for whatever reasons, with *The Sound Of Music* this incomparable team looked for fresh inspiration – not so much in locale, for with its 'foreign' setting and fusion of different cultures, it was essentially no different from *Flower Drum Song*, *The King And I* or *South Pacific*; in this instance, the fresh inspiration was creative, in that Oscar Hammerstein did not participate in the writing of the book on which the musical was based. In *The Sound Of Music*, Rodgers and Hammerstein worked for the first

time with Howard Lindsay and Russel Crouse who together wrote the book.

The book was not, however, an original idea: in turn, it was an adaptation of *The Trapp Family Singers*, an autobiographical work by Maria Augusta Trapp. This tells the remarkable story of a family who achieved fame as a group of Austrian folk-singers who managed to escape from their country following the Nazi invasion, the Anschluss, in March 1938. The original idea of dramatising the book was to make it into a play, in which the authentic Austrian folk-songs in the Trapp family repertoire would be interpolated. Howard Lindsay and Russel Crouse, who had enjoyed considerable success as a play-writing team on Broadway with *Life With Father* and the Pulitzer Prize-winning drama *State Of The Union* amongst other plays, began work on the stage adaptation. They had also worked on such famous musicals as *Call Me Madam*, *Red, Hot And Blue* and *Anything Goes*.

As the dramatised version of the book proceeded, it gradually became clearer that it needed a full-scale musical treatment, and a treatment that was wholly original, not based upon folk-songs.

In this way, first Oscar Hammerstein II and

Julie Andrews as Maria in 20th Century-Fox film of *The Sound Of Music*, 1965.

then Richard Rodgers, almost immediately afterwards, were brought into the project. A by-product of this provenance was that this saved Hammerstein the trouble of writing the book from scratch. In view of his health, the removal of this additional creative strain was clearly an added bonus for the team.

Another aspect of Rodgers and Hammerstein's working methods which ought to be remarked upon here is that the first thing to be written was the finished lyric of the song. Hammerstein would send this to Rodgers, who would then – often with the barest of changes – set the words to music. In this regard, there was no soul-searching 'collaboration' such as have bedevilled other song-writing partnerships, jointly seeking inspiration at the piano in the small hours, a glass or two to hand. Nor is there anything inherently wrong in such collaborative working-methods – the only thing that matters is the result, not how it is obtained. But as Rodgers and Hammerstein had been together for 18 years by this time, and had got to know each other's work-pattern intimately, it was for them a comparatively simple matter to write their songs in this way.

Richard Rodgers also admitted that he found himself directly inspired by words: he would get the lyric, read it a couple of times, mull over it in his head, perhaps go for a short walk, and then sit down at the piano to find the music almost ready, virtually complete in his mind, to be played and then worked on in terms of harmony and the like, enabling him to work quite quickly and always come up with a tune that fitted the words perfectly. It is also true that on occasion, Rodgers would have a tune for which there were no words, and the reverse would take place, but this was very much the exception.

These factors – the book was written by another experienced team, and Rodgers and Hammerstein's song-writing had been, as a craft, developed into a fine art – go a long way in explaining how it was that the show opened on Broadway less than a year after *Flower Drum Song* had opened. *The Sound Of Music* had done the usual round of try-outs, this time in New Haven and in Boston, prior to the final touches being applied in readiness for the New York opening: already, during the out-of-town previews, word had spread that here was something wholly exceptional in the Rodgers and Hammerstein canon: the show-business newspaper *Variety* had announced "a sensational musical is on its way to Broadway" and in the *New York Journal-American*, critic John McClain wrote of *The Sound Of Music* being "...the most mature product of the Rodgers-Hammerstein team. It has style, distinction, grace and persuasion; it may not have the popular appeal of *Oklahoma!* or *South Pacific*, but it has more importance. It seemed to me to be the full ripening of these two extraordinary talents. The whole production has exquisite good taste. The music, which at times becomes almost operatic, is wonderfully in the mood of the story." Whatever reservations John McClain had of the show were not shared by Frank Aston, writing in the *New York World Telegram & Sun*, who called the show "...the loveliest musical imaginable. It places Rodgers and Hammerstein back in top form. The dialogue is vibrant and amusing in a plot that rises to genuine excitement." Walter Kerr, writing in the *Herald Tribune*, said that "...the show is handsome, has a substantial plot, and it is going to be popular".

It was quite clear from these few plaudits out of many, that here was a brilliant success on a grand scale. But the success – largely due to the magnificence of Rodgers' score – could not necessarily have been so confidently predicted when one considers the plot in isolation. *The*

Sound Of Music, coming so soon after West Side Story, which marked a new development in musical theatre, and so soon before the death of one of its incomparable creators, may be felt by many to be the last great musical in the 'traditional' manner. Whether it was or not, it was the last great musical of Rodgers and Hammerstein.

The story begins in 1938, in the Nonnberg [the mountain of the nuns] Abbey in Austria. As the show opens – wholly without an orchestral overture, still very exceptional in Broadway shows at that time – the nuns of the Abbey are proceeding about their daily tasks and supplications; from a distance, they chant Psalm 109, Dixit Dominus. It is morning, and it has come to the attention of the Reverend Mother Abbess that the postulant (candidate) nun Maria Rainer is not in the building, nor in its grounds. She is, in fact, outside on the mountain, communing with nature and loving every minute of the spectacular view and the fresh, clean air. It transpires that she has the permission of the Mother Abbess to walk on the mountains, but she has stayed out much longer than she ought to have done, and at last returns, the others becoming concerned as to her fate. This is not the first time that Maria has wandered in this way, and the Abbess is reluctantly forced to conclude that the life of a nun is not for Maria – at least, not yet.

But the Abbess is very sympathetic to Maria – they sing a splendid duet 'My Favourite Things' in which the Abbess shares a few of the younger postulate's enthusiasms – but explains that she has decided to send her from the Abbey to become a temporary governess to the children of a Captain von Trapp, whose wife has recently died, leaving their children without a loving maternal figure at home.

Captain von Trapp, who has recently retired from the Austrian Navy, is himself unsuited to take over his wife's role as well as his own, and has indeed become something of a stickler for discipline at home. Maria arrives, and introduces herself to the children, who do so in turn to her: she soon realises that some lightness and, dare one say it? – fun – has to enter their lives, at the same time as respecting the wishes of Captain von Trapp. This part of the story may seem to many to bear a striking resemblance to the arrival of Anna Leonowens in *The King And I*, but here it is handled with sufficient originality and difference as to be no more than a passing allusion. After all, the children in the earlier show were far more in number, and in need of being taught Western manners – in *The Sound Of Music*, the children need to be taught how to relax.

The von Trapp children are seven in number, and Maria soon teaches them to sing the musical notes of the scale ('Do-Re-Mi') to a quite brilliant Oscar Hammerstein lyric. The oldest, Liesl, who is 16 (going on 17) is in the wonderland of her first love. He is a village boy, Rolf Gruber, and she manages to steal away to meet him. On her return, a thunderstorm is heard, and Maria is able to calm her and all the other children by singing her charming song 'The Lonely Goatherd'. After this demonstration of her care and love for the children, they all come to adore her.

Captain von Trapp now arrives from Vienna, accompanied by his new fiancée, Elsa Schraeder, and a friend Max Detweiler. Max has a been-around view of life, and cannot believe that the Captain and Elsa will be happy together, as they appear to have no differences. The Captain, very surprised to find the children singing, at last joins in their song, and Elsa – touched by the scene – cajoles the Captain into giving an impromptu party for the children. This is a rare moment in a Richard Rodgers score, for this is set to a purely orchestral Austrian-type Laendler.

In the distance, the sounds of the German invasion are heard as they retire for the night, but during the evening Maria becomes convinced that she is in love with Captain von Trapp. Afraid of her feelings, she runs back to the Abbey, and confesses her love to the Abbess. The Reverend Mother gently reproves Maria for not facing up to life, but running away from it: she tells her that love is holy and it is up to us all to 'Climb Ev'ry Mountain'.

Maria returns to the von Trapp household, to find an argument going on between the Captain, Elsa and Max. The quarrel is about the accommodation they are forced to give to the Nazis: the Captain and Elsa recognise that they are, in fact, incompatible, and agree mutually to end their engagement. This frees the Captain, who almost at once realises his own feelings for Maria. Two weeks later, they are married in the Abbey, blessed by the Abbess, and leave for their honeymoon.

On their return, they find that the Germans have successfully incorporated Austria within greater Germany, and they are now effectively ruled by the Nazis from Berlin. They are shocked to discover that even Rolf, Liesl's boy-friend, has joined the Nazis; the Captain is also non too pleased on learning that, in his absence, Max has arranged for the children to sing at a music festival. But as the Captain has served in the Austrian armed forces, he is to be pressed into service once more by the Germans, and his presence is now required in Berlin.

Maria is very alarmed at this turn of events, and manages to gain a little time for her husband by persuading him (and the Nazis) that the whole family – including the Captain – should sing at the Festival. The Germans agree, on condition that he leaves at once after the performance with an

escort. During the concert, they sing the beautiful waltz-song 'Edelweiss', and as they sing their final song, each member of the family takes their bow and leaves the stage, one by one. Max manages to delay the Nazi escort, as the family, now reunited, are able to hide in the gardens of the Abbey while the storm troopers search fruitlessly for the Captain.

Once the soldiers have gone, the entire family can make their escape, over Maria's beloved mountains – the terrain which she knows intimately – to freedom, set on their way by the nuns singing a stirring reprise of 'Climb Ev'ry Mountain'.

Thus does this magnificent show end, and it has to be said that although some commentators noted the thin dividing line between sentiment and sentimentality may have been crossed on occasion, the sheer dramatic force of the main thrust of the story and the inspired magnificence of the music are sufficient to silence any criticism on this front.

The cast assembled in New York was brilliant. The legendary Mary Martin was Maria and the casting of Theodore Bikel as Captain von Trip was positively inspired: a fine actor, he was also a noted folk-singer (apparently able to sing folk-songs in 17 languages!), and his creation of the role was quite magnificent. Patricia Neway, the fine dramatic soprano – who created the role of Magda Laszlo in Menotti's opera *The Consul* in 1950 – played the Mother Abbess; Kurt Kasznar was Max, Marion Marlowe was Elsa, and Lauri Peters and Brian Davies played Liesl and Rolf.

The production was directed by Vincent J Donehue, the musical numbers were staged by Joe Layton, scenic production was by Oliver Smith, and costumes were designed by Lucinda Ballard (Mary Martin's clothes were designed by Mainbocher); the lighting was by Jean Rosenthal and the musical director Frederick Dvonch. Whilst it is almost an irrelevance to state that the orchestrations were by Robert Russell Bennett, an interesting sidelight on the musical aspects of the production is that the choral arrangements, that added so much to the effectiveness of the piece, were by Trude Rittman. *The Sound Of Music* won six Tony Awards in the 1959-60 season, and ran for no fewer than 1,443 performances. It also was given a special award from the National Catholic Theatre Conference in 1961.

But by this time Oscar Hammerstein II was dead. This great man of the theatre passed away in August 1960, unable to see the release of the films of his final shows with Rodgers – *Flower Drum Song* and *The Sound Of Music*, and before what would have been a special pleasure for him, the opening of the London production of *The Sound Of Music*. This last event took place on May 18, 1961, at the Palace Theatre, when it was supervised and directed by Jerome Whyte. From Broadway, Joe Layton staged the musical numbers, and the musical director was Robert Lowe.

Jean Bayless created something of a sensation in her assumption of the role of Maria Rainer, for this was her first starring role in the West End. Roger Dann was Captain von Trapp, and, following the Broadway example, a famous British soprano, took the part of the Mother Abbess – Constance Shacklock, who for many years was a stalwart of the famous Henry Wood Promenade Concerts in London, leading the singing of Arne's 'Rule Britannia' in the last night programmes. Eunice Gayson was Elsa Schraeder, and Harold Kasket played Max Detweiler. Liesl was Barbara Brown,

and Rolf was played by Nicholas Bennett. In London, *The Sound Of Music* ran for 2,385 performances.

Following Hollywood custom, the stage was now literally set for a film version of the musical. The movie was made by 20th Century-Fox, and was released on March 2, 1965. It was produced and directed by Robert Wise, and starred Julie Andrews as Maria and Christopher Plummer as Captain von Trapp. It ran for a little under three hours, and proved to be one of the biggest-grossing films of all time. The RCA sound-track album was Number One in the charts for almost 70 weeks, and Julie Andrews was presented with a double gold disc for album sales in the UK alone in 1977. It does not require much imagination to realise that the film of *The Sound Of Music* was one of the finest screen portrayals of a stage musical ever.

The film won Academy Awards for Best Picture, Best Direction and Best Musical Direction; nominations for Academy Awards were for Julie Andrews, Peggy Wood (Best Supporting Actress), and Ted McCord for Best Photography in Todd-AO and DeLuxe Color – the opening sequence, one of the most memorable in cinematographic history, in which Julie Andrews is shown atop an Alpine mountain photographed from the air, deserved an Academy Award by itself. Christopher Plummer was quite superb as the widower father, but the film belongs, utterly, to Julie Andrews. Such is the quality of the original show that *The Sound Of Music* remains, in a suitable production, both a great theatrical experience and a magnificent film.

Chapter 33

Tommy

One of the more remarkable consequences of the world-wide rock music explosion of the 1960s, as the 'Baby Boomer' generation reached maturity, was the realisation that the best rock music deserved to be taken seriously, and not treated as fashionable, merely ephemeral, 'throwaway' noise.

One of the elements that contributed to this was the rise of the importance of the album, as opposed to the single: the long-playing record could accommodate up to an hour's music (although, in popular music terms, it hardly ever did), and whereas earlier composers were confined to (at most) three or four minutes or so for one song – the maximum playing time of one side of the old 10" 78rpm disc, which became the 7" 45rpm single – the better creative pop musicians of the late 1960s realised that they were no longer confined to such restrictions.

One of the leading British groups of the late 1960s was The Who, a band whose members were individually and collectively highly gifted. Amongst their number was the quiet and sensitive Pete Townshend, and the band astonished the music world in 1969 by issuing a double-album, *Tommy*, described as a 'rock opera'. It is a moot point as to whether *Tommy* was the first 'opera' to be written entirely in the rock idiom but it is undoubtedly an opera, and grand opera at that, as there is no dialogue – just music: songs, ensembles, and instrumental interludes tell the story.

The music world's astonishment was that this concept was so new that most people – probably the creators included – did not know what to do with it. If it were truly an opera – which it clearly was, fulfilling those criteria we have just outlined – then it deserved production. How was this production to be achieved? Confining the instrumentation mainly to electric guitars and drums, with the occasional keyboard, meant that *Tommy* was entirely outside the scope of a traditional opera house. Quite apart from anything else, the musical idiom would be far outside the experience of virtually any opera house musician in the world.

If this opera could not be produced in an opera house, then it would have to be produced somewhere else. The success of the music – the single, 'Pinball Wizard' provided The Who with their ninth Top Ten out of their first 14 releases, and came to be regarded as an anthem for many young people of the day, and the double-album

The Pinball Wizard (Elton John) competes against Tommy for the World Championship title.

became a multi-million seller throughout the world – demanded that the concept of *Tommy* could not be ignored. In 1975, six years after the double-album was released, the British film director Ken Russell turned *Tommy* into a film; yet despite Russell's eminence and enthusiasm this was not the last word on the subject. If *Tommy* could not be staged as an opera, and did not wholly successfully translate into film, what was to become of this music that would not go away?

A number of stage productions of the music were attempted, with varying degrees of success – mostly owing to the staying power of the original music – but it was not until March 1996, 27 years after the release of the double-album, that *Tommy* was finally shown to be a fully-coherent work of art in a London production at the Shaftesbury Theatre that did full justice both to the music and, equally significantly, to the opera's underlying 'message'.

Perhaps one of the main reasons as to its unsuitability as a vehicle for stage production was that it was 'about' a character who was deaf, dumb and blind, and whose only skill was his ability on arcade pinball machines. It has to be admitted that it is difficult to cast any singer in such a role, especially the title role, for it is not until well over half-way through the opera itself that the character is able to be freed from the horrendous confines of his disabilities. Indeed, so forward-looking was *Tommy* as a conceptual spectacle that the public – to say nothing of theatrical producers and casts – would have to wait until technology caught up with the creative imagination of Pete Townshend and the other members of The Who before the work could adequately be realised in a staged production. This lay behind the success of the 1996 production, which was given in two acts, the first an astonishing modern-day recreation of the old theatrical concept of the 'ballet-chanté' –

the sung-ballet, a concept which is almost 300 years old and more.

The first act of *Tommy*, lasting just over an hour, is continuous music: there is no break whatsoever. Much of this is choreographed, and – if not initially written to be danced to – is therefore ballet music. But there are songs, of course – the act ends with the spectacular 'Pinball Wizard' sequence – but not in the manner of an 'opera'; the songs help the story along, but do not wholly 'tell' the story. Therefore, what we experience in this first act is a type of musical theatre that briefly flourished in the second decade of the 20th-century in Paris – Milhaud's *L'Homme Et Son Desir* and Stravinsky's *Pulcinella* being two outstanding examples – the ballet-with-singing, the sung-ballet. To some people, it may seem strange to consider *Tommy* in these terms, but that is precisely what the first act is.

The second act is somewhat different – but only because, early on, Tommy himself is freed, reborn if you like, and becomes a singing, talking, seeing individual – so the nature of the theatrical realisation changes. The speech element, so long delayed, makes a profound theatrical effect – as it does at the conclusion of Benjamin Britten's opera *Gloriana* (but to very different use, where in that work the ageing Queen Elizabeth I speaks intimately to herself, not like the public communication of Tommy) – and the reconstruction of the spectacle to take account of his metamorphosis demands a new view of our perception of the story.

Tommy is a parable. So direct and powerful is this parable that it may well prove to be one of the more enduring of popular art in the latter third of the 20th-century, and it may well also be that this element has ensured the work's survival rather more than the music.

The boy Tommy was conceived in wartime; his

father is called up to fight away from home and, captured as a prisoner of war, he misses the formative years of his son's upbringing. Tommy's mother takes up with another man, but her husband is released at the end of the war and returns home to find his wife in the arms of the other man, and his 4-year-old son witness to her understandable infidelity. In a rage, Tommy's father kills the man – an act which Tommy also witnesses, and which sends him into a profound traumatic shock, manifesting itself in his deafness, dumbness and blindness. Tommy withdraws into his inner self, a private uncommunicative world, whose only later contact with the outside world comes through the pinball machine – still the only archetypical interactive modern-day sociological entertainment piece of machinery. In other words, Tommy can only communicate through machinery, not through people, but he can do it to such a degree that it sets him further apart – in an admirable sense – from his contemporaries. In this, Tommy is a child of his time.

As he has grown up and matures, the mirror at home through which he witnessed the killing also contains his earlier self. For, as "a deaf, dumb and blind kid", he was consoled by his future persona. A man's adult personality is formed by the time he is five years old; we see that young Tommy was given insights into his present life by his future persona, as reflected in the mirror.

Now, as a teenage boy, he sees himself as a child, and hears – through the child – those things which, as a child, he was unable to express. Therefore, Tommy is at all times the personification of now and the past and the future, and when his mother smashes the mirror – freeing him from the confines of his past and future, and catapulting him into the now – his all-seeing, all-hearing, all-feeling experience has created in him an all-knowing individual who is

only able to express himself best through the machinery of modern-day popular music yet who, because of this, remains – however guru-like he becomes – once more the outsider. His only redemption is love, which he finds through Sally, and whose simple adoration of him causes Tommy to shed the trauma of (present-day) life and find his true destiny.

This is not a simple story. It contains deep psychological under-tones in addition to its parabolic relevance. It is a tremendous creative achievement, and – musically – it made an equally tremendous impact at the end of the 1960s. What raises *Tommy* far and above the level of almost all other rock-based music of the time is that, decades later, the music still possesses that power to shock and move. It may not be insignificant that – also in 1996 – the British government chose 'I'm Free' as a theme song for its anti-smoking television campaign – aimed at young smokers.

The essential song in *Tommy* is 'Pinball Wizard' – so new for its time that the notion that it could have been written ten years earlier is absurd. It obeys none of the so-called 'rules'. 'Pinball Wizard' is constructed along the lines of a Bach Toccata – reflected in a distorting mirror – but its combination of lyric, harmony, rhythm and melodic virtuosity is such as occurs rarely in music; the total is far more than the sum of its parts.

If it was not until 1996 that *Tommy* was finally shown to be – as mentioned earlier – a coherent work of art that up to now has worked best in a staged version, then that staging could not have come about if it were not for the Ken Russell filmed version of 21 years before. This film has to be seen in relation to its own age.

The director's following and technical brilliance demanded that it be taken with some seriousness, but it has dated, badly. Some commentators have dismissed the film as a self-

Roger Daltrey – Tommy – in glorious 1970's glam.

indulgent piece of Russellese, but his exuberance matches the subject-matter; others have found it astonishingly exciting, yet it reeks of 1970s glam-rock, with a whole succession of stars giving their all: Ann-Margret, Oliver Reed, Elton John, Tina Turner – and Roger Daltrey and Keith Moon from The Who, especially.

The central, inescapable, fact is that the music has been shown to have qualities that have outlasted its earlier interpretations – the cheering first-night audience in London in 1996 was not wholly made up of nostalgic middle-aged people, anxious to recapture the excesses of their 1960s youth: for this was not a 1960s show.

It was a show for today, with a timeless story expressed through music of undimmed power. It will surely be the case that well into the 21st-century, *Tommy* will still be seen to have those essential characteristics of art – transcendence and relevance. It is time for a new *Tommy* film.

Chapter 34

West Side Story

The opening night of *West Side Story*, on September 26, 1957 at the Winter Garden Theatre at 1634 Broadway – following try-outs in Washington and in Philadelphia – was a watershed in the history of the American musical theatre. In the previous year, audiences had seen the incredibly successful *My Fair Lady* open, and, with these two masterly shows, which could hardly be more different in their treatment or their subject-matter – although they both shared a curiously similar provenance – the nature and character of the stage musical was changed for ever.

Their 'curiously similar provenance' is that they each emanated from classic stage plays – *My Fair Lady* from George Bernard Shaw's *Pygmalion* and *West Side Story* from Shakespeare's *Romeo And Juliet*. Many felt that with these two shows, twin peaks of equal achievement, it was *My Fair Lady* which on the one hand signalled that the era of the classic stage musical was being brought to a magnificent end, while with *West Side Story*, on the other hand, a new chapter of the modern verismo musical had opened.

It would be wrong to claim that this was an entirely clean break, but a consideration of the respective creators and their varied backgrounds serves to indicate their different approaches. As we have seen earlier, Frederick Loewe, the composer of *My Fair Lady*, was in 1956 in his early 50s, having been born in Europe and having studied music with an impeccably impressive pedigree – he was a pupil of Busoni, Reznicek and Eugen d'Albert. Loewe's musical world was essentially European, the world of Planquette, Friml, Romberg and Victor Herbert. Leonard Bernstein, however, was much younger (in his late 30s); born in the USA, like Gershwin, Richard Rodgers, Jerome Kern, Cole Porter (and, stretching a point, Irving Berlin – who came to America at the age of 5), and Richard Adler. Although Bernstein nevertheless came under the influence of European teachers – especially Dmitri Mitropoulos, Fritz Reiner and Serge Koussevitsky – he did not possess a personal nostalgia for Europe. In addition, he was of the generation that succeeded those of the pioneering American composers – the generations of Charles Ives, of Aaron Copland, Roy Harris and, perhaps, Samuel Barber, most notably – and could therefore build on their achievements. Although it was for some time believed that Bernstein was the first native-born American (he was born in Lawrence,

In *West Side Story* the choreography used jive and rock 'n' roll to breathtaking effect.

Massachusetts, in 1918) ever to be appointed to the position of musical director of an American symphony orchestra – he was not – his was certainly the first most significant, and lasting, such appointment.

Whilst Bernstein's career – as symphonic and operatic conductor, concert pianist, composer of concert and musical stage works, to say nothing of his enormous gifts as a communicator and educator – was so utterly unique, it also remains true that in the case of his contribution to the Broadway musical, precisely the same situation applied.

For, in the preceding three decades, the American musical had been brought to a high level of sophistication, and, generally speaking, that level of such entertainment had been essentially escapist. These were, perhaps, natural reactions to the miseries of the Depression and World War II, the uncertainties of the immediate post-war years which saw the descent of the Iron Curtain, the Berlin Airlift, the Korean War, the Communist Revolution in China, the McCarthyite witch-hunts within the USA – following a series of spy trials, of which the Alger Hiss and Whittaker Chambers case was the most sensational – and the earlier ordering by President Truman of the production of the hydrogen bomb after the discovery that Soviet espionage had succeeded in acquiring the means of producing atomic weapons. The decade following peace in Europe was a troubled one, but by the mid-1950s a new generation, the first post-war youth generation, had arrived, and it was in the USA that they found their voice and most lasting expression.

The generation that embraced the rise of Marlon Brando, of James Dean, of Elvis Presley and Jack Kerouac, early rock-n-roll and the first protests of the Beat Generation, was therefore prime material – given its own musical language –

to be reflected in a stage work in a modern setting, and dealing with a serious contemporary social problem – in this case, the drama is played out against the background of teenage gang rivalry in the West Side district of Manhattan, a social phenomenon that is with us still and shows no signs of abating. If a cynical observer might argue that the subject-matter of *West Side Story* was hardly calculated to appeal to a sophisticated theatre-going Broadway audience, that audience would, by 1957, certainly have been aware of that subject-matter – and, as it impinged upon their daily lives (even at a distance), it would have possessed far greater 'relevance' to such an audience than the adventures of a pre-World War I professor of phonetics in London had done in 1956. The 'conception' of *West Side Story*, as the title-page of the full score has it, was by Jerome Robbins, the distinguished New York-born choreographer, who was almost two months younger than Bernstein, and who had been associated with the composer since the beginnings of both of their careers. Leonard Bernstein's first ballet score *Fancy Free* (which was written in 1944) was also the first ballet to be choreographed by Robbins. As we have also seen, this ballet was to become the film musical *On The Town* five years later – which manifestation might well have been also the inspiration that same year for Robbins to conceive of *West Side Story*. Bernstein's second ballet, *Facsimile*, of 1946, was also choreographed by Jerome Robbins – this is perhaps a better score, considered purely as music, than *Fancy Free*. Later, in 1950, Robbins choreographed Bernstein's second symphony *The Age Of Anxiety* and as late as 1974 they collaborated on a third original ballet, a return to their roots, *The Dybbuk*.

Given the locale of the works on which Bernstein and Robbins were collaborating in 1949

– aspects of modern-day New York – the proximity of the idea of *West Side Story* to their then-current efforts explains a great deal. It is frequently, but somewhat erroneously, assumed that the plot of *West Side Story* is a modern-day retelling of Shakespeare's *Romeo And Juliet*. It could hardly be maintained that *West Side Story* is a reproduction of the story, but the musical takes the play's elements of fratricidal strife, together with the doomed pair of young lovers from opposing 'families' – in this case racial, Puerto Rican and Italian – as its starting-point.

It was eight years before *West Side Story* came to fruition. The delay, however uneasy it may have seemed at the time, was wholly beneficial: in the intervening period, besides building an enviable career as one of the world's most significant young symphonic conductors, Bernstein had demonstrated his mastery in four very different works, each of which contains some of his best music.

The first was *Trouble In Tahiti* of 1952 – a chamber opera in a few scenes, about the emptiness of much modern-day suburban married life, with story, libretto and music by Bernstein: a somewhat curious subject to have essayed from a man who had just married for the one and only time in his life. Be that as it may, *Trouble In Tahiti* is a magnificent, humorous and moving work, and an interesting point for us is that the female character's main aria is concerned with her annoyance at having seen a 'terrible movie', the title of which is *Trouble In Tahiti* – not a million miles from *South Pacific*.

Bernstein's three other outstanding works at this time include the score for the Elia Kazan movie *On The Waterfront*, another contemporary New York piece, for which music Bernstein was nominated for an Academy Award (the picture itself won seven Academy Awards, but, regrettably,

the music did not). The third outstanding composition is Bernstein's 'Serenade' for solo violin, strings, and percussion which also dates from 1954 (the year of *On The Waterfront*), and which is arguably his finest serious concert piece.

However, early in 1953, before the first of these three varied compositions appeared, his next Broadway musical, *Wonderful Town* (yet another New York piece) had opened. This score has – to some extent – been eclipsed by that for *West Side Story*, but the show has considerable merit on its own, and contains one beautiful song – 'I Love a Quiet Girl' – which was inexplicably omitted from the 'Overture'. The conductor for *Wonderful Town* (which opened in New Haven in January 1953, prior to transferring to Broadway) was the great Lehman Engel, and whilst the show enjoyed a respectable run, with Carol Channing as the star, it was as nothing compared with the sensational success that attended *West Side Story*.

Another benefit of the delay in the arrival of *West Side Story* was that it enabled the protean talents of another soon-to-become great man of the musical theatre, Stephen Sondheim, to be employed in writing the lyrics. In spite of the cult status *On The Waterfront* has come to enjoy, Sondheim had written of the movie as being "a medley of items from the Warner gangland pictures of the 30s, brought up to date".

Perhaps the main reason for the delay was a factor we have hinted at earlier: Bernstein's growing career as a conductor. In addition, he may have sensed, however subconsciously, that *West Side Story* was to be an important piece, and he could only devote the necessary time to it (remembering that he had collaborators with whom he had to confer – in his own music, he had no-one else to consider in the creative process), when he was reasonably free of outside encumbrances and engagements. 'Reasonably free' in Bernstein's instance being a relative term: the demands on such a talented man's time were literally super-human.

However, it seems that such an opportunity afforded itself in the early part of 1957, and the music was written quite quickly. In view of the remarkable cohesion the entire musical score exhibits it is very likely that the music had been welling up in Bernstein's mind for some time, waiting for the chance to be put down on paper. The almost symphonic integration and unity the score possesses is one of its most remarkable features, considered solely as music. Indeed, it is another measure of the unique nature of this show that we can speak of it in these terms.

Large parts of the stage action of *West Side Story* reflect Jerome Robbins' balletic inclination: 'action' is literally the keynote here, for the opening music discards the convention of musicals – there is no overture, no pot-pourri of 'hits', no pleasant background music as the audience settles comfortably for an evening's escapist entertainment, and no opening chorus as the curtain rises upon an opening sequence, a 'Prologue', that is entirely *danced,* not sung. The wholly balletic opening was a very new departure for a musical, but it sets the scene on the lower West Side of New York against which the story will be played.

In *West Side Story*, we are plunged head first into the world of today, a world unknown up to then in 'musicals', and the music that accompanies the opening balletic sequence as the gangs assemble contains many of the melodic germs from which the entire score grows.

The opening dozen bars or so encapsulate this superbly. The background to the work is the key of C major, which Bernstein uses brilliantly. After a sudden, discordant call to action, the very opening chords, shuffling yet not dragging,

encapsulate the image of a youth walking down the block, his shoulders slightly hunched in the surly manner of Dean or Brando – these crunchy chords cut across the key of C major, in a couldn't-care-less manner, above an oscillating, almost modern-day evolution, of the walking bass. As the chords cut across the key of C, a dramatic *musical* tension has thus been set up, which can only be resolved in strict musical terms by the establishment of a clear C major at the very end of the work. Nor is this all – during the first bar of the score, we hear the tension of what the Medievalists called the *diabolus in musica,* the very interval which cannot be incorporated into traditional diatonic harmony.

At the very outset, therefore, Bernstein has thrown down a disturbing challenge, and it is fascinating to see how he tackles this problem in the course of the score. *West Side Story* as a stage work, is in two acts, the first of which gravitates from C major to E flat. 'Gravitates', for the music certainly does not modulate in the generally accepted sense of the word – it could hardly do so, given the opening harmonic challenge. The non-musical reader need not bother with these technicalities, but they are important musically and the reader ought to be aware of what is going on in the musical background as well as in the foreground, and should take it on board as a concept.

As the first act has gravitated from C major to E flat, the second act reverses this process, from E flat to C major. The present writer well remembers Bernstein's astonishment when he pointed this out to the composer – Bernstein had not realised it himself, certainly not when writing his music, that the second act of *West Side Story* harmonically reverses – almost as a mirror-image – the harmonic journey undertaken in the first act.

Therefore, in order to establish some form of

pacification or resolution at the end of the show, the E flat has to be got rid of – and this is dramatically achieved, near the beginning of Act II, when it comes at the point of most delight in the song 'I Feel Pretty'. The song does not stay in this key for very long, but uses this 'unwanted' tonality as a starting-point; this therefore reflects the brief appearance of E flat at the end of Act I. Dramatically, as well as musically, this key is essentially, exactly, right.

Why? Because Maria's happiness is to be short-lived. Dramatically, it cannot endure, and so – musically – neither can the key with which the song begins. In addition, the basic tonality of the whole score, C major, does not want the key of E flat anyway, and so we have come full circle.

The opening theme – a sleazy saxophone solo in 6/8 pulse – shows this organic cohesion in melodic terms. The almost careless way in which the tune slides around, upwards and backwards, landing on C almost by chance finally, shows the harmonic tension writ large. The bass line oscillation delineates the harmonic problem from another angle. The non-technical reader, without wading through a lengthy paragraph of harmonic analysis, will have to take it as read that by the end of the show we realise that even if this particular story may have finished, the underlying causes of the drama remain. Bernstein's extraordinary ability to mirror such dramaturgical matters in his score, and at the same time make the show wholly organic as music – and not as some kind of clever scene-painting – goes some way to explaining the continuing vitality of the music and his own mastery as a composer in this genre, for the central point about this is to demonstrate the great care and compositional skill which clearly went into the creation of this work. Underneath the surface, the foundations of *West Side Story* are particularly strong, and virtually indestructible.

However, whatever underlying linking threads we can find in the music of this work, it is the distinctive melodic and rhythmic qualities – the top layers – which perhaps strike the listener first. And here again Bernstein demonstrates his cunning; let us consider the rhythmic structure first. We have noted that the first pulse we hear is 6/8 – but it is unlikely that even the most musical of listeners would at first have perceived it as such. It is only with the saxophone theme that this pulse becomes apparent, for at this point both melody and rhythm open out for us at the same time.

The advantage for Bernstein of using a basic 6/8 pulse is manifold – in the first place, it permits a basic duple rhythm; secondly, it permits a jazz-inflexion in melodic shapes without upsetting the basic pulse (as the saxophone solo immediately shows). In addition, it can embrace two kinds of triple metre – two-bar phrases each of three quavers, and/or a basic 3/4 in the same time as the underlying 6/8. In other words, Bernstein has given himself an amazingly rich rhythmic palette whilst at the same time as allowing himself to preserve the underlying pulse – and such preservation is essential if the harmonic basis is not to be dislodged by other factors. The rhythmic flow is brilliantly demonstrated by the segue into the first 'Jet Song' – much of the music of the 'Prologue' is here subsumed into an accompanying role, preserving the basic 6/8, but the song itself is sung in 3/4 against this rhythm.

The 3/4 now takes over as the accompaniment for 'Something's Coming' (the next song) sung by Tony, who in turn changes the pulse into 2/4, without altering it at all! In this way, Bernstein brilliantly, musically, demonstrates 'change' in the very song which sings of such immediate expectation and change – at the same time as preserving the basic pulse.

This is an astonishing achievement, a

remarkable piece of very subtle composition, and as one goes through the score, the rhythmic structure of the work overall becomes apparent: the secondary ballet sequence, the dance at the gym, brings together all the rhythmic elements heard so far, and changes them into a new guise, for 'America' is a thrilling use of 6/8 in myriad forms; 'Cool' combines the jazz rhythmic structure within a 4/4 (that is, two bars of 6/8) basic time-signature. 'One Hand, One Heart' is the slow version of 3/4; the 'Rumble' (the third ballet sequence) returns to 6/8 but in a far harsher, grinding manner than the easy-going nonchalance we heard before. 'I Feel Pretty' actually is in 3/8 and 'Gee, Officer Krupke' is now a harsher 4/4 than 'Cool', at the same time preserving the three quavers in its refrain (to the word 'Officer') – and so on.

Only at the end of the show, as the realisation of the awfulness of the senseless murder dawns, does the music solidify, statuesque-like, into gestures of stunned immobility.

If the harmonic and rhythmic layers of *West Side Story* are very subtle and fully integrated, then no less so is the melodic. The very first music we hear is that rising *diabolus in musica*, which – although we certainly do not realise it at the time, forms part of a traditional chord in C major – and this extraordinary interval is the cell from which all the main themes grow, for it can be found at virtually every climactic moment all the way through each song in the show.

It even possesses harmonic implications which are not lost on this composer. For example, the 'Jet Song', which begins in B flat then gravitates towards C major. Technically, there are more examples of songs in *West Side Story* moving to what might at first appear to be the supertonic (that is, the next whole-tone key above, as in this instance) but which turns out to be the tonic major, the song having in reality begun on the flattened seventh.

Such extraordinary compositional skills as Bernstein exhibits in this work verge on genius, and there is little doubt that – quite apart from the freshness and vitality of the ideas themselves and the memorability of such songs as 'Tonight' and 'Maria' – the utterly organic whole created musically at every level by Leonard Bernstein raised his score of *West Side Story* to the level of a masterpiece.

It is a magnificent score for dancing, as well as for singing, and for those who recall the original cast productions in New York and in London, the choreographic treatment by Jerome Robbins was quite breathtakingly new in its utilisation of jive and rock-n-roll dance steps within a Broadway musical. In this score, and in this particular treatment of it, the East and West Sides of New York met together. Of course, with such a contemporary treatment of young working-class life, no other type of dance was possible, but it is always exciting to see the essence of what a later generation would call 'street dancing' transferred so aptly and successfully to what was termed the legitimate musical theatre.

The choreography, however, was not Robbins' sole contribution to the show – as we have seen, it was his concept originally. Indeed, the famous complete recording of 1985 conducted by Bernstein himself makes no bones about it: 'Entire Original Production Directed and Choreographed by Jerome Robbins' is written more than once – and deservedly so, as it was on the original cast recording (on the original sound-track recording, the box design is omitted, the wording remains) yet the facts are that the music is by Leonard Bernstein, and the words are by Stephen Sondheim.

In 1982, Bernstein recalled the origins of the

work. On Thursday, January 6, 1949, he wrote in his diary: "Jerry Robbins called today with a notable idea: a modern version of *Romeo And Juliet* set in slums at the coincidence of Easter-Passover celebrations. Feelings run high between Jews and Catholics... Juliet is Jewish. Friar Lawrence is a neighbourhood druggist. Street brawls, double death – it all fits. But it's all much less important than the bigger idea of making a musical that tells a tragic story in musical-comedy terms, using only musical-comedy techniques, never falling into the 'operatic' trap. Can it succeed? It hasn't yet in our country. I'm excited. If it can work – it's the first. Jerry suggests Arthur Laurents for the book. I don't know him, but I do know *Home Of The Brave,* at which I cried like a baby. He sounds just right."

From this opening idea, within three months the project had proceeded apace, but six-and-a-half years were to pass before, on August 25, 1955, Bernstein and Arthur Laurents were again able to discuss the idea in depth. However, Bernstein continued in his recollections: "...now we have abandoned the whole Jewish-Catholic premise as not very fresh, and have come up with what I think is going to be it: two teenage gangs, one the warring Puerto Ricans, the other self-styled 'Americans'. Suddenly it all springs to life. I hear rhythms and pulses, and – most of all – I can sort of feel the form."

Jerome Robbins was enthusiastic about "our gang idea", and in New York on November 14, Bernstein met Stephen Sondheim for the first time: "A young lyricist named Stephen Sondheim came and sang us some of his songs today. What a talent! I think he's ideal for this project, as do we all. The collaboration grows."

At the time Sondheim and Bernstein met, the lyricist was 26 years old. *West Side Story* was to be Sondheim's first show. Sondheim had been taken under the wing of Oscar Hammerstein II as a youth and had actually written four complete shows by the time he was 21, although none actually came to production. He had also studied composition with Milton Babbitt, and additionally had written television scripts, and one other mature (and also unperformed) show by the time of his meeting with Bernstein.

But Sondheim was not the sole collaborator making his Broadway debut with this show; Arthur Laurents, who wrote the book, was also engaging upon his first musical production with *West Side Story*; if one considers that Bernstein and Robbins were the only two seasoned Broadway creators within the collaboration, then the result is all the more astonishing.

The story opens with the balletic sequence referred to earlier, in which the warring gangs, one made up of 'native' New Yorkers called the Jets and the other, named the Sharks, are of Puerto Rican extraction – a relatively new immigrant group in post-war New York. Riff is the leader of the Jets, and – once the danced prologue is over – the gang members sing of their desire to clear the Sharks from the streets. Riff decides to challenge the Sharks' leader, Bernardo, to a fight at the coming dance at the gym, and asks his old friend Tony for help. Tony had been a co-founder of the Jets with Riff, but recently he has loosened his ties with the gang: he has a job and hankers after new experiences, but at last he agrees to help Riff and anticipates the dance.

Also looking forward to the dance is Maria, Bernardo's sister, who has recently arrived from Puerto Rico, ostensibly to marry Riff's friend Chino. As the gang members assemble and the dance gets under way, at first all is well, but then Tony and Maria see each other and for Tony it is love at first sight. The dance takes place against the undercurrent of hatred between the rival gangs and the growing feelings Tony has for Maria, and, once the dance is over, Tony walks the streets to visit Maria on the fire escape of her apartment. They meet, and declare their love for each other and arrange to meet again the following day at the bridal shop where Maria has a job.

In the meantime, the gangs have chosen a place and the weapons for their coming fight; as Tony leaves Maria, the Sharks escort their girl-friends home and go to the drug-store, where Anita and two of the other girls sing of the difference between life in America and in Puerto Rico. Some Jet gang members are a little nervous about the coming fight with the Sharks, but Riff enjoins them to play it cool, and when the Sharks at last arrive, Tony persuades everyone to settle their differences over one fight between the two best fighters from each gang only, to take place the following evening. They all agree.

The following day, at the bridal store, Tony meets up with Maria, and they enact their own wedding ceremony amongst the bridal gowns in the shop. Maria is worried that Tony will be hurt in the fight and extracts a promise that he will not fight her brother, but the plans for the fight have gathered their own momentum, and in the magnificent sequence for 'Tonight', which ends Act I, Bernstein writes a full-scale operatic quintet with each character singing of their own feelings as the fight approaches. This is arguably the most involved vocal music ever written for an ensemble in a stage musical, and it works superbly.

Later that night, the rival gangs assemble in preparation for the fight; Tony rushes in and tries to persuade Riff and Bernardo not to fight each other, as he has promised Maria. Bernardo is furious to learn that Tony has been seeing Maria and a fight begins in earnest, during which a knife is pulled and Bernado stabs Riff fatally. Tony grabs a weapon and knifes Bernardo in revenge.

Suddenly a police whistle sounds, and the youths disappear into the night, leaving the two bodies.

Back in her room, Maria is looking forward to meeting again with Tony; unaware of what has happened. She is stunned when Chino bursts in to tell her that her lover has killed her brother. Grabbing a gun, Chino rushes out, vowing revenge, but Tony has come to Maria's room via the fire escape. Despite what has happened, she cannot send Tony away; as one, they dream of a place for them to be together somewhere.

On the streets, the police have arrested and questioned two gang members who, now released after questioning, tell the others how to cope with the experience of being arrested by Officer Krupke.

Tony and Maria are still in her room, and when Anita calls he slips away. Anita remonstrates with Maria for allowing herself to go with Tony, but Maria answers that she loves Tony, and nothing can change that. Anita grudgingly accepts the situation, and agrees to warn Tony that Chino is after him with a gun. She goes to the drugstore to see him, but she is racially abused there by the Jets, and, enraged, she snarls that Chino has shot Maria in revenge. Tony is dazed on hearing this news, and, numb with shock, wanders aimlessly into the streets.

In the distance he sees Maria, but their moment of reconciliation is brief; they are with each other again for only a few moments before Chino sees the couple and, stepping from the shadows, he shoots Tony, who dies in Maria's arms. The rival gang members, shocked by the senseless killings, are at last united in their tragedy and both groups together lift Tony's body and carry him away.

It has been said, albeit with some exaggeration, that *West Side Story* contains more music in terms of playing time than any other stage musical: this element of the show is not only of high quality, and provided a number of hit songs, but also raised the standard of the work overall. If the conception was by Jerome Robbins, his choreography would mean nothing without the music; similarly, Stephen Sondheim's lyrics, fine though they are – even if their author has spoken disparagingly of his own work in this instance – would remain unknown if it were not for the instant memorability of the music. Leonard Bernstein's music for this show is not, in length, so very much greater than that for others – what has ensured the show's immortality is not the conception, the choreography or the lyrics, but the music.

The show took Broadway by storm when it opened in September 1957; the conductor was a classical musician, Max Goberman, who was the first to plan to record all of the symphonies of Haydn – a project which was brought to a sudden end by his untimely death in the 1960s, and the cast – necessarily all young – included a mixture of youthful singers from the world of opera, such as Reri Grist, and others from more popular fields – Carol Lawrence, Chita Rivera and Larry Kert. The show's run was unusual, for it enjoyed 734 performances before touring the USA for six months before coming back to Broadway where it ran for another 249 performances.

In London, *West Side Story* opened on December 12, 1958 at Her Majesty's Theatre in the Haymarket, and ran longer than on Broadway – 1,039 performances. The conductor for that run was another classical musician, Lawrence Leonard, and a curious piece of music is found on the original London cast recording, which Leonard conducts, which is not to be found on any other recording of this score.

This is described as 'Overture (America)' but it is no such thing – it was neither the overture to the show, nor does it contain any reference to the song 'America'. It is, in fact, a brilliant orchestral montage of three parts of the score – the 'Tonight' ensemble that ends Act I, the 'Somewhere' closing music, and the 'Mambo' from the dance at the gym – entirely without any singing at all. This music – which is superbly performed by the London orchestra, certainly better playing than can be heard on either the original cast or original sound-track recordings – was added only for the London run. It appears that it was played after the show – the exact opposite of an 'overture'! – so as not to leave the last music the audience heard as the increasingly immobile and statuesque quiet ending as Tony's body is carried off to the final curtain.

When Bernstein came to London for the rehearsals with Lawrence Leonard, he was astonished at the quality of the musicianship and how well the London players had captured the idiom; he was also puzzled by this additional music and did not want anything to be heard after the curtain fell, but there was nothing he could do about it, and so the London cast recording remains the only one ever made of this extra orchestral music. Not even the much-vaunted 'complete' recording that Bernstein himself conducted in 1985 with a clutch of operatic singers contains this music, a recording that fails to capture the essence of the original in many ways, not least in the arch and unsuitable 'operatic' singing. The orchestral playing in Bernstein's own recording is no more than adequate and sadly also fails to generate the tingling excitement that both Max Goberman and – best of all – Lawrence Leonard extracted from this brand new music of 40 years ago.

The extra music for the London run is interesting as Bernstein was required to provide additional music for the film version – and did not

Gang warfare, a theme of West Side Story, brought to the attention of theatre-going society a contemporary reality.

use any of the 'London' piece. That the film was more than likely to be a success could have been expected from those assembled to make it, rather than all of those who starred in it. The direction was by Robert Wise and Jerome Robbins, whose choreography tends to put this film in a class of its own. In this instance, Jerome Robbins was able to make a permanent record of his work, and excelled himself: the visual element of this film is fully the equal of the musical and the dramatic, and the visual element is contained, first and foremost, in the dancing. Another part of the visual element is the actual street locations of New York City – such locations make it difficult to film under any circumstances, but much more so when group dancing is involved; after all, the City had to go about its business whilst this film was being made in the heart of it.

The film was made by Mirisch Pictures and released through United Artists. For his choreographic work, Robbins demanded – and got – an unprecedented (for Hollywood) ten weeks of rehearsal time; in the London production George Chakiris played Riff, but for the film he was chosen as Bernardo – Riff was played by Russ Tamblyn. The part of Tony went to Richard Beymer and Natalie Wood – like Bernstein, of a Russian immigrant family – was Maria. The screenplay, by Ernest Lehman, changed certain aspects of the story, but not by much, and actually made more filmic sense – as the changes should have done.

But three of the roles had to be dubbed. These were for Richard Beymer – who was dubbed by Jim Bryant – and Natalie Wood, whose singing voice was recorded by Marni Nixon. As we have seen, Miss Nixon was also to dub the voice of Audrey Hepburn in *My Fair Lady*, and Natalie Wood again for the film of *Gypsy*. The other dubbed role was that of Anita, played in the film by Rita Moreno whose singing voice was provided by Betty Wand. The film was shot in Panavision 70, in Technicolor of course, a process from which Robert Wise extracted almost limitless possibilities and which technical opportunities thus provided were utilised to the full.

Leonard Bernstein's additional music was confined to extending certain numbers – notably the 'Prologue' – and he was obliged to shorten others; his score had also to be reorchestrated for the far larger orchestral forces demanded by the sound-track. This task was done with Bernstein's approval by his long-time associate Saul Chaplin. The score was conducted by Johnny Green. The film was 18 months in the planning, and was a triumph, garnering ten Academy Awards. If certain parts have inevitably dated with the passage of time, the essence of the story remains sadly as relevant today as it always was, with the exception that *West Side Story* took place before the insidious drug culture of the 1960s had taken a stranglehold on large parts of society.

Part III
Yesterday, Today And Tomorrow

Chapter 35

Postlude

In the Summer of 1976, almost exactly 20 years ago as I write these words, within a few days of returning from a trip to the USA, I had lunch with the late Hans Keller. This great man, who was tragically to die from motor neurone disease nine years later, was one of the greatest musicians – certainly the greatest musical thinker – it has ever been my good fortune to meet. Hans, who had been born in Vienna in 1919, escaped from the Nazis after the Anschluss and fled to England. He became an indispensable figure in British musical life: as an outstanding writer and sometimes trenchant commentator on classical music, his energy and output were prodigious, and from his noble, lively and enquiring mind those who knew him could learn much. Hans's genius was such that he was able to encourage people to learn equally from themselves as from others, and yet his mind – which was neither narrow nor hidebound in any way (or so it seemed to me) – would range widely over fields other than music.

Hans Keller was one of the first people in England to take George Gershwin as a seriously gifted composer. The shock that ran through the English classical music establishment when it read, under his byline and in his inimitable prose, that Gershwin was not only a genius but also a great composer, was considerable. Those who had been born after Gershwin's death knew nothing at first hand of those years when he was alive, and known as an individual to his contemporaries, when through the sheer force of his natural genius his music was performed as equally in the concert-hall as in the night-club. All each later generation has to go on, is the music itself. Those who were alive when a new work by Gershwin appeared, and were therefore at one with the social and aesthetic milieu of the day, could not but help bring their own contemporary experiences to an appreciation of the work in question. As much of Gershwin's output was in the ephemeral media of stage shows and films, it naturally appeared to many people that he was, first and foremost, an ephemeral artist.

We have all been attracted by a 'catchy' tune which enjoys some temporary success but which, in the nature of things, has been elbowed to one side by newer tunes, equally 'catchy'. Each of us cannot but help belong to a certain generation, and any generation will bring its own experiences to society when it is old enough and able to do so. At one level, therefore, as the distance between Gershwin's life and death and the experience of hearing his music for the first time increases for later generations, we are forced – if we believe that his music is worth playing at all – to consider the inherent musical qualities which have ensured its lasting success, and not regard it as a legacy of someone who was tragically cut off in his prime, in which our natural sympathy for the tragedy might over-ride our more rational feelings.

Hans Keller, being both a great musician and a great thinker, knew that Gershwin was a genius. Gershwin had made it somewhat easier for Hans to think that because he wrote a half-dozen works or so that were intended for the concert-hall – four works for piano and orchestra, a full-length grand opera, a symphonic poem and an overture – with which someone, like Hans, whose life was mainly lived in classical music, would at some point be likely to come into contact. There are always going to be – indeed, in the 1950s in England, such people were very much in the majority – those who feel that a composer like Gershwin who wrote commercially successful popular music could not, therefore, be taken seriously as a creative artist.

If Gershwin's concert music was the genre which kept his music alive for serious musicians the same was not true for almost every other popular music composer. Not having written for the concert-hall, their concert music did not exist, and so Hans Keller, for all his pioneering crusade in getting Gershwin accepted, would often be unfamiliar with the best work of Cole Porter, Irving Berlin, Richard Rodgers and other composers.

Hans Keller was not alone, however; he worked at the BBC for 20 years from 1959 until his retirement on the Third Programme, which later became Radio 3. One has to say that Radio 3 in the mid-1990s is very different from the Third Programme or Radio 3 as it was in Hans Keller's

day – the main difference being one of the fields for which Hans was responsible, namely music talks. One of his innovations in this field was an occasional series of talks on music called *In Short*. These were broadcast talks on one or other aspect of classical music, which would not last for more than about ten minutes. These were sometimes used as interval 'fillers' during broadcast concerts, and would more often than not be related to some aspect of the music in the concert. Hans was always on the look-out for new, and preferably polemical, subjects for his talks, and during this lunch I took the plunge and said I should like to be considered for such a talk, to be called 'Are Musicals Musical?'.

I could see that the title immediately appealed to him, and I outlined the kind of thing I would like to talk about. It so happened that Hans was a member of the European Broadcasting Union committee, which chose one big work to be broadcast simultaneously throughout the member countries of the union each year. He told me that the committee was considering that the next broadcast should be of Gershwin's musical *Lady, Be Good* – of which plans I was unaware – and that my timely suggestion of a talk should proceed the broadcast. I replied that I did not envisage talking much, if at all, about Gershwin – my talk would concentrate upon those composers who seemed never to be taken seriously outside of a small coterie of devoted followers.

The point I was trying to make, and about which I had convinced Hans, was that music which may, in the first place, have been written purely for entertainment, purely for the audiences of the day, could possess lasting qualities. As an example, why was it that, even in the 1970s, one of the more successful programmes on the BBC's Radio 1 popular music station was 'The Golden Hour' which played only hits from the past.

What was it about those old popular songs – apart from nostalgia, which in an increasing number of cases could not have been the reason for their undimmed popularity, if a large part of the audience was not around at the time the songs first became hits – what musical qualities did these songs possess that ensured their relative immortality, when so much popular music of the day had sunk without trace?

If this were true of old rock-and-roll records and other pop singles, then it was equally true – and more so – I argued, of the continuing success of revivals of shows from the hey-day of the American musical theatre. It is to be hoped that the main body of this book has detailed many of the purely musical qualities of the great musicals, for, without the music, such works do not exist. As we have seen, the musical theatre, 'musicals' for short, has been essentially, and remains so, an American phenomenon of the 20th-century.

Yet, as we have also seen in casting our net a little wider, if the words 'Broadway' and 'Hollywood' might only suggest 'America', the 'musicals' phenomenon has not been exclusively so, and is not necessarily one which will remain so, in so far as modern communications will permit.

There is a similar parallel between 20th-century American composers of musicals and 19th-century German classical composers, a parallel which shows that genius can only flourish when it is given the environment in which to do so. We have noted that many of the more notable American practitioners of the Broadway musical were of Russian extraction, but the notion that Russia in the 20th-century would have provided a sympathetic environment in which the popular musical theatre could flourish is nonsense.

Nor is the provision of the environment any guarantee that genius will flourish, because you have to have the genius in the first place, and the genius has to be recognised in the second place. Therefore, as it is largely the fruits of genius about which we have concerned ourselves in this book, only if these two demands have been met will we know that such fruits have lasting qualities which can speak afresh to future generations.

The genius also has to adapt to new circumstances, at the same time as forcing circumstances to adapt to the demands of his genius. To paraphrase a character in Bernard Shaw's *Man And Superman*: the reasonable man adapts himself to the world as he finds it, but the unreasonable man spends his time getting the world to adapt to what he wants the world to become – therefore, advances in human endeavour come about through the actions of unreasonable men.

As we said in Chapter 1, 100 years ago few people would have given the flickering peep-show or the stage show with music the consideration of being new art-forms, but it was not just films and musicals that were being born then. The internal combustion engine, the motor-car, was another coming thing at that time. If the majority of transportation, apart from rail, was horse-drawn in those days, to be replaced within 30 years by motorised vehicles, then what happened to all of the blacksmiths? Did they sit around, bemoaning the fact that there was no demand for their services any more? Perhaps some did, and they would have been left behind by the march of time, but others adapted to the coming of the motor-car; Benz was the genius, but the many petrol and filling-stations which, in the early years of motorised transport, were adjuncts to blacksmiths' workshops, came about as the result of decisions taken by reasonable men.

Immigrants to America at the dawn of the 20th-century had one priceless chance: opportunity.

For many, they had to learn a new language, and in so doing added elements of their own languages to spoken English, enriching it in the process. The American Declaration of Independence, as we have had occasions to mention before, held several things to be self-evident, including the truth that all men are created equal – and if in the process that truth was not always practised by those in positions of power, nonetheless it was enshrined as an ideal which all could understand and to which all could aspire. No such declaration would be enshrined in the independence of any European.

In short, the millions of immigrants to America in the early years of the 20th-century learned one lesson very quickly: if you don't work, you don't eat. The lesson applied equally to musicians as it did to everyone else, apart from the children of millionaires. The changes in society which were forced upon these immigrants, by the fact of coming to a new world, equally offered them new opportunities – as the coming of the automobile had done to the blacksmith. The rise of the film, the inventions of gramophone recordings and the telephone, the supply of electricity and gas nationwide, the invention of television – each of these things, and more – must have seemed to many, particularly those in America because of its size and 'newness' to be the fruits of a new Jerusalem.

Immigrant musicians could find work in movie houses, in theatres and in vaudeville, as well in orchestras and opera houses across the country. In theory, they could also find similar work in many European countries, but not in all, certainly not if they were Jewish. In America, no such anti-Semitism prevented musicians from obtaining work in its burgeoning economy, but the coming of sound to movies threw many musicians in movie houses out of work at a time when the Wall Street Crash of October 1929 and the following years of Depression sent seismic shock-waves across the entire world.

If many now found themselves close to despair, the entertainment business boomed, as people turned to music and movies and theatres to forget the grind of their daily lives. It remains a curious paradox that when the economy falters, the entertainment business usually does well by comparison, and when the economy is doing well, the entertainment business does better. But what makes the entertainment business less than a sure-fire bet for investors is what the London *Financial Times* concluded after a big survey of the music industry in the mid-1970s: "The only certain thing about the music business is that it is uncertain."

The success of the entertainment business in the 20th-century surely demonstrates that popular entertainment – or popular 'culture' as it is sometimes rather grandly described, principally by journalists keen to make mountains out of intellectual molehills – fulfils a deep-seated social need. The best of this popular entertainment, as we hope to have shown with regard to film musicals, contains qualities that lift it out of the ordinary, and is capable of continuing to fulfil that need across the generations. Simply said, as we noted near the beginning of this book, it is an aid to many in their pursuit of 'Happiness'. For some people also, the best film musicals personify the Happiness they have pursued.

As human beings, we instinctively know that happiness of one kind or another is good for us, and that unhappiness is not. We also know that, given the right circumstances, such happiness tends to be contagious, for our happiness is best experienced in the company of others, and our unhappiness generally tends to be a solitary experience. Although to experience happiness we do not always have to laugh, it is more often than not the case that when one person in a small group laughs, the others do also. If this is true of a small group, then how much more true is it of a larger audience, whose main purpose in being in the theatre in the first place is to pursue happiness?

The point is that the overwhelming majority of the musicals that were filmed in Hollywood were conceived for, and first given in front of, a paying audience. The filming, also, produced movies that were shown before audiences: the public's consumption of these musicals – as with all films, of course – took place in public. But today, with the world-wide growth of video film, pre-recorded video discs and the great explosion of viewing choice from many satellite movie channels, the films of these musicals are seen on comparatively miniature screens, often of the wrong relative size and frequently on the small mono speaker of the average television set, at home. These are, it need hardly be said, not the conditions under which the movies – or the musicals in the first place – were meant to be seen.

A film, such as the 1953 movie *Kiss Me Kate* is, as we noted in the chapter on this musical, a splendid piece of cinematic art in its own right. It deserves to be seen in a cinema – and even in its original intended form, in three-dimensional format – for it to make its full and proper impact. But, realistically, this is not the way in which anyone today is likely to view the movie, to the chagrin of the film's admirers. They are going to see it at home, on a television screen.

Which is better than nothing, for as this is the medium by which all films are seen in the home, the viewer will have adjusted to the smaller screen in the way in which all television programmes are experienced. If it were not for the existence of pre-recorded formats or satellite channels then these films would hardly be seen at all, for the chances of them being re-released for cinema distribution are virtually non-existent.

Some may feel that this is an argument for not filming musicals, but such an argument would apply to not showing any films at all on television, which is absurd. On the other hand, it does raise the question of what, precisely, the cinema can achieve in realising the potential of, say, a musical. As an aside, having noted that the average television set has a comparatively small speaker, a technical disadvantage of this is that, for example, an important film innovation – so important that it is not a visual one – by Stephen Spielberg can only be appreciated in the cinema.

This is Spielberg's use of more than one conversation at the same time. In *Jurassic Park*, this device has a considerable dramatic function, and its use can be noted in such relatively early work of Spielberg as *Jaws*. But in a television broadcast of a film which contains this device, one conversation is completely obliterated by the other. In the cinema, we may be aware of two conversations going on at the same time – coming from opposite speakers, or in surround-sound from behind us – but at home, we hear only one, to the inevitable loss of a gifted film-maker's cinematic innovation, and our own loss through our inability to experience thereby what it was he wanted to convey.

If the fact remains that we are stuck with the video film or disc and a minuscule screen-size should we wish to view old films – it being a practical impossibility for the majority of us who are not millionaires to view old films in the conditions for which they were made to be seen – then we should console ourselves with the thought that this is the only practical way in which we can see these movies. As that is the case, we tend to make allowances in our viewing, in much the same way as we do when listening to a recording of a symphony, which is not the same as hearing the orchestra live in the concert hall.

There would seem to be no market in showing old movies of musicals in modern cinemas, yet has the market ever been adequately tested? The public, of course, can only see what is screened, and the pressure on distributors' screen time is as strong today as it has always been, for there are many worthwhile films made today which do not get distribution – if this is true, and it is, then what chance does the older movie, especially an 'unrestored' one, stand?

If commercial pressures prevent us today from experiencing that collective pursuit of happiness that cinema audiences regularly knew, from the mid-1930s to the mid-1970s, then – still assuming that it is better to experience such emotions as part of an audience – where can we still do so today? The answer is: for the time being, in the theatre. In this regard, therefore, theatre audiences have the edge over cinema-goers: for if films of musicals are not made, then not only will there be no audience in the cinema for them, but also there will be no future audience for video releases, or for television showings. In other words, we could be at a time in history when the musical is in limbo.

But as we noted earlier, anything is possible in art given two criteria: imagination and technical ability, and one of the more exceptional things about stage musicals of the past quarter-century or so is that the two leading composers in the genre have written musicals that have resisted what one might call traditional movie-making: Sir Andrew Lloyd Webber and Stephen Sondheim. Now, it is true that films have been made of some of their work: in Sir Andrew's case, a film of *Jesus Christ Superstar* was made in 1973 by Universal, but this could hardly be described as a success –

either as a film or as a film of a musical. We have earlier noted the filming of Sondheim's masterly *A Little Night Music* and the sad failure that resulted.

In Sir Andrew's case, we should remember that *Jesus Christ Superstar* was amongst the first of his musical shows, and at the time the film was made one could not be entirely certain that the piece itself – which has subsequently shown itself to possess an inherent, lasting vitality, and therefore longevity – was as well treated as it could have been. Consequently, it is of no little import that his subsequent shows have not been filmed, nor have they appeared to lend themselves to filming. If we consider *Cats*, *Starlight Express*, *Phantom Of The Opera*, *Aspects Of Love* and *Sunset Boulevard* – although this list does not constitute anything like the complete Lloyd Webber canon – they would appear to have been so comprehensively conceived as stage vehicles as to render their filming to be almost insuperable.

On the one hand, this is because they have been so spectacularly successful as theatre pieces, but on the other Sir Andrew is one of those rare creative artists who is prepared to bide his time and who also wishes to have a by no means insignificant personal input into aspects of the realisations of his work. Perhaps the film of *Jesus Christ Superstar* was a cautionary tale. But the one show not mentioned in the above list, *Evita*, whilst being a considerable theatrical success in its own right, began life as a gramophone record – a double-album of an opera which had not been staged. There were a few raised eyebrows at the claim that *Evita* was an 'opera' – but it was, as there was no dialogue: in fact, in strict theatrical terms, this was grand opera.

The commercial success of the double-album (naturally, of the complete opera) led to a production, and at last we were able to see the work in something like the concept that the composer and lyricist, Tim Rice, had in mind when they wrote it. Of all of Sir Andrew's works, *Evita* would seem to be the one that most readily lends itself to filming. But one must applaud the tenacity of the film-making itself when one considers that Madonna, who had been selected to play the title role in 1990, and who had seen two delays in the production (the last in 1991) actually got her chance to make the film in 1995-6. At the 1996 Cannes Film Festival, in May 1996, a ten-minute excerpt from the film was shown: the result by all accounts exceeded all expectations, and it would seem that the film of *Evita* has been well worth the wait.

But what of *Cats* or *Starlight Express*? Surely, these are virtually unfilmable: but the clue lies in the word 'virtually'. There are now plans afoot to film these shows, using the latest technology in moving images – not as 'cartoons' in the generally–accepted sense of the word, but as moving images, in which the considerable fantasy and imagination that went into the staging of the shows in the first place have been re-translated into modern-day filmic terms.

Quite clearly, as these films have not yet been made, it would be nonsensical to write about them as if they were, but the recognition of the problems they pose – and the likely solutions being considered – is itself an indication of their profound originality in theatrical, dramatic terms.

The filming of Sir Andrew Lloyd Webber's musicals is an exciting prospect, and all the indications we have is that they will be a success. We must hope so, not least for the fascination of seeing one art-form recreate another, but because if they are successful, they will undoubtedly re-open the gates for films of musical shows.

One of the more frustrating aspects of *Broadway To Hollywood* is the lack of interest by Hollywood in Broadway shows; yet today we have filming technology at a level far and away superior to anything available to film-makers in the past. All they need, it would seem, is the material from which to make movies.

Yet the material is there: we know, from brilliantly successful revivals of Broadway shows, that there is a large public for musicals; why should this public not be equally drawn to films of those self-same shows, the more so in modern terms and made with modern techniques? There would appear to be every indication that the public would so respond. For lovers of the musical, both theatrical and on film, it would be wonderful if the fastidious work of Sir Andrew Lloyd Webber were to usher in a new Golden Age of film musicals, utilising the finest shows of the past, and the modern-day masterpieces of the genre. There is no reason why this should not be so, and we should look to the future with keen anticipation and no little excitement.